The Professionalization of Pastoral Care

The Professionalization of Pastoral Care

The SBC's Journey from Pastoral Theology
to Counseling Psychology

T. DALE JOHNSON JR.

WIPF & STOCK · Eugene, Oregon

THE PROFESSIONALIZATION OF PASTORAL CARE
The SBC's Journey from Pastoral Theology to Counseling Psychology

Wipf & Stock
An Imprint of Wipf and Stock Publishers
199 W. 8th Ave., Suite 3
Eugene, OR 97401

www.wipfandstock.com

PAPERBACK ISBN: 978-1-7252-6492-2
HARDCOVER ISBN: 978-1-7252-6491-5
EBOOK ISBN: 978-1-7252-6493-9

Manufactured in the U.S.A.   07/20/20

To Summer, my bride,
you have sacrificed as Christ,
loved as Christ,
encouraged as Christ,
persevered as Christ,
you are my true gift and treasure,
and to
Easton, Titus, Will, Ellie, Annadale, and Caroline,
you are a heritage from the Lord and
you make my heart glad.

Contents

Introduction

In 2002, a resolution entitled, "On the Sufficiency of Scripture in a Thera-peutic Culture" was adopted by the Southern Baptist Convention (SBC). The resolution called "on all Southern Baptists and our churches to reclaim practical biblical wisdom, Christ-centered counseling, and the restorative ministry of the care and cure of souls,"[1] and it stimulated a revision in the pastoral care approach taught at Southern Baptist Theological Seminary.[2]

In 2009, Dr. Russell Moore, former Dean of The Southern Baptist Theological Seminary's School of Theology, cited the resolution in an un-published document written as a rationale for a curriculum change in favor of Biblical Counseling.[3] A shift toward a Biblical Counseling model for pastoral care was necessary because the therapeutic model had been the es-tablished approach at Southern Baptist Theological Seminary (SBTS) since at least 1947.[4]

The SBC presently is divided regarding the methodology of soul care. As recently as June 2013, at the convention meeting in Houston, Texas, a resolution was passed entitled "On Mental Health Concerns and the Heart of God." This resolution invoked "all Southern Baptists and our churches to look for and create opportunities to love and minister to, and develop methods and resources to care for, those who struggle with mental health concerns and their families."[5] The language of the resolution seems to align with the psychological model, utilizing the diagnostic categories of the

1. Resolution No. 5, "Sufficiency of Scripture," Southern Baptist Convention.

2. Moore, "Counseling and the Authority of Christ."

3. Moore, "Counseling and the Authority of Christ," 11–13.

4. Oates, "Gaines S. Dobbins," in Dobbins, *Great Teachers*. The Department of Psychology of Religion began in 1947; Oates claimed that Dobbins actually began the concept in 1937. Throughout this book Southern Baptist Theological Seminary may also be referred to as SBTS or Southern Seminary.

5. Resolution No. 5, "On Mental Health Concerns," Southern Baptist Convention.

Diagnostic and Statistical Manual for Mental Disorders.[6] There are conflict-
ing views on how to define the phrase "mental health," and a divergence in
ministry models to care for those enduring such mental, emotional, and
soulish anguish.

The SBC at large is conflicted in its way forward regarding the issues
of soul care and mental illness. Historically, there was a major transition
within the SBC that contributed to the confusion regarding the role of the
church in soul care. Theological education at Southern Seminary made
drastic strides in adopting the social sciences as an authority on human nature causing ministers to yield to the therapeutic culture that was dominant
in America.

BACKGROUND

The advances of enterprise and intellect were felt during the turn of the
twentieth century in the United States of America and many benefited from
the economic growth.[7] Intellectual acumen was gaining ground on American soil, especially within higher education in New England. The advent
of Darwinism brought about new ways of considering the metaphysical
foundations of every discipline, as many were adapting their disciplines to
fit the new framework of proposed origins of life.[8] The field of education became disheveled as newly developed philosophies and psychologies arose.[9]
Some considered evangelicalism to be the primary hindrance to intellectual
growth in America in the same way the Mosaic worldview was said to have
shackled scientific growth before evolutionary theory was born.[10] The advent

6. American Psychiatric Association. *DSM-IV-TR*. The *DSM-5* was not published
until May 2013, only a month prior to the resolution being presented at the SBC Annual Meeting in June.

7. Callahan, *Education and the Cult of Efficiency*, 2.

8. Grinder, *History of Genetic Psychology*, 1–30. Grinder provided the explanation
for Lamarckian and Darwinian influence in the realm of biology and psychology. The
primary sources of John Dewey, George A. Coe, G. Stanley Hall, and E. L. Thorndike
demonstrate the influence of Darwinian origins on child development and philosophy
of education, which Dobbins utilized.

9. James, *Varieties of Religious Experiences*. Dewey, *Democracy and Education*. Dewey, *School and Society*. Thorndike, *Educational Psychology*. Thorndike, *The Principles of
Teaching*. Hall, *Adolescence*.

10. Hofstadter, *Anti-Intellectualism in American Life*, 82–83. Grinder, *History of
Genetic Psychology*, 2. Joncich, *Psychology and the Science of Education*, 5–10, 48–54.
Hofstadter acknowledged that the Mosaic system hindered the birth of evolutionary
theory, but the shift in metaphysical foundations made way for the new theory. According to Grinder, the psychological worldview was hindered in growth by evangelical

of psychology in the latter half of the nineteenth century gained influence within evangelicalism, in part because some Christians sought to maintain intellectual credibility with the scientific progression of the west.[11] The social sciences began to infiltrate the theory and practice of pastoral care.

In 1970, with the publication of *Competent to Counsel*, Jay Adams, former Professor of Practical Theology at Westminster Theological Seminary, alerted Christians to the dangers found in the philosophical underpinnings of psychiatry. His argument revealed the anti-scriptural polemic of psychiatric medicine and its counterpart from the social sciences, psychology.[12] The opposition to Adams was substantial and his principal adversaries were evangelicals who desired to integrate the discipline of psychology with theological principles.[13] Due to competing approaches, the practice of Christian counseling has become convoluted as demonstrated in Eric Johnson's *Psychology & Christianity: Five Views.*[14]

During the one-hundred years prior to Adams, churches and seminaries pursued a philosophical openness to integrate psychology with the practice of soul care.[15] The Industrial Revolution, rapid urbanization, and emphasis on business efficiency contributed to an alteration upon the cultural and religious terrain of America.[16] Christian leaders permitted the

---

beliefs; they were even competing. Thorndike claimed that religion to be a hindrance to the growth of intellectualism, especially in the area of human learning.

11. Aden and Ellens, *Turning Points in Pastoral Care*. Holifield, *A History of Pastoral Care in America*. Clinebell, *Basic Types of Pastoral*. Oates, *The Christian Pastor*. Collins, *Christian Counseling*. Johnson, *Foundations of Soul Care*.

12. Adams, *Competent to Counsel*. Adams is founder of Institute for Nouthetic Studies, Association of Certified Biblical Counselors (formerly National Association of Nouthetic Counselors), and Christian Counseling and Education Fountation. His works attempted to distinguish a biblical or Christian approach to counseling from the integrated model of Christian psychology.

13. Dobbins, "Capturing Psychology for Christ," 427–36. Dobbins, "The Minister Learning from the Psychiatrist," 60–71. Dobbins, "Pastor as Counselor," 421–29. Collins, *Can You Trust Psychology?*. Collins, *Psychology & Theology*. Collins, *The Rebuilding of Psychology*. Collins's books were a part of the intense dialogue with Adams over the usefulness of psychology.

14. Johnson, *Psychology & Christianity: Five Views*. Johnson was formerly the Lawrence and Charlotte Hoover Professor of Pastoral Care at Southern Baptist Theological Seminary. This volume presents five divergent and intricately nuanced views of Christian counseling.

15. Spencer, *A Pastor's Sketches*. See Holifield, *A History of Pastoral Care in America*, 107–11. Lambert, *The Biblical Counseling Movement After Adams*, 25–26.

16. Wills, *Democratic Religion*, 26–36. Lambert, *The Biblical Counseling Movement After Adams*, 31–48. Callahan, *Education and the Cult of Efficiency*.

voice of experts in psychology as authorities on human nature—a position once firmly held by the church and its leaders.[17]

In 1984, Thomas Oden, a Methodist theologian, wrote *Care of Souls in the Classic Tradition* and acknowledged a trend that demonstrated the dependence upon secular psychologists by the major contemporary contributors to pastoral counseling.[18] Pastoral care had once been firmly rooted in the theological rather than in the psychotherapeutic version of reality.[19] Oden defined the classic tradition of pastoral care as historically rooted in theology and Scripture; and he identified Augustine, Gregory the Great, Luther and others as part of this tradition. Oden demonstrated that the continuity of the use of Scripture for pastoral care had been broken and writers of modern pastoral care were utilizing another source. Oden then concluded that since the 1920s the classic tradition of pastoral care had not been consulted as the primary source of theory or practice.[20] Moreover, Oden sounded a clarion call for modern theologians to recover the lost identity of pastoral care by studying significant historical figures and their contributions to soul care built upon a theological basis.[21]

Oden and Adams focused primarily on the broad causes and effects of the shift in the practice of pastoral care. In contrast, I will detail the root causes of this same shift specifically within the Southern Baptist denomination. In order for a recovery of the sort that Oden suggested to be advanced within the SBC, it would be helpful to understand how the denomination began to accept principles from secular psychology as authoritative. I will demonstrate that Gaines Stanley Dobbins,[22] former Professor of Church Ef-

17. Vitz, *Psychology as Religion*. Holifield, *A History of Pastoral Care in America*, 15–31. Holifield demonstrates the major transition in America from the late 1800s to the 1960s, see: 175–230. Lambert, *Biblical Counseling Movement After Adams*, 26–36. Kemp, *Physicians of the Soul*, 3–68. Powlison, *The Biblical Counseling Movement*, 51–71. Deckard, *Helpful Truths in Past Places*. Oden, *Care of Souls in the Classic Tradition*, 11–74. Purves, *Pastoral Theology in the Classic Tradition*. Clebsch and Jaekle, *Pastoral Care in Historical Perspective*, 1–75.

18. Oden, *Care of Souls in the Classic Tradition*, 26–42.

19. Oden, *Care of Souls in the Classic Tradition*, 18–21.

20. Oden, *Care of Souls in the Classic Tradition*, 32–34. Holifield, *A History of Pastoral Care in America*, demonstrated agreement with Oden, but gives a much more in depth explanation of the influences that affected the shift from classic pastoral care to the modern focus upon self-realization and personality development.

21. Some of the following resources demonstrate a response to Oden's call. Purves, *Pastoral Theology in the Classic Tradition*. Deckard, *Helpful Truth in Past Places*. Beeke and Pederson, *Meet the Puritans*. Lundgaard, *The Enemy Within*. Tappert, *Luther: Letters of Spiritual Counsel*.

22. Dobbins has been called "Mr. Southern Baptist," "Mr. Administration," and the father of pastoral care for his influence as a professor and writer. Dobbins was raised in

ficiency and Religious Education at The Southern Baptist Theological Seminary, synthesized ideas from various disciplines that invigorated the shift in practical ministry from reliance upon Scripture to secular psychology.

In the early twentieth century, due to the rise of Darwinism and the applications of evolutionary theory and the scientific methods to more fields of study, theological disciplines lost academic respectability within intellectualism, and many theological educators sought a more substantiated and respected form of study.[23] Dobbins and others did not abandon theology, but were in need of a more reputable discipline.[24] The scientific status of the methods of psychology was a respectable means by which religious education was promoted within the discipline of theology.[25] Dobbins, along with other religious educators, attempted to integrate the scientific view of human nature with the theological.

Theology had been a discipline firmly rooted within the realm of philosophy.[26] A movement was underway at end of the nineteenth century and into the twentieth century that brought about a shift in interpretation of religious experience. Several men and their works were germane to creating the scientific category for the new discipline. The work of G. Stanley Hall (*Adolescence: Its Psychology and its Relations to Physiology, Anthropology,*

Mississippi after his birth in 1886. His parents and grandparents were farmers. Once he was old enough, Dobbins began working in a printing shop, which began his love for reading and journalism. After his undergraduate work at Mississippi College aspiring to be a Christian journalist, he moved to Louisville, Kentucky to study at Southern Seminary. Upon his graduation in 1914, Dobbins pastored a few rural churches in the south. In 1916, only two years after graduation, he was called to join the editorial staff of the Sunday School Board of the Southern Baptist Convention, a position he held until 1932. Amid his responsibilities as a journalist, in he became a professor of Church Efficiency and Sunday School Pedagogy in 1920 at Southern Baptist Theological Seminary in Louisville, Kentucky. He served on faculty for thirty-six years at Southern Seminary and then for another ten years on the faculty of Golden Gate Baptist Theological Seminary. Throughout his life, Dobbins was also involved in the Sunday School Board of the SBC as a journalist and a writer of Sunday School curriculum. After teaching at Golden Gate Seminary, Dobbins retired to Birmingham, Alabama where he died in 1978 and is buried.

23. Dobbins, *Great Teachers Make A Difference*, 80.

24. Dobbins, *Great Teachers*, 58–59 and 80. Dobbins, "Theological Education in a Changing Social Order," 181–96.

25. Holifield, *A History of Pastoral Care in America*, 221–28.

26. James, *Varieties of Religious Experience*. Adams, *Competent to Counsel*. Pearcey, *Total Truth*, 41–205. Pearcey and Thaxton, *The Soul of Science*, 17–56. Schaeffer, *Escape From Reason*. Vitz, *Psychology as Religion*. Vitz argued that rather than religion becoming scientific, the social science of psychology was merging into the realm of the philosophical and becoming more of a religion than a scientific discipline. He went so far as to claim that psychology was a competing religion in which self-worship was the pinnacle.

Sociology, Sex, Crime, Religion and Education), William James (*Varieties of Religious Experience*), E. D. Starbuck (*The Psychology of Religion*), and George Albert Coe (*The Spiritual Life: Studies in the Science of Religion*) attempted to classify religion as scientific. Psychology of religion was the new category formed to study the incorporeal in scientific terms.

The penetrating influence of each of these men and their works is seen repeatedly in works by Dobbins as he tried to legitimize the practical disciplines of religious education and pastoral care in an effort to capture psychology for Christ.[27] Dobbins synthesized his views of religious education, church organization, and pastoral care from his encounters with these influential people. Not only can these influences be seen in Dobbins's writings but also in his lecture notes, to which his students referred as, "Dobbinology."[28]

Four dissertations have been written about Dobbins or his impact on religious education at Southern Seminary.[29] These works addressed specific aspects of his teaching, but have remained unused to demonstrate his contribution to pastoral care. His views of efficiency and the origins that influenced him have been revealed by James Ryan in, "A Study of the Administrative Theory of Gaines Stanley Dobbins in Relationship to the Scientific Management, Human Relations, and Social Sciences Emphases in Administration." Stephen Combs's study, "The Course of Religious Education at The Southern Baptist Theological Seminary 1902–1953: A Historical Study" chronicled the influence of secular psychology on the practice of religious education. William Hacker emphasized the effect of Thorndike's educational psychology on the curriculum of Southern Baptists, evidencing the dependence upon secular psychology for educational methods.[30]

27. Dobbins, "Capturing Psychology for Christ," 427–36. Dobbins, "The Minister Learning from the Psychiatrist," 60–71. Dobbins, "Pastor as Counselor," 421–29. Dobbins, *Working Together in a Spiritual Democracy.* In *Great Teachers Make a Difference*, Dobbins paid a special tribute to the influence of Coe and his methods, which depended upon psychology, for his own work.

28. Oates, "Gaines S. Dobbins," in Dobbins, *Great Teachers*, 89. Dobbins Papers, Box 9, Folders 9.10, 9.11, 9.12, 9.14, 9.15, 9.16, 9.21, 10.14. Findley B. Edge Papers, Box 14, Folders 7, 8, 16, 17; Box 15, Folders 1–5; Box 17, Folders 1–5; Box 24, Folders 26–34.

29. James Ryan, "Administrative Theory of Gaines Stanley Dobbins." Combs, "The Course of Religious Education." Moore, "Biblical Fidelity to Organizational Efficiency." Hardin, "Retailing Religion." Both Moore and Hardin have also completed significant research in this area.

30. McGee, "The Place of the Bible," 85–99. I will focus on Thorndike's influence specifically upon Dobbins. Hacker, "Learning Theories of E. L. Thorndike." Hacker demonstrated the significance of my argument by showing the breadth of Dobbins's influence and use of Thorndike as it spread convention wide.

Although William McGee's "The Place of The Bible in the Curriculum of Religious Education" was written before the previously mentioned dissertations, he foresaw the resulting view of the Bible after the new methods of psychology had been applied.[31]

No one has addressed in detail Dobbins's influence within the arena of pastoral care and counseling. The completed research regarding origins of Clinical Pastoral Education (CPE)[32] among Baptists tends to focus primarily on the work of Wayne Oates.[33] Edgar's "Pastoral Identity in the Thought of Wayne Oates" and Jeane's "An Analysis of Wayne Edward Oates' Phenomenological Method of Diagnosis in Pastoral Counseling" are representative in demonstrating Oates's role in utilizing CPE for training pastors.[34] The present study will question Oates's role as the lone pioneer in pastoral care in order to unveil Dobbins as the protagonist in transition

---

31. McGee, "The Place of the Bible," 85–99. McGee explained the anthropocentric shift toward human need as the focal point of educational curriculum. His work was completed at the recommendation and under the supervision of Gaines Dobbins. McGee said, "Our educational methods have been improved, but we are not yet free from the old craze of memorization. There is still a widespread conception that the important thing is to get the words of the Bible into the minds of the pupils. It has been only a short time since the writer was in a class of adults in a city church of high standing. An intelligent woman in the class expressed belief that we would be following more effective educational method by having boys and girls memorize the Ten Commandments and recite them each Sunday to keep them fresh in mind, rather than giving the pupils opportunity to express Christian principles in life situations. She thought that the words of the Bible would magically transform the lives of boys and girls, and that nothing else was needed. Any view which insists that only biblical material be used in religious instruction is a wrong view. It is wrong because it puts primary emphasis on the materials used rather than on the end to be accomplished. The end does not always justify the means; but a good end justifies any good means, so long as the expenditure is not too great for the returns." McGee, "The Place of the Bible," 150–51. This is quintessential pragmatism at its height and the reason for the eclecticism of Dobbins in choosing varied methods for education and pastoral care.

32. Clinical Pastoral Education, as credited to Anton Boisen and Richard Cabot, began around 1925. CPE was a distinct methodological approach to theological training in conjunction with medical facilities to care for those who were labeled as mentally ill patients. This presented an opportunity for clergy to become part of the "healing team," for those with deep mental anguish. CPE is discussed further in chapter 3 of this book.

33. Wayne Oates was the first professor of Psychology of Religion and Pastoral Care in the Southern Baptist Convention. This department was organized by Dobbins and began in 1947. Oates was chosen to lead the new department in the clinical training of pastors. Oates remained at Southern Seminary until 1974, when he took a position at Louisville Medical School. He is well-known for his contributions to the new pastoral care movement, which is discussed in greater detail in chapter 3 of this work.

34. Thornton, "Critique of Clinical Pastoral Education." Edgar, "Pastoral Identity in the Thought of Wayne Oates." Jeane, "Wayne Edward Oates's Phenomenological Method."

from traditional pastoral care to dependence upon the psychology of religion, which led to the importance of clinical training for pastoral counseling among Southern Baptists.

Oates's Th.D. dissertation "The Significance of the Work of Sigmund Freud for the Christian Faith" detailed the psychologically dependent trajectory of pastoral counseling under the leadership of Dobbins.[35] As demonstrated by Boisen, Dicks, and Sherrill, secular psychological theory was favorably viewed within the arena of pastoral care and counseling during Oates's time as a student at Southern Seminary.[36] Edward Thornton's "A Critique of Clinical Pastoral Education" was written in 1960 under the supervision of Oates.[37] Thornton's work demonstrated that the direction which began under Dobbins continued into a third successive generation of scholars at SBTS.[38] To the detriment of a distinctly theological perspective, traditional pastoral care had transitioned to a clinical based model of counseling as the primary component of pastoral counseling methodology. During this time the curriculum at the Southern Baptists seminaries affirmed that the path toward a clinical model had been clearly established.[39]

Dobbins was trained in a theological milieu at SBTS that was showing signs of being influenced by intellectualism, modernism, and liberal criticism.[40] Edgar Young Mullins was appointed as president to help the seminary move beyond the effects of Crawford Toy, Landmarkism, and the Whitsitt Controversy.[41] Dobbins came to the campus in 1909 amid the residual effects of these controversies and studied with several men who wielded distinct influence in his life and ministry. President E. Y. Mullins, Charles Spurgeon Gardner, A. T. Robertson, and John Sampey certainly shaped the thought of Dobbins as evidenced in his book, *Great Teachers*

---

35. Oates's dissertation was supervised by Dobbins.

36. Oates, "Gaines Dobbins," 102. Dobbins was responsible for introducing Oates to Anton Boisen, Spafford Ackerly, Lewis Sherrill and others who led the Clinical Pastoral Education movement. Boisen, *Exploration of the Inner World*. Boisen, *Religion in Crisis and Custom*. Sherrill, *Understanding Children*. Sherrill, *Struggle of the Soul*. Cabot and Dicks, *Art of Ministering to the Sick*.

37. Dobbins also chose Oates to lead the new Department of Psychology of Religion and Pastoral Care in 1947.

38. Thornton, "Critique of Clinical Pastoral Education," 1960.

39. Cox and Allen, *Encyclopedia of Southern Baptists*, 1073–79. Southern Baptist Theological Seminary Annual Catalogue, 1908–1956. An observation of the curriculum changes, course descriptions and required text demonstrate the growing influence of the social sciences in the fields of Ethics, Sociology, Sunday School Pedagogy, Pastoral Theology, Ecclesiology, and Church Efficiency.

40. Wills, *Southern Baptist Theological Seminary*.

41. Wills, *Southern Baptist Theological Seminary*, 230–350.

Make a Difference.[42] Dobbins dedicated a chapter to each man highlighting their influence at SBTS. *Axioms of Religion* by Mullins and *Psychology and Preaching* by Gardner made the ideas of pragmatism and psychology common. This seemed to grant Dobbins permission to explore those disciplines and their application in his writing, teaching, and formation of pastoral duties.[43]

This study will proceed to the work of Dobbins's most well-known student, Wayne Oates. Oates is significant as the individual who employed much of Dobbins's theory in the field of pastoral care. *Pastoral Counseling, The Christian Pastor,* and *The Bible in Pastoral Care,* all by Oates demonstrate the integration of psychological theory with theological principles. Oates became a leader in the CPE movement, and his works are crucial to the thesis of this study in order to prove the modification of historical pastoral care in favor of specialized pastoral counseling saturated with psychological theory and clinical practice.[44] In "Organizational Development and Pastoral Care," Oates clearly credited Dobbins as responsible for the alteration in pastoral care at Southern Seminary.[45]

STATEMENT OF THE PROBLEM

Since the middle of the 1940s there has been a clear dependence upon the psychology of religion and CPE reflected in the courses offered by the seminaries of the SBC.[46] Among the most noted Southern Baptist leaders to promote the clinical theory of pastoral counseling as helpful in pastoral care was Wayne Oates. Oates taught at The Southern Baptist Theological

42. Dobbins, *Great Teachers.* See the corresponding chapters named for each individual.

43. Dobbins, *Great Teachers,* 28–29 and 64.

44. Babler, et al. *Counseling by the Book,* 28–33. Dobbins introduced Oates to Boisen, Ackerly, Sherrill and Dicks, who were influential in the CPE movement. See *Great Teachers,* 102–3.

45. Oates, "Organizational Development and Pastoral Care," 349–60. This issue of the *Review and Expositor* is a *Festschrift* in honor of Dobbins's service at Southern Seminary. The other essays in honor of Dobbins will be valuable in understanding the scope of his contribution to theological education in the SBC.

46. Southern Baptist Theological Seminary, *Catalogue of The Southern Baptist Theological Seminary, Forty-Eighth Session, 1906–1907,* 36–37. Southern Baptist Theological Seminary Annual Catalogue, 1948. Although the psychology of religion was taught prior to 1947, the new department was not official until Wayne Oates completed his PhD. Oates et al., "Pastoral Care," in Cox and Allen, *The Encyclopedia of Southern Baptists,* 1073–79. This encyclopedia explains the dependence of the SBC seminaries' training upon Psychology of Religion. Oates, *An Introduction to Pastoral Counseling, v.*

Seminary in Louisville, Kentucky, from 1947 to 1974.[47] He is most remembered for his cross-disciplinary approach to pastoral care, especially the utilization of CPE. He is viewed by many as the man who shaped pastoral counseling in the Southern Baptist Convention.[48] Oates, however, credited Gaines Stanley Dobbins with the redirection of pastoral care within the SBC, referring to him as "the father of the pastoral care movement at Southern Baptist Theological Seminary."[49] What impact did the methodology and ideology of Gaines Dobbins have upon the practical ministry of pastoral care within Southern Seminary and, consequently, Southern Baptist churches?

THESIS STATEMENT

This work will demonstrate that Gaines Stanley Dobbins synthesized an ideology and methodology from business efficiency, progressive education, psychology of religion, and educational psychology, which he implemented through religious education, and, in so doing, he inaugurated professionalized counseling within the Southern Baptist Convention.

DEFINITION OF TERMS

Pastoral Care and Pastoral Counseling

The two phrases to describe the pastoral function of care and counseling will be used synonymously in this book unless expressly stated as being different in the immediate context. Dobbins and Oates used the two phrases at times synonymously. In the work of Oates pastoral care was considered as the broad category of pastoral ministry and pastoral counseling became a specialty function of pastoral care. Pastoral counseling has morphed in meaning from the traditional promotion of self-denial to self-realization,

---

47. Babler, et al., *Counseling by the Book*, 28. Oden, *Care of Souls in the Classic Tradition*, 30. Moore, "Counseling and the Authority of Christ," 6. Southern Baptist Theological Seminary may be referred to as Southern Seminary or SBTS throughout this prospectus.

48. Babler, et al., *Counseling by the Book*, 28. Moore, "Counseling and the Authority of Christ," 6. Thornton, *Professional Education for Ministry*, 155.

49. Oates, "Organizational Development and Pastoral Care," 349. Dr. Gaines Dobbins was the man who organized the Department of Psychology of Religion and Pastoral Care which infused a new philosophy for practical ministry and sought to professionalize the pastorate.

conforming to what has been referred to as a therapeutic culture.[50] Oates distinguished pastoral care or pastoral work as "informal" and pastoral counseling as "formal," but in essence the philosophy, technique, and practice of the two remain the same.[51] When pastoral care and pastoral counseling are used in their generic and non-technical sense, Oates's definition will be utilized: "Pastoral counseling may be said to be a systematic effort to apply inductive, clinical, and scientific method to the accepted function of the minister as he confers with persons about their personal problems and life destiny."[52]

I will, on occasion, refer to pastoral care in a distinct form referring to it in the classic tradition. When used in this way the phrase will be stated in context and will be referring to the classic tradition in pastoral care as discussed by Thomas Oden, Andrew Purves, and E. Brooks Holifield.[53] Broadly, Oden described pastoral care as, "that branch of Christian theology that deals with care of persons by pastors."[54] Oden also offers a more complete definition:

> Pastoral care is a unique enterprise that has its own distinctive subject-matter (care of souls); its own methodological premise (revelation); its own way of inquiring into it subject-matter (attentiveness to the revealed Word through Scripture and its consensual tradition of exegesis); its own criteria of scholarly authenticity (accountability to canonical text and tradition); its own way of knowing (listening to sacred Scripture with the historic church); its own mode of cultural analysis (with worldly powers bracketed and divine providence appreciated); and its own logic (internal consistency premised upon revealed truth).[55]

50. Holifield, *A History of Pastoral Care in America*, 12. Reiff, *Triumph of the Therapeutic*. Clebsch and Jaekle, *Pastoral Care in Historic Perspective*.

51. Oates, *Pastoral Counseling*, 100–119 and 123.

52. Oates, *Pastoral Counseling*, 56. This does not assume that everything that Oates said or did is an imitation of Dobbins. However, Oates clearly credited Dobbins with his introduction to CPE and psychology of religion. Dobbins offered a similar definition in, *Building Better Churches*, 27–28.

53. Oden, *Classical Pastoral Care*. Oden, *Care of Souls in the Classic Tradition*. Purves, *Pastoral Theology in the Classic Tradition*. Holifield, *A History of Pastoral Care in America*.

54. Oden, *Classical Pastoral Care*, 5.

55. Oden, *Classical Pastoral Care*, 4. While Oden is a bit more ecumenical in the authority he grants to church traditions and ecumenical councils, this is an acceptable definition, since pastoral care is seen as the task of the church to care for souls by means of God's Word.

As Purves described it, classic pastoral care, he was concerned with "the fundamental connection between the Christian doctrines of God, redemption, and hope, and the pastoral ministry of the church."[56]

Efficiency

The concept of business efficiency was crucial in Dobbins's development of specialized counseling as a function of the local church. The definition used for efficiency in this work will be from Dobbins's own pen. "Efficiency," wrote Dobbins, "therefore, is the quality of producing effective results; or it is a quality of mind, or of body, producing, or capable of producing, maximum result with a given effort, or a given result with minimum effort."[57]

Psychology of Religion

The purpose of this book is not to pursue a history of the psychology of religion as a discipline, as many have had difficulty identifying its origins.[58] I will utilize the definition proposed by E. D. Starbuck and affirmed by George A. Coe, "The Psychology of Religion has for its work to carry the

---

56. Purves, *Pastoral Theology in the Classic Tradition*, 4.

57. Dobbins, *The Efficient Church*, 12. James Ryan, Allen Graves and Austin Dobbins report the degree to which the business models of efficiency and scientific management of Harrington Emerson, Frederick Taylor and Roger Babson influenced Dobbins's methods of church efficiency. Ryan, "Administrative Theory of Gaines Stanley Dobbins." Dobbins, *Gaines S. Dobbins*, 64.

58. Drakeford, *Psychology in Search of a Soul*, 1–15. Drakeford tended to trace the psychology of religion to men like Hegel, Freubach, and James as formalizers of the discipline. He attempted to explain that Jonathan Edwards was the first man to truly observe religious experience in a scientific manner, 11–15. Oates, *What Psychology Says About Religion*, 77–81. Oates utilized Kierkegaard and Schleiermacher as the inaugurators, especially as it pertains to understanding religious experience, 77–81. Coe, *The Psychology of Religion*, 1–13. Coe, however, seemed to clarify the use of these men in developing the ideology, since they would fit categorically within the philosophical history of religion, rather than the scientific understanding of psychology of religion, as defined above. Coe explains this transition of understanding coincided with the scientific shift in the definition of psychology, which, in turn, provided another way to explain religious experience from the scientific vantage point, rather than from a philosophical or theological dogma. Coe believed, "a distinctly new departure was made when systematic, empirical methods were employed in order to analyze religious conversion and thus place it within the general perspective of the natural sciences," and therefore, psychology of religion truly began with G. Stanley Hall, A. H. Daniels, J. H. Leuba, E.D. Starbuck (*The Psychology of Religion*), and W. James, *Varieties of Religious Experience*. See Coe n1, 1.

well-established methods of science into the analysis and organization of the facts of the religious consciousness, and to ascertain the laws which determine its growth."[59]

Clinical Pastoral Education

This book will depend upon Oates's definition of CPE:[60]

> Clinical Pastoral Education is an opportunity in a church, hospital, or other clinical facility for persons in church-related vocations to relate theological studies to interpersonal relationships through personal supervision by a pastoral supervisor within the framework of a theological education and in relation to the ministries of the church.[61]

SIGNIFICANCE OF THE SUBJECT FOR RESEARCH

The study of Gaines Stanley Dobbins is not a new topic for study. As mentioned in the literature review, there have been several doctoral theses written on differing aspects of his life and work. Dobbins was most well-known as a church administrator and religious educator, based on his innovative contributions in these two disciplines. Dobbins was mentioned within

59. E. D. Starbuck, *The Psychology of Religion*, 1. Starbuck wrote the first full-length book on the subject. Coe, in, *The Psychology of Religion*, affirmed Starbuck's definition as the scientific study of the nature of religious experience. But, Coe clearly stated that the science of psychology cannot achieve the fullness of the religious experience or the process of self-realization; he leaves the interpretation open to personal interpretation. See n1, 13. Oates, *Psychology of Religion*, 15. Oates said, "The psychology of religion is an effort to identify the human experience of the divine, to identify and purge the distinctly idolatrous distinctions of religious experience, and to unmask the elements of human deceptiveness in what otherwise would seem to be lofty, transcendental religiosity. As such, the psychology of religion is a combined effort to appreciate the idea of the holy in human life and to keep the experiences of the religious consciousness down to earth." Drakeford, *Psychology in Search of a Soul*, 1 and 4. Drakeford, first stated that, "Psychology of religion is seen as a returning to the historic function and thus is 'psychology in search of a soul.'" He later seemed to clarify with a more generic definition relating to the new science: "Psychology of religion more specifically examines the influence of religion on individuals and their adjustment to life."

60. Oates, "Gaines S. Dobbins," in Dobbins, *Great Teachers*, 102. Boisen, *Exploration of the Inner World*. Hiltner, *Preface to Pastoral Theology*. Wise, *Pastoral Psychotherapy*. These works help to understand the history of CPE. See also, Thornton, "Critique of Clinical Pastoral Education," 1960.

61. Oates, *An Introduction to Pastoral Counseling*, 325.

discussion regarding the development of pastoral care and counseling in the Southern Baptist Convention; however, he is mentioned most often as a tertiary contributor to the body of knowledge and development of the discipline. This work will be used to alter that opinion by presenting evidence placing him within the top tier of contributors in the expansion of pastoral care and counseling as a professional pastoral duty within the SBC.

It is not that pastoral care had not been done before 1920. Martin Luther, Washington Gladden, Richard Baxter, Ichabod Spencer, Puritan authors, and many earlier church leaders believed that one of the primary roles of the pastor was to minister the Word of God in the care and cure of souls.[62] E. Brooks Holifield has written the foremost work demonstrating the shift in mode and means of soul care in America.[63] He demonstrated the dependence upon psychology and chronologically traces its steady influence upon the churches in the United States. Thomas Oden, in *Care of Souls in the Classic Tradition*, identified Wayne Oates as the leading literary contributor regarding soul care from the ranks of Southern Baptists.[64] His assertion is true, but he does not identify the specifics of the transition from classic soul care to modern pastoral counseling in the SBC, since this was not Oden's intention. My goal is to present an argument identifying Gaines Dobbins as the primary Southern Baptist responsible for promoting the ideology and methodology that led to the psychological and clinical focus for the specialization of pastoral care.

The current debate regarding mental illness within the SBC may benefit from such a work that attempts to explain the origins of psychologically motivated training for pastors and care for parishioners of SBC churches. The task force chosen to raise awareness of mental illness in churches and the means to minister to those labeled as mentally ill may benefit from the body of knowledge compiled in this work. The implications of the arguments in this particular work will dispute a number of assumptions that are considered to be *scientific* or *empirical*, based on the origins of these terms as used in the early twentieth century in the convention. The words, *scientific* and *empirical*, were used to describe reliable sources of knowledge and were motivating terminology in the expansion of curriculum for theological training in efficiency, religious education, and pastoral counseling. The word *empirical* was used to intrude upon the primary position of the authority and sufficiency of Scripture. This and other works may at least

---

62. Tappert, *Luther: Letters of Spiritual Counsel*. Baxter, *The Reformed Pastor*. Gladden, *The Christian Pastor*. Spencer, *A Pastor's Sketches*. Deckard, *Helpful Truths in Past Places*.

63. Holifield, *A History of Pastoral Care in America*.

64. Oden, *Care of Souls in the Classic Tradition*, 28–32.

raise the question regarding the degree of faith Christians choose to place in the philosophy of psychology, as an assumed empirical science, and its dominating grip on western culture and religious thought.

CHAPTER SUMMARIES

The first chapter provides the immediate historical setting. Dobbins attended Southern Seminary as a student prior to being called as a professor. E. Y. Mullins, Charles Spurgeon Gardner and John R. Sampey introduced him to several philosophies that later, as a professor, structured his views of ecclesiology and pastoral theology. Mullins held considerable influence over Southern Seminary as its president and called for a new direction in the teaching of education and church efficiency. Mullins urged Dobbins to lead the new department, a position he held for thirty-six years at SBTS. Discontent with his methods of teaching, Dobbins wanted to resign after his first year. This chapter will explain, chronologically, how Mullins encouraged Dobbins to seek new methods of pedagogy from progressives who taught a person-centered approach to teaching and learning.

Chapter 2 familiarizes the reader with key figures within progressive education, psychology of religion, religious education, and the scientific management of efficiency. Through Dobbins's writings, this chapter will demonstrate the foundations of his religious education and pastoral care as other than Scripture. I will highlight the influence of George A. Coe, Harrington Emerson, John Dewey, and E. L. Thorndike whose theories helped Dobbins coalesce his view of pastoral care with the new science of psychology.

Chapter 3 shifts the focus to the influence of Dobbins as professor. "Dobbinology," was the term used by Dobbins's students to describe his lecture notes, containing progressive methodologies for practice within church ministries. Dobbins's course notes and books are examined to determine the ideology and methodology behind his pedagogy and pastoral care. The subsequent sections of the chapter will highlight the subtle, but identifiable dependence upon methodology and practice over orthodoxy. Due to the nature of the symbiotic relationship between belief and practice, I will demonstrate the erosion of orthodox pastoral care, in favor of the new practices of professionalized pastoral counseling.

Chapter 4 chronicles the emergence of the first department of psychology of religion within the Southern Baptist Convention. This chapter relies upon the work of Wayne Oates, whose methodological approach to pastoral care became the fruition of the specialized philosophy promoted by Dobbins. The value of this chapter hinges upon my ability to demonstrate the influence of Dobbins's ideologies and influence within the work of Oates. It will be revealed in this chapter that Oates clearly identified Dobbins as the father of pastoral care in the Southern Baptist Convention.

The conclusion will demonstrate a few of the deleterious effects of professionalized pastoral care within the Southern Baptist Convention. Special attention will be given to explain the academic approach to pastoral care and counseling within the seminaries supported by Southern Baptists cooperation. The chapter will conclude with a brief synthesis of the arguments supporting the thesis and provide suggestions for further research.

Chapter 1

The New Department of Practical Studies

INTRODUCTION

Gaines Dobbins joined the faculty of Southern Seminary during the presidency of E. Y. Mullins, in 1920.[1] Dobbins remained at the seminary in Louisville, Kentucky for thirty-six years until his retirement in 1956.[2] During his time on campus, he was influenced by many of the faculty members and thereby began to formulate his philosophy relative to theology, education, and ministry. While the majority of his learning experiences at Southern Seminary were positive, it should be noted that a few significant influences were negative. These later prompted his determination to search for alternative methods of pedagogy and modern innovation in theological education.

Dobbins enrolled as a theological student on the heels of major discord at Southern Seminary.[3] Controversies sparked in the denomination

---

1. Dobbins, *Gaines S. Dobbins*, 57–58.

2. Dobbins, *Zest for Living*, 119. Dobbins, upon his retirement from Southern Seminary in 1956, would serve at Golden Gate Baptist Theological Seminary as a distinguished professor for ten more years.

3. Dobbins, "Oral History Interviews," 10. Dobbins described in his "Oral History Interviews" that the residue of the controversy was still alive and well when he arrived on campus as a student. This was about ten years after Whitsitt's resignation and the election of Mullins to the presidency.

between Baptists who were aligned with traditional theological positions and those considered modern or progressive in their thinking. It seemed as though the price of stability for the seminary was to allow the academic liberty of a small portion of progressive thinkers. Nevertheless, the seminary began to stabilize as an institution under the new leadership of E. Y. Mullins.[4]

In order to gain proper context for Dobbins's methodological approach to education and pastoral care, the reader will benefit from a brief understanding of the personalities and teaching methods that were prominent at Southern Seminary during his years as a student.[5] While the epistemological position of Scripture at Southern Seminary did not appear to be any different than in previous days under the leadership of James Boyce and John Broadus, there were hints of theological liberalism and of a breach in the firmly held doctrine of Scripture's authority as a small number professors began to consider other sources of truth.[6]

MULLINS AND THE SOUTHERN SEMINARY FACULTY[7]

The Southern Baptist Theological Seminary began in 1859, the same year as Darwin's *Origin of the Species* was published. After a brief hiatus during

4. Dobbins, "The Southern Baptist Theological Seminary," Dobbins Papers, Box 10, Folders 15, 9.

5. Dobbins did not become the educator he was simply through his own independent study. As several of his works describe, his professors at SBTS had deep influence on his life and thinking. See Dobbins, *Great Teachers*, as an example of the tribute Dobbins paid to his professors.

6. The scientific revolution was beginning to demand intellectual ascent from academic institutions in the West. Theological educators also began to experience the pressure to succumb to alternate sources of authority as an explanation of origins of man, human nature, conscience of man, and theories of learning. The faculty from Southern Seminary tended to follow the cultural current sweeping higher education in America. As will be evidenced in the discussion to come, psychology and pragmatism made scriptural authority questionable and experiential knowledge to be on par with scriptural truth. Geisler, *Christian Apologetics*, 65. Geisler said that, "experientialism offers experience as the final court of appeal. The experience may be special or general, private or available generally, but it is the self-attesting character of experience which verifies the truth-attached claim." Geisler identified Schleiermacher as creator of one of the major forms of experientialism (68–72). As reported in the following section, the work of Schleiermacher had significant impact on Mullins. If experience is the "proof" of truth, the Scripture is only subjective in nature, describing the experiences and truths of other men. This idea made pragmatism seem all the more enticing as a methodology to have religious experiences that prove truth.

7. The men discussed in the following section best represent the influences upon Dobbins at Southern Seminary in relation to the thesis of this book. The men were

the Civil War, the new seminary reconvened in November 1865.[8] In a short time, the young school would reap consequences from the influence of evolutionary biology through the teachings of one of its own professors, Crawford H. Toy. The historical criticism of Julius Wellhausen influenced Toy's interpretation of the creation narrative, and the issue did not go away when Toy was advised to resign at the trustee meeting in May of 1879.[9] The leadership of Southern Seminary continued to have difficulty navigating through liberal leaning scholarship with some professors.

The Whitsitt Controversy in the closing years of the nineteenth century formed battle lines for many associated with the seminary and the denomination. Lines were formed in relation to a published position of Baptist origins by President William H. Whitsitt of Southern Seminary. A corollary of the debate was whether the seminary would allow academic freedom of research. Whitsitt's administration "was marked by controversy" and had nearly "wrecked the institution," according to Dobbins, "The evident issue was the origin of Baptists and of immersion as a mode of baptism, but personal matters also were involved."[10] Southern Baptist historian William A. Mueller said the issue of liberty in academic research was a primary factor in the dispute.[11] Wills agreed, but explained the legitimate fear of many within the denomination:

> The Whitsitt Controversy revealed a deepening rift within the denomination. Although tensions between Landmarkers and non-Landmarkers set the controversy in motion, this rift was of a different character. It was a rift between traditional orthodoxy and the new progressive evangelicalism of many seminary graduates. Many were "evangelical liberals" who demanded freedom from denominational and creedal constraints. Whitsitt

chosen intentionally because of the nature of their influence upon Dobbins. This is not to say that Mullins, Gardner and Sampey were the only men to influence Dobbins during his time as a student at SBTS. A. T. Robertson, W. O. Carver, and B. H. Dement all had considerable influence in the life of Dobbins and the future shape of his ministry. Dobbins wrote a tribute chapter to Robertson in *Great Teachers* demonstrating that fact. Dobbins also wrote a chapter in tribute to Carver which did not make the book, but appeared as an article: Dobbins, "William Owen Carver," 2–6. Dement was hired as the first professor of Sunday School Pedagogy at Southern Seminary and his story and influence will be briefly addressed in a separate section of this chapter: The Need for Efficiency.

8. Dobbins, "The Southern Baptist Theological Seminary," 4.

9. Wills, *Southern Baptist Theological Seminary*, 127.

10. Dobbins, "The Southern Baptist Theological Seminary," 8. Dobbins Papers, "Pen Pictures of Southern Seminary Personalities," Box 10, Folders 15, 4.

11. Mueller, *A History of Southern Baptist Theological Seminary*, 179.

became the accidental martyr to their cause. The controversy set the trajectory of twentieth-century theology at the seminary in a progressive direction.[12]

Whitsitt first came under fire when he anonymously published his opinion regarding Baptist history. He was of the persuasion that Baptists found their beginnings with English Baptists in the seventeenth century. The sentiment of the SBC was that Baptists had succeeded since the days of the New Testament as the true church.[13] For many, this issue of Landmarkism was at stake, but for those on the side of Whitsitt there was a greater battle at hand.[14] The battle was, at least partially, for academic liberty within the seminary. Would a professor be allowed to write his opinion regarding his scholarly findings without fear of reprisals from the trustees and the convention at large?

Academic freedom was not a concern to many of the grassroots Baptists, but they feared that such freedom could become a license to pursue the progressive liberalism that was prevalent around the turn of the twentieth century. The expansion of academic freedom would allow liberal scholarship to enter the seminary in days to follow. For that reason, B. H. Carroll, a trustee at Southern Seminary who would later become the founder and first president of Southwestern Baptist Theological Seminary (SWBTS), stood vehemently against the stance of Whitsitt and pled for his resignation.[15] John Sampey and A. T. Robertson, both faculty members during the controversy, initially supported Whitsitt; but in 1898, Sampey finally convinced Whitsitt to resign at the end of the 1899 academic session.[16]

E. Y. Mullins

The installation of Edgar Young Mullins as the fourth president of Southern Seminary came amid the lingering controversy. Mullins was elected in 1899, at a crucial time in the direction of the institution, to help calm the

12. Wills, *Southern Baptist Theological Seminary*, 228–29.

13. In order to gain a cursory understanding of Landmarkism see Pendleton, "An Old Landmark Reset," in White, *Selected Writings*, 273–321. Also see Pendleton, *Church Manual*.

14. Pendleton, *Church Manual*, 194–210 and 215–29. Mueller, *A History of Southern Baptist Theological Seminary*, 155–78.

15. Both Wills and Mueller stated Carroll's influence as a decisive factor leading to Whitsitt's resignation. T. T. Eaton is reported among the first men to bring attention to Whitsitt's articles and his position as being "heretical" and anti-Baptist.

16. See Mueller, *A History of Southern Baptist Theological Seminary*, 172–73. Also Wills, *Southern Baptist Theological Seminary* 224–25.

dueling sides.[17] Residual effects from Landmarkism, Crawford Toy, and the Whitsitt Controversy remained as he began his tenure.[18] Dobbins said, "President Mullins came to the seminary following the stormiest episode in its history."[19] Mullins was called out of the pastorate to lead the denomination's seminary through its most trying and critical times. Thomas Nettles has aptly called Mullins's presidency, "a theological pivot."[20]

The trustees moved forward in electing Mullins as a compromise and as an attempt for peace, not only for the seminary but for the denomination. According to Dobbins, "Mullins was the unanimous choice of the trustees," he continued, "There was very little debate. They wanted an outsider. They wanted a peacemaker. They wanted a man who could regain the confidence of grassroots Baptists."[21] This is not to insinuate that Mullins was an unqualified candidate, but that the trustees believed him to be the man who could help them move beyond such controversy. Whether or not the trustees were fully aware of Mullins's position regarding the Whitsitt Controversy is difficult to know, but Mullins had not been neutral during the disputes. Instead, he had written multiple articles in the *Religious Herald* supporting Whitsitt's position.[22] Wills suggested that the trustees were willing to overlook Mullins's support for Whitsitt based on the simple fact that he was not a Landmarker.[23]

Mueller and Wills disagree regarding the loyalty of the faculty after Mullins was elected. Mueller proposed, "The faculty was wholeheartedly behind its new leader,"[24] while Wills argued that, "The division of the faculty did not fully heal."[25] Wills's position is the more plausible of the two based on the personal letters he cited from the faculty at that time.[26] He reported that F. H. Kerfoot and E. C. Dargan had been opposed to Whitsitt and, therefore, were on opposite sides of the matter from Sampey, Robertson,

17. Mohler, "Baptist Theology at the Crossroads," 4–22.

18. Mohler, "Baptist Theology at the Crossroads," 5–6.

19. Dobbins Papers, "Pen Pictures of Southern Seminary Personalities," Box 10, Folders 15, 4.

20. Nettles, "E. Y. Mullins: Reluctant Evangelical," 24.

21. Dobbins, "Oral History Interviews," 10.

22. Mullins, "A Roman Catholic Party among the Baptists," 1. See Mueller, 179–80 and Wills, 234. Also see, Ellis, *A Man of Books*, 32–35.

23. Wills, *Southern Baptist Theological Seminary*, 231–36.

24. Mueller, *A History of Southern Baptist Theological Seminary*, 181.

25. Wills, *Southern Baptist Theological Seminary*, 235–36.

26. Wills, *Southern Baptist Theological Seminary*, 233–36. See n10–18.

McGlothlin, and Carver. Moreover, Kerfoot left the faculty the same year
Mullins was elected and Dargan resigned only seven years later.[27]

Student enrollment had dropped during the controversy, but rebound-
ed to over three hundred soon after Mullins began, which indicated relative
stability at the institution.[28] He claimed a medial position being both "progressive as well as conservative," in his theology.[29] Wills reported, "Before
Mullins, Southern Baptist theologians, with traditional Protestants generally, began with the reliability of the Bible and then established Christian
doctrine from it."[30] Mullins in his book, *Why is Christianity True?*, introduced his views on experience as an,

> . . . innovation in general discussions of Christian evidences and
> have employed Christian experience as an important evidence
> of Christianity. This form of evidence appeals with irresistible
> force to men and women who "know whom they have believed";
> and at the same time it is, as Mr. Romanes asserted, a class of
> facts open to investigation of all seekers for the truth, and
> should be allowed its proper weight in determining the result.[31]

27. Wills, *Southern Baptist Theological Seminary*, 236.

28. Dobbins, "The Southern Baptist Theological Seminary," Dobbins Papers, Box
10, Folder 15.

29. Edgar Y. Mullins to Charles S. Gardner, May 4 1907, Letterbook 31, 1906–1908,
The Southern Baptist Theological Seminary, 340. This compromised position of Mullins
confirms Yarnell's argument that, "Mullins's first objective was to reconcile the warring
parties among Southern Baptists. His second was to reconcile Southern Baptists with
mainline Protestantism." Yarnell, "Changing Baptist Concepts of Royal Priesthood,"
in Lovegrove, *The Rise of the Laity*, 245. Mullins's success in the latter category mentioned by Yarnell provided sufficient evidence that Southern Seminary paralleled in
progression to mainline Protestant America in their pursuit of Religious Education and
Pastoral Care. The course taken by mainline Protestants in America regarding Pastoral
Care has been best demonstrated and explained by E. Brooks Holifield in *A History of
Pastoral Care in America*. It will be argued briefly in chapter 4 and more fully in chapter
5 that the Southern Baptist denomination followed a similar path as the mainline protestant denominations toward specialization of pastoral care.

30. Wills, *Southern Baptist Theological Seminary*, 247.

31. Mullins, *Why is Christianity True?*, 17. The Mr. Romanes to whom Mullins referred to in this quote is, evidently, George John Romanes. He was one of the men who
carried the mantle of the evolutionary biology of Charles Darwin. He believed in a similar cognitive processing between animals and humans. The scientific study of behavior
and mental processing based on phylogenetic history and development of behavior, he
termed comparative psychology. Mullins used Romanes as an authority throughout the
book, utilizing his book *Thoughts on Religion*, edited by Charles Gore in 1895. In chapter twenty of Mullins's *Why is Christianity True?*, he discussed the relation of Christ to
Christian experience. He positively rejects an "idealistic" Christ from the Gospels and
a "Ritschlian Christ," which seemed positive until he promoted, "the Christ of recent
psychology," to explain the validity of Christian experience. In this chapter he relied

The works of Friedrich Schleiermacher, William James, and Borden Parker Browne contributed to the compromise in Mullins's thinking relative to traditional beliefs in the truths of Scripture.[32] "Mullins," Mohler wrote, "led Southern Baptists to adopt a new approach to theology. He reconstructed Christian doctrine on the basis of experience."[33] In other words, the Personalism of Browne led Mullins to a "critical appreciation for the centrality of the person as the starting point for theological understanding," rather than the Scriptures.[34] This seems to be a dynamic modification in the epistemological basis for theology that affected the form of theological education at Southern Seminary for years to come.

According to Mullins, experience constricted the Scripture's functional authority for believers. Wills said, "Mullins's experientialist approach limited the sense in which the Bible could be the Christian's objective authority."[35] For Mullins, experience was true in an objective sense.[36] Mullins led the seminary in the very direction that had caused such controversy under Whitsitt.[37]

W. T. Conner from Southwestern Seminary held similar convictions to that of Mullins.[38] "I do believe," said Conner, "in the infallibility of the fundamental teachings of the Bible. I believe we can depend on these and realize them in our own experience, and after all, as I see it, that is what we need and all need."[39] Conner also said of the inspiration of the Bible: "inspiration acted not as an external clamp to put on man's mind . . . it acted

---

upon Romanes, William James, E. D. Starbuck, G. Stanley Hall and George Albert Coe as experts that should shape one's understanding of Christian experience and empirical study of that experience. With the exception of Romanes, the other men are significant in the formation of Dobbins's approach to ministry. It is here that the reader can see the greatest influence of Mullins upon Dobbins. As will be discussed later, Mullins encouraged Dobbins to go study with each of the above mentioned men in order to build his view of church efficiency and religious education.

32. See Mullins, "Pragmatism, Humanism and Personalism," 501–15. Mohler, "Baptist Theology at the Crossroads," 8. Wills, *Southern Baptist Theological Seminary*, 237–47. Crouch, "The Influence of William James." Crouch said, "Mullins's published works, produced later during his years as president of SBTS, reveal the influence of Friedrich Schleiermacher's liberal theology, Borden Parker Bowne's personalism, and William James's works on religious experience, philosophy, and psychology" (172).

33. Wills, *Southern Baptist Theological Seminary*, 242.

34. Mohler, "Baptist Theology at the Crossroads," 8.

35. Wills, *Southern Baptist Theological Seminary*, 248.

36. Wills, *Southern Baptist Theological Seminary*, 248.

37 Dobbins, "Oral History Interview," 10.

38. Sutton, *The Baptist Reformation*, 410.

39. Conner, *Revelation in God*, 86–90.

rather as a liberating and releasing power," enabling, "each man to be his best self."[40] It was under the leadership of Mullins that Conner completed his ThD degree; his thesis was written on "Pragmatism and Theology."[41] The topic selected by Conner is not surprising considering Mullins was his supervisor. As Mohler explained,

> The central thrust of E. Y. Mullins's theological legacy is his focus on individual experience. Whatever his intention, this massive methodological shift in theology set the stage for doctrinal ambiguity and theological minimalism. The compromise Mullins sought to forge in the 1920s was significantly altered by later generations, with personal experience inevitably gaining ground at the expense of revealed truth.[42]

The epistemological convictions of Mullins led to experience as much or more than Scripture, as a legitimate source of authority. This influence was not contained in Mullins alone, but most agree that its roots within Southern Baptist doctrine began with him.[43]

Dobbins was affected by Mullins's writings while enrolled at Mississippi College. He even attributed a small portion of credit to Mullins for his salvation experience, even though the two were not acquainted at that time. A self-proclaimed agnostic when he entered college, Dobbins was faced with the claims of Christ.[44] Prior to his conversion in his college Bible class with H. F. Sproles, Dobbins was required to read *Why is Christianity True?* as a course text. He remained a skeptic, but after his conversion, he would write in a private journal words from Mullins that aided him through his skepticism, "The glory of Christianity is that it does not force the will. Men must choose for themselves [conclusion] in order to reach their highest

40. As found in Sutton, *The Baptist Reformation*, 411. Conner, "Letter to E. B. Atwood."

41. George and Dockery, *Theologians of the Baptist Tradition*, 205–7. James Leo Garrett authored the chapter on Walter Thomas Conner and he demonstrated E.Y. Mullins's profound impact upon his theological convictions. Garrett reported that Mullins was Conner's major professor in theology, W. O. Carver was his minor professor in the philosophy of religion and B. H. Dement was his minor professor in psychology of religion.

42. Mohler, "Baptist Theology at the Crossroads," 17.

43. Wills, *Southern Baptist Theological Seminary*, 230–72. Sutton, *The Baptist Reformation*, 409. Sutton says Mullins, "was probably the most influential theologian in the history of Southern Baptists." The repercussion of Mullins's ideology is evident in W. T. Conner, a prominent former professor at Southwestern Baptist Theological Seminary, who demonstrated the percolating effects of Mullins's view of pragmatism and Christian experience.

44. Dobbins, *Gaines S. Dobbins*, 20.

attainments. Moral sonship cannot be imposed on an evil and sinful nature. Christianity respects personality, individuality."[45]

Once Gaines Stanley Dobbins became a student at Southern Seminary, he was among the men deeply indebted to the work of Mullins.[46] He recounted, "As I seek to recall the teachers who influenced me the most during a more than ordinary period of schooling and then a long lifetime of theological teaching, I am constrained to put at the head of the list Edgar Young Mullins."[47] As a student, Dobbins took both Systematic and Biblical Theology with Mullins. "[Mullins] stirred the smoldering inner fire," said Dobbins, "into a blaze that ever after continued to burn more brightly."[48] By Dobbins's recollection, these were the theology lectures that became one of his mentor's most famous works, *The Christian Religion in Its Doctrinal Expression.*[49] Malcolm B. Yarnell, III, called this work in systematic theology by Mullins his *magnum opus.*[50] Although a general consensus would agree the work maintained Southern Baptist orthodoxy,[51] Yarnell, asserted an interesting nuance:

> Although its theological content was generally conservative, his methodological dependence on experience paralleled the employment of religious consciousness in the liberal agenda established by Schleiermacher. Mullins sought to ground doctrine first in personal experience but without denigrating Scripture.[52]

Yarnell is not alone in his critique of Mullins's thought. Mullins's contemporaries saw the seed of pragmatism and experientialism in his teachings and writings.[53] Dobbins testified to the pragmatic bent of Mullins in his tribute chapter from *Great Teachers Make a Difference:*

---

45. Dobbins, *Gaines S. Dobbins*, 29.

46. Dobbins, *Great Teachers*, 23–35.

47. Dobbins, *Great Teachers*, 25.

48. Dobbins, *Great Teachers*, 24.

49. Dobbins, *Great Teachers*, 27.

50. Yarnell, "Edgar Young Mullins," in Larsen, *Biographical Dictionary*, 459.

51. Weaver, *Axioms of Religion*, vii. Mohler, "Baptist Theology at the Crossroads," 4–22. "In the eyes of some conservatives, Mullins was attempting to save Christianity from science by forfeiting its very foundation of truth," 10. Russell Moore in this same issue of the journal claimed that Mullins did not favor the "new orthodoxy."

52. Yarnell, "Edgar Young Mullins," in Larsen, *Biographical Dictionary*, 459.

53. Mohler, "Baptist at the Crossroads," 10. According to Mohler, J. Gresham Machen was more concerned with the way Mullins distinguished science, religion, and philosophy into three separate categories.

Dr. Mullins possessed in rare degree the quality which we speak of as "insight." There are two obvious ways of arriving at truth. One is by the process of research, analysis and synthesis, and of painstaking observation and experimentation. The other is by insight, the quick intuitive perception of truth that lies beyond and above the plodding search of the investigator. The two processes are not incompatible. A moment of insight may mean years of research for verification; and the long pathway of research may suddenly be rewarded by the flash of insight that illuminates the pathway of the tedious climb. The truly creative thinker and teacher is the one who combines both processes and is at once the pragmatist and the idealist.[54]

As scholars are further removed in time from Mullins, they have been less reluctant to reveal the seeds of his pragmatism. Modern authors appear compelled to reveal the fruits of his teaching that placed experience and results on level ground with the authority of Scripture. Their compositions have been in effort to unveil the negative effects of Mullins's philosophy and theology upon the SBC.[55] Thomas Nettles, evincing a conclusion similar to that of Yarnell, described Mullins's view of the Scripture relative to experience:

As a theologian, Mullins worked energetically to create a new theological paradigm for the defense of evangelical Christianity. Receiving Scripture primarily as the transmitter of genuine religious experience, Mullins concluded that attempts to explain "textual errors, scientific, or historical deviations from exact truth, discrepancies of various kinds" was an attempt to do more than faith required. In religion, Scripture is "final and authoritative" but we must avoid debate on the grounds of history and criticism so that our representation of Christian faith will not be merely intellectual. Truth must be assimilated experientially, not "imposed by authority of any kind, whether pope or church or Bible."[56]

54. Dobbins, *Great Teachers*, 30. Dobbins alluded to the process of insight as having the ability to illuminate the pathway of the tedious climb toward truth. This seems to refer to insight and experience as the illuminator of truth rather than the Scriptures or the work of the Holy Spirit alone. Dobbins also affirmed the pragmatic approach of Mullins toward understanding Christian experience and therefore, truth.

55. Schreiner, "E. Y. Mullins in Retrospect," 1–88. The journal contains articles by Mohler, Nettles, Thornbury and Moore, Sean Lucas and two articles by Mullins. Crouch, "The Influence of William James." Crouch described in detail the effects in curriculum and pastoral theology due to Mullins's influence.

56. Nettles, "E. Y. Mullins: Reluctant Evangelical," 29. In this reference Nettles

Dobbins clearly associated Mullins with the pragmatic philosophy and psychology promoted by William James. Dobbins said, "As teacher of Systematic Theology, Dr. Mullins made a bold departure from the text-proof method. He came under the influence of William James, the noted Harvard philosopher and psychologist, whose *Varieties of Religious Experience* had opened a new avenue of approach to theology."[57] In his writings, Dobbins often highlighted the influence of James upon the Southern Seminary president.[58] In the following example, Dobbins described how the influence of James led Mullins to exalt experience as a proper source of authority:

> [Mullins] was deeply influenced by William James's philosophy of pragmatism and was fascinated by his book *Varieties of Religious Experience*. Here he found his clue to a vital approach to theology. To him the Bible was the inspired record of personal experiences with God, God's dealings with men, and men's experiences with one another. He sought to establish theological truths with human values as the frame of reference.[59]

The existential and pragmatic thrusts of Mullins's foci were conspicuous to Dobbins. Theological truths were dependent upon and even revealed by the experiential. Dobbins's understanding of Mullins is not contrary to the modern Baptist scholars cited above.[60] The difference is that Dobbins did not see the danger in the ideology and the practices that resulted.

Dobbins was also appreciative of Mullins's expression of the Baptist faith through his book *Axioms of Religion*. Dobbins heard first-hand the lectures that outlined the individual axioms, "His *Axioms of Religion* undertook to state in the form of axiomatic truths the fundamentals of the Christian faith as it finds expression both in the biblical revelation and in human reaction to this revelation."[61] That which Dobbins used to praise Mullins is now viewed by some SBC scholars as detrimental to orthodoxy. Stan Norman penned the following caustic view of Mullins:

is quoting portions from, Mullins, *The Christian Religion in its Doctrinal Expression*, 10–11.

57. Dobbins Papers, "Pen Pictures of Southern Seminary Personalities," Box 10, Folders 15, 3. In *Great Teachers*, 28.

58. Dobbins, "Oral History Interviews," 42. "I think Mullins's key source, and he made reference again and again to it, was William James." Dobbins, *Great Teachers*, 28. Dobbins Papers, "Pen Pictures of Southern Seminary Personalities," Box 10, Folders 15, 3.

59. Dobbins, *Great Teachers*, 28.

60. See n50 and n55 above. Yarnell, Mohler, Moore, Nettles, Wills and Schreiner are the scholars referred to here.

61. See n50 and n55 above.

Writings on Baptist distinctives that affirm Christian experience as the core distinctive embrace the Enlightenment assumption of individual autonomy. This profound emphasis upon the individual is often expressed in terms of individual freedoms, individual rights, and individual morality. This strand of distinctives can be called "Enlightenment Baptist distinctives." This tradition was birthed in Edgar Young Mullins' *The Axioms of Religion: A New Interpretation of the Baptist Faith*. As indicated by the title, Mullins intentionally sought to redefine the existing "Reformation Baptist distinctives" tradition. He wanted to stress that both Christian experience and biblical authority are equal and necessary for developing Baptist distinctives. He did not, however, achieve this balance. His understanding of Christian experience overshadowed his understanding of biblical authority. Christian experience became for Mullins the core distinctive that shaped his understanding of biblical authority.[62]

The authority of experience began to erode the authority of Scripture. In turn, the epistemological standard of Scripture was replaced with the ever modernizing pace of human experience.

Norman is not alone in his important assessment, as Mohler and Yarnell exhibit agreement.[63] Yarnell is concerned that Mullins was "redefining Baptist theology to meet twentieth-century concerns."[64] Mohler attributed a portion of the shift in Baptist identity to Schleiermacher's influence on Mullins. According to Mohler, "Schleiermacher's emphasis on religious experience over revealed knowledge so shaped Mullins's theology that, though points of continuity remained, his teachers could not have recognized their own theological system behind that of their student."[65] For Mullins, this led to focus on soul competency, perhaps, his key axiomatic doctrine.[66]

---

62. Norman, "Fighting the Good Fight," 8–9.

63. Mohler, "Baptist Theology at the Crossroads," 19. Mohler says, "The emphasis on soul competency is, as Mullins must have both hoped and expected, the most enduring element of Mullins's legacy. The concept does underscore the necessity of personal religious experience—including repentance and faith—to the Christian life. But soul competency also serves as an acid dissolving religious authority, congregationalism, confessionalism, and mutual theological accountability." Yarnell, "Changing Baptist Concepts of Royal Priesthood," in Lovegrove, *The Rise of the Laity*, 243 and 249.

64. Yarnell, "Changing Baptist Concepts of Royal Priesthood," in Lovegrove, *The Rise of the Laity*, 243.

65. Mohler, "Baptist Theology at the Crossroads," 12.

66. Mullins expressed soul competency as it relates to the church in this way: "Because the individual deals directly with his Lord and is immediately responsible to him, the spiritual society must needs be a democracy. That is, the church is a community of autonomous individuals under the immediate lordship of Christ held together by a

Mohler continued, "The focus on autonomous individualism led to another theological development that would form the central thrust of Mullins's conception of Baptist identity."[67]

Soul competency was an assertion by Mullins to provide for individualism and freedom of the soul. Yarnell helped to place this axiom in proper perspective:

> Where Landmarkers defined Baptist "distinctives" in terms of a "high church ecclesiology" centered on local churches, Mullins redefined the primary distinctive as "soul competency," a concept for which he offered no biblical support. This was a classic liberal move, using traditional language in a new way.[68]

The individual soul for Mullins was, therefore, exalted by the focus of, "all truth and meaning in the autonomous individual."[69] Yarnell likened the doctrine of soul competency to Nietzche's *ubermench* saying that, "Regeneration in Christ is correlated with 'self-realization,' 'self-determination,' and a Nietzchean 'will to believe.'"[70] Elsewhere, Yarnell asserted that Herschel

---

social bond of common interest, due to a common faith and inspired by common tasks and ends, all of which are assigned to them by the common Lord. The church, therefore, is the expression of the paradoxical conception of the union of absolute monarchy and pure democracy. This we might say is the formula of the church. Every form of polity other than democracy somewhere infringes upon the lordship of Christ." Mullins, *Axiom of Religion*, 129.

67. Mohler, "Baptist Theology at the Crossroads," 12.

68. Yarnell, "Changing Baptist Concepts of Royal Priesthood," in Lovegrove, *The Rise of the Laity*, 245.

69. Mohler, "Baptist Theology at the Crossroads," 17. Mohler is summarizing thoughts from Bloom, *The American Religion*, 200–206. Bloom described Hobbs as, "very much of the moderate school of E. Y. Mullins." (202) Bloom claimed that Hobbs's primary principle used in the *Baptist Faith & Message* was soul competency. In summary, Bloom said, "But all Southern Baptist spiritual experience, as represented by Mullins, finds its center in one doctrine alone . . . the competency of the solitary soul confronting the resurrected Jesus." (206) Bloom characterized himself as a self-appointed religious critic. He recognized soul competency as an "unassailable" doctrine, which had its roots in Mullins. His conclusion demonstrates the danger in the experiential focus of soul competency as later revealed in Dobbins, Hobbs and others who might be considered moderate Southern Baptists. The authority of Scripture is compromised by the search for truth in the experiential. Bloom concluded, "If soul competency is simply a description of an absolutely unmediated and intimate relationship with Jesus, then what precisely is the function of reading and interpreting Scripture?" (207).

70. Yarnell, "Edgar Young Mullins," in Larsen, *Biographical Dictionary*, 460. Yarnell, "Changing Baptist Concepts of Royal Priesthood," in Lovegrove, *The Rise of the Laity*, 246. The language Yarnell used to describe Mullins is portent to the objective advocated by the humanistic psychology of Abraham Maslow and Carl Rogers. This could explain why Dobbins embraced the psychology of Rogers in pastoral care. Nietzche,

Hobbs, chairman of the 1963 *Baptist Faith & Message* Committee, "collapsed all the axioms into 'self-determination in every area of life.'"[71]

With a focus on self-determination and self-realization, Mullins began to shift toward person-centered pedagogy and pastoral function at Southern Seminary. If Yarnell is correct in his assertions, then Mullins's influence upon Dobbins was an accessory that permitted his acceptance of the third force psychology, which expressed similar goals toward self-realization.[72]

The exaltation of man in the doctrine of soul competency of Mullins also affected ecclesiology. Referring to soul competency as a myth, Russell Moore and Greg Thornbury asserted that, "Mullins's myth has been

Beyond Good and Evil, 25. "The non-free will is a piece of mythology; in real life there is only *strong* will and *weak* will. It is almost always a symptom of what the man lacks when a thinker feels something of constraint, necessity, having-to-obey, pressure. And lack of freedom in all his 'casual connections' and 'psychological necessities.' It is revealing to feel these things: the personality betrays itself." Nietzsche, *Thus Spoke Zarathustra*, 309. "Before God!—Now however this God had died! Ye higher men, this God was your greatest danger. Only since he lay in the grave have ye again arisen. Now only cometh the great noontide, now only doth the higher man become—master! Have ye understood this word, O my brethren? Ye are frightened: do your hearts turn giddy? Doth the abyss here yawn for you? Doth the hell-hound here yelp at you? Well! Take heart! Ye higher men! Now only travaileth the mountain of the human future. God hath died: now do *we* desire—the Superman to live." Nietzsche spoke of the superman, or sometimes translated overman, describing that man, as is known now, is to be surpassed. According to Nietzsche, man is to be a bridge to something greater, which is possible through the power of the will. A more progressive definition of the will, which takes into account the theories of modern psychology have been stated by Gardner, "Syllabus of Lectures on Homiletics," 17. He said, "The will is the intelligent reaction of the organism to stimuli." The language of genetic and educational psychology, as well as evolutionary thought is evident in Gardner's definition.

71. Yarnell, "Changing Baptist Concepts of Royal Priesthood," in Lovegrove, *The Rise of the Laity*, 248. Hobbs and Mullins, *The Axioms of Religion*. Hobbs wrote, "The inner impulse to personal and social development under Christ is like an endless spring fixed in the machinery of man's faculties and uncoiling itself through the centuries in ever-increasing vigor and power" (118). Hobbs later added that "Freedom is self-determination . . . Freedom is self-determination in every area of life . . . To have intellectual freedom means to be intellectually self-determined." He added that, "In religious freedom is exemption from State compulsion, social coercion, ecclesiastical or priestly authority, creedal binding, or parental acts" (120). For a basic understanding of Herschel Hobbs and his significance as a Baptist theologian see George and Dockery, *Theologians of the Baptist Tradition*, 216–31. Mullins wrote and Hobbs later revised a statement of Southern Baptists distinctives entitled, *The Axioms of Religion*.

72. Rogers, *Counseling and Psychotherapy*. Rogers, *On Becoming a Person*. The first of the three "forces" of psychology was the psychotherapy of Sigmund Freud. His ideals were followed by the behaviorism most associated with B. F. Skinner as the second "force." Carl Rogers, Rollo May, and Abraham Maslow are most noted as leaders of the third "force" promoting self-realization. This wave of psychological theory is also known as humanistic psychology.

harmful," because, "it provides no basis for ecclesiology."[73] Yarnell agreed, "Mullins's high anthropology and low Christology lead to an impoverished ecclesiology."[74] A person-centered approach to ministry exalts individualism and demotes the functionality of the corporate church body. At the same time, if proper ecclesiology is diminished, the role of the pastorate naturally will be skewed due to the biblical relationship of the pastor to the church as servant-leader.

As will be shown below, low ecclesiology did allow for the redefining of pastoral duties to be more akin to business principles and specialization than the historical view of ministerial calling and duties.[75] The low view of ecclesiology resultant from Mullins could have begun a trickle-down effect favoring Dobbins's formation of the professional pastorate within the SBC, including the specializing of the pastoral duty of soul care.[76]

Before Gaines Dobbins became a professor, Southern Baptist men already were espousing psychology and sociology, attempting to reconcile the theological with the empirical.[77] However, no one had quite synthesized the methodology learned from the two disciplines the same way as Dobbins would during the next forty years. J. M. Price, as Dobbins's contemporary,

73. Moore and Thornbury, "The Mystery of Mullins," 51.

74. Yarnell, "Changing Baptist Concepts of Royal Priesthood," in Lovegrove, *The Rise of the Laity*, 246. The low ecclesiology allowed for a redefinition of pastoral duties, including the care of souls. The church once held as its duty the care of souls, but the pursuit of the clinical practice has abated the classic practice.

75. In chapter 4 I will discuss the trend in curricula at Southern Seminary as evidenced in the seminary catalogues. The catalogues reveal that the separate course in ecclesiology was combined with Sunday School Pedagogy and only given brief attention in that course. Pastoral Theology was also a separate course that combined with Sunday School Pedagogy in the new department under Dobbins, "Church Efficiency and Sunday School Pedagogy." Pastoral Theology cannot be separated from a proper understanding of ecclesiology, but the minimal attention given to both subjects in a combined format fails to represents the importance of the subjects for the minister. See Crouch, "The Influence of William James."

76. As will be demonstrated in subsequent chapters, an appeal to modernity for adaptation of pastoral methodologies was a consistent pattern of Dobbins, possibly learned from Mullins. Norman said, "This strand of distinctives can be called "Enlightenment Baptist distinctives," because of the assumption of individual autonomy, whereas Yarnell likens Mullins's proposals to principles characteristic in humanistic psychology. See Norman, "Fighting the Good Fight," 8–9. See Yarnell, "Changing Baptist Concepts of Royal Priesthood," in Lovegrove, *The Rise of the Laity*, 246, particularly his discussion relative to self-realization as the metaphysical end of soul competency.

77. George and Dockery, *Theologians of the Baptist Tradition*, 205. Walter Rauschenbusch, William O. Carver, B.H. Dement, Charles S. Gardner, Weatherspoon, Mullins, etc., were among the men introducing the social sciences into Baptist education. Dobbins, *Gaines S. Dobbins*, 36. Dobbins, *Great Teachers*, 59–67.

was influenced by many of the same people and taught in parallel and pioneering form at SWBTS.[78] Early on in Dobbins's career Mullins helped to create the foci of practical experience and efficiency in church administration, rather than the traditional tenets of pastoral theology. The following figures represent other major contributors to Dobbins's formal theological education.[79]

Charles Spurgeon Gardner

Upon the retirement of E. C. Dargan, Professor of Ecclesiology and Homiletics, the seminary hired Charles Spurgeon Gardner in 1907. His assignment was to teach Homiletics and Ecclesiology. Gardner never achieved an earned doctorate, but received several honorary doctorates for his work in the ministry. One such degree was the Doctor of Divinity given by Union University. Gardner did have experience with twenty-three years serving different churches in pastoral ministry.[80]

Gardner's influence seems to lack proper recognition among certain scholars and does not adequately represent the same degree of importance described by Dobbins and Weatherspoon, who were among his contemporaries.[81] Gardner's influence is essentially missing from Wills's account of Southern Seminary's history, as he is almost without mention.[82] Mueller slightly referenced Gardner regarding his involvement as a trustee during the Whitsitt Controversy and then again, briefly, as an elected faculty member.[83] E. Brooks Holifield suggested that the influence of psychological theory at Southern Seminary began with Dobbins and Oates while he left unaddressed Gardner's use of the social sciences.[84] Gardner and Mullins, however, gave significant credence to these new sciences of human nature.

Gardner was best known as a pastor and a preacher, but was also a trustee of Southern Seminary during the Whitsitt Controversy. As a pastor

78. Maguire, *J. M. Price: Portrait of a Pioneer*, 82–83.

79. The primary source for the following sections will be Dobbins's own writings as he remembered each of these men. Secondary sources will be used to confirm Dobbins's recollections of the men he revered.

80. Weatherspoon, "Charles Spurgeon Gardner," 186–87.

81. Dobbins, *Great Teachers*, 59–67. Weatherspoon, "Charles Spurgeon Gardner," 183–98.

82. Wills mentions Gardner once, but his mention has nothing to do with his influence as a professor. Wills highlights the near absence of doctrinal preaching from Gardner. See Wills, *History of Southern Seminary*, 241.

83. Mueller, *A History of Southern Baptist Theological Seminary*, 173–74, 206–7.

84. Holifield, *A History of Pastoral Care in America*, 225–27.

in South Carolina, Gardner was an open supporter of Whitsitt. Sampey confided in Gardner and sought his advice on how to proceed once Whitsitt had resigned.[85] Gardner's position regarding the controversy seemed to side him with progressives. Mueller affirmed that Gardner was "a progressive evangelical, who was fully aware of the great changes going on in the society of his day. Consequently, he strongly emphasized the relevance of sociological insight, psychological acumen, and ethical motivation to life-centered preaching."[86] Weatherspoon wrote of Gardner, "his students recognized in him that attitude of mind which he recommended to others—'open-minded conservatism.' His moral and social interpretation of Christian experience differed widely from conventional orthodoxy."[87] Dobbins seemed to affirm the claim that Gardner was more progressive, alluding to his "pioneering in the application of the Christian gospel and ethic to social issues."[88] Dobbins also described Gardner as "soul-hungry and controversial."[89]

The controversy to which Dobbins referred was the accusation that Gardner was preaching the "social gospel."[90] Dobbins reported that a resolution was presented on the convention floor demanding Gardner be fired from the seminary.[91] The criticism raised against Gardner might be substantiated based upon Weatherspoon's report regarding Gardner's dependence upon the social sciences:

> The criticism was that his courses had too much sociology and too little ethical interpretation, and that his book on "Psychology and Preaching" had too much psychological analysis and too little illustration and application to preaching. Today that might be valid criticism, for many students have had good courses in these sciences in college, and all have had the opportunity . . . What was the professor to do when he felt so deeply the value of those things for intelligent communication? Dr. Gardner's answer was to introduce enough sociological knowledge to reveal

85. Mueller, *A History of Southern Baptist Theological Seminary*, 173–74.

86. Mueller, *A History of Southern Baptist Theological Seminary*, 207.

87. Weatherspoon, "Charles Spurgeon Gardner," 192.

88. Dobbins, *Gaines S. Dobbins*, 36.

89. Dobbins, *Gaines S. Dobbins*, 35.

90. Dobbins, "Oral History Interviews," 28.

91. Dobbins, "Oral History Interviews," 28. Gardner preached the convention sermon in 1911 at Jacksonville, FL, according to Barnes, *The Southern Baptist Convention 1845–1953*, Appendix A. Dobbins also added that Gardener was under fire during the same year he preached this sermon. See Dobbins, *Great Teachers*, 64. This researcher could not identify evidence, other than Dobbins's statements, that an official resolution was brought to the convention floor regarding Gardner's teaching of the social gospel.

the ethical task and problem, and enough of psychological facts to reveal the problem of communication and give guidance in persuasion.[92]

Henry Wilder Foote in *Harvard Theological Review* wrote a review of Gardner's book *Psychology and Preaching*. He claimed that Gardner focused primarily upon the "psychological factors" related to the subject of preaching, a topic given little attention by previous teachers of homiletics.[93] Foote further explained that the contents of the book could be learned from any basic course in psychology.[94] Gardner sanctioned this indictment made by Foote in the preface to *Psychology and Preaching*:

> But so far as my knowledge extends there have been few serious efforts to apply modern psychology to preaching. Indeed, the statement might be made even more nearly absolute without doing violence to facts. There have been homiletical works almost without number, applying the formal rules of logic and rhetoric to sermon-making, and books on elocution are even more numerous. But the works discussing the preparation and delivery of sermons rarely, if ever, approach the subject from the standpoint of modern functional psychology. The psychological conceptions underlying most of these treatises belong to a stage of psychological thought long since past.[95]

The controversy surrounding Gardner and the criticism from the so-called fundamentalists seemed to be justified. Gardner's progressive ideas enmeshed with the social sciences led to an epistemic compromise. His writings and lectures reflect a deep dependency upon more ulterior sources of authority.[96] Following the path permitted by Mullins, Gardner's writings reflected the psychology of his era, "which gathered about the study of instincts, faculties, stimulus and response, the emotions, attention, and suggestion."[97] "Dr. Gardner," said Dobbins, "explored the extant literature with great thoroughness and derived from his wide reading many keen insights for the preacher and his preaching. In all of this he was twenty years ahead of his time."[98]

92. Weatherspoon, "Charles Spurgeon Gardner," 193.

93. Foote, Review of *Psychology and Preaching*, 203.

94. Foote, Review of *Psychology and Preaching*, 203.

95. Charles Spurgeon Gardner, *Psychology and Preaching*, Preface.

96. Charles Spurgeon Gardner, *Psychology and Preaching*, Preface. Also see, Gardner, "Syllabus of Lectures on Homiletics."

97. Dobbins, *Great Teachers*, 65.

98. Dobbins, *Great Teachers*, 65.

These various reports regarding Gardner's pedagogy revealed his epistemology. Like Mullins, Gardner valued human experience at least equally to Scripture, if not also to validate the sacred writings. Gardner's "Syllabus of Lectures on Homiletics: Third Quarter" demonstrated his dependence upon psychological principles to dictate his style of preaching.[99] Weatherspoon indicated that Gardner,

> . . . was in no way bringing in strange fire into the temple of theology, or forgetting the purpose of the Seminary. He was simply filling a gap in ministerial education, a gap that he discovered in his own early ministry and which he set out by main strength and awkwardness to fill by private study.[100]

Weatherspoon may be correct in asserting Gardner's intentions, which are not in question. There may have been inadequate teaching on pastoral duties during that time in seminaries at large and at Southern Seminary in particular. The point is that he appended to pastoral training the modern teachings of psychology and sociology that were entangled with atheistic tenets and assumptions promoting a biologically determined and environmentally driven understanding of anthropology.[101]

The entirety of Gardner's third quarter lectures resonated the psychological jargon of his day. His epistemological stance was affirmed with the last sentence of his lecture notes, "Science is coming more and more to confirm [Jesus] in all respects; and the scientific spirit, reinforcing the teaching of Jesus, will ultimately be effective in correcting the lax tendencies of the present day without reverting back to the austerity and puritanical rigor of former standards."[102] Gardner believed the puritanical ethic to be austere and binding. He believed, however, that ethics were necessary so that man did not become lax. The rules of Jesus are not petty, but "appeals to that which is deepest and most universal in man, the primal instincts, and sets

---

99. Gardner, "Syllabus of Lecture on Homiletics: Third Quarter." These notes were found in Southwestern Baptist Theological Seminary's Library. This particular copy seemed be to be J. M. Price's copy of notes when he was a student of Gardner's at Southern Seminary. The date "1/28/14" (January 28, 1914) is inscribed along with Price's signature inside the front flap.

100. Weatherspoon, "Charles Spurgeon Gardner," 198.

101. See Gardner, *Psychology and Preaching*. Grinder, *History of Genetic Psychology*. Vitz, *Psychology as Religion*. Gardner argues for the use and adoption of psychology and the social sciences, whereas Vitz argues that psychology is acting as a pseudo-religion. Grinder traces the history of genetic psychology, using excerpts from primary sources that demonstrate a contrary metaphysic to a Christian's view of God and man.

102. Gardner, "Syllabus of Lectures on Homiletics Lecture," 48.

up standards of universal application."[103] According to Gardner this is how science will confirm Jesus—discovering proper stimuli that will aid man's adherence to his primal instincts.[104]

Gardner was reliant upon science and pragmatic effectiveness as primary sources of truth. Dobbins acknowledged the epistemology of Gardner by explaining the source material for his professor's book on preaching: "Out of a study of general psychology and psychology of religion came Dr. Gardner's *Psychology and Preaching*. Educational psychology had found a firm place in the study and practice of teaching."[105] Dobbins agreed with Gardner's use of the social sciences. He relied especially upon psychology to dictate his methodology in ways consubstantial to Gardner's method of homiletics.[106]

Dobbins was captivated also by Professor Gardner's concern with modern social issues, "Dr. Gardner at once introduced the class to Walter Rauschenbusch, who was then at the height of his career as a leader of the Christian social movement in America."[107] This was important to Dobbins because he was also keenly aware of the "little concern for social righteousness" within the churches. "Imagine my surprise and delight, then," continued Dobbins, "when I enrolled at Southern Seminary in a Christian Sociology class taught by Dr. Charles S. Gardner. Here was a man after my own heart—a transparent and committed Christian, with as sensitive social conscience as a Lincoln Steffens or a Mark Sullivan or an Upton Sinclair."[108] Dobbins grew to be person-centered in his approach, which apparently meant a focus on peripheral human needs.[109] As human needs could be

103. Gardner, "Syllabus of Lectures on Homiletics Lecture," 47.

104. Gardner, "Syllabus of Lectures on Homiletics Lecture," 47–48.

105. Dobbins, *Great Teachers*, 64.

106. Especially chapters 2 and 3 of this work will demonstrate Dobbins's level of agreement with Gardner in his use of psychological theory as a legitimate source of epistemology.

107. Dobbins, *Great Teachers*, 60. Walter Rauschenbusch was known as a "tireless critic of excessive capitalism," and as a "standard-bearer of Christian socialism." Stephen Brachlow said, "Rauschenbusch turned to the Bible to support his vision of a social system based on Christlike love for the poor and oppressed." See Brachlow, "Walter Rauschenbusch," in George and Dockery, *Baptist Theologians*, 366–83.

108. Brachlow, "Walter Rauschenbusch," in George and Dockery, *Baptist Theologians*, 60. Steffens, *The Shame of the Cities*. Steffens, *The Auto-Biography of Lincoln Steffens*. Sullivan, "A Year of the Government," 308–21. Sinclair, *The Jungle*. Each of these men were leaders of the social movement in America and wrote to expose social injustices. Dobbins said that Gardner introduced him to *The Jungle* by Sinclair. See Dobbins, "Oral History Interviews," 28–29. Also see Dobbins, *Great Teachers*, 59.

109. This is a paramount issue that provided Dobbins with the permission and encouragement necessary to study the teaching methods, motivated by psychological

identified through the means of the "empirical science" of psychology, the Scripture would be molded to meet those human needs rather than playing its historic roles of defining true human need and providing the methods by which those needs would be met.[110]

The trajectory of the material taught by Gardner was sustained and refined after his years as a professor. Gardner was hired to teach homiletics, the art of preaching, and ecclesiology, the study of the church. Gardner was responsible for the new department called Christian Sociology begun in 1916, although he preferred the title Sociology of Christianity.[111] The "Southern Seminary Catalogue" of that same year indicated that Gardner also taught Homiletics and Elocution: The Theory and History of Preaching and Elocution, and Psychology of Religion as a special study course. His lectures spanned the spectrum from homiletics and ecclesiology to educational psychology and psychology of religion. However, the social sciences were the core around which Gardner would construct his courses, no matter the topic.[112]

Dobbins described Gardner as, "a profound student of sociology and psychology." Gardner introduced a course in Christian Sociology which was "one of the first to be offered in any theological institution in America."[113] Dobbins would add that, "This combination of homiletics, sociology, and psychology gave unique character to Dr. Gardner's teaching."[114] Dobbins's

learning theories, promoted by Coe, Kilpatrick and Dewey. The person-centered approach to teaching and learning was also applied to counseling in Clinical Pastoral Education.

110. Dobbins, *Deepening the Spiritual Life*, 17–43. Dobbins discussed growth and experience in relation to understanding human nature according to the studies of psychology. Dobbins said, "The spiritual is the higher realm, hence its laws can supersede, though they do not contradict the laws of nature. Science sets itself up to the discovery of the natural law and controls experience through the utilization of the powers of nature. Education investigates and states the laws of learning, and controls experience through the application of psychological principles to mental development" (38–39). Also see Dobbins, *Building Better Churches*, 161–95.

111. Southern Baptist Theological Seminary, *Catalogue of The Southern Baptist Theological Seminary, Fifty-Eighth Session, 1916–1917*, 38. See Weatherspoon, "Charles Spurgeon Gardner," 190.

112. Southern Baptist Theological Seminary, *Catalogue of The Southern Baptist Theological Seminary, Fifty-Eighth Session, 1916–1917*, 38–46. The course descriptions indicate a dependence upon the framework of psychology as a venue through which to teach each subject.

113. Dobbins Papers, "Pen Pictures of Southern Seminary Personalities," Box 10, Folders 15, 13.

114. Dobbins Papers, "Pen Pictures of Southern Seminary Personalities," Box 10, Folder 13.

description of the course content affirmed his belief in the importance of psychology and psychology of religion both in religious education and preaching. Weatherspoon acknowledged that Gardner had a share "in creating the tone and character of two other future departments: Religious Education and Psychology of Religion."[115]

> Although on the point I have no documentation, I am quite sure there was an understanding that he would introduce into the course of study the subjects to which he had given himself for a number of years and which he felt were essential to a minister's preparation in our time: sociology, psychology, and ethics in their joint relationship to preaching.[116]

The use of these social sciences impressed Dobbins as a student. Dobbins called Gardner his favorite teacher because he was more contemporary in his style and method of teaching.[117] Based upon Dobbins's recollection and the content of his courses, one can see Gardner's profound impact. "He contributed to me," Dobbins said, "the ideal of teaching as stimulating rather than transmitting thought."[118] As Dobbins remembered, Gardner not only had thorough influence upon him, but also the Convention, "In his 22 years of service, Dr. Gardner did much to influence the preaching and teaching ministry of the men who largely shaped the present course of Southern Baptist life and thought."[119]

John R. Sampey

John Sampey was a steady figure at Southern Seminary. He entered as a student in 1882, studying under the iconic personalities of Boyce, Broadus, and Manly. Sampey certainly won the favor of Broadus as he began to assist him in his Greek courses in 1885. He was elected president of Southern

---

115. Weatherspoon, "Charles Spurgeon Gardner," 190. The departments of Religious Education and Psychology of Religion later began under the direction and leadership of Dobbins. Weatherspoon sees cohesion between the teaching of Gardner and the later work of Dobbins in the two fields.

116. Weatherspoon, "Charles Spurgeon Gardner," 189.

117. Dobbins, "Oral History Interviews," 28.

118. Dobbins Papers, "Pen Pictures of Southern Seminary Personalities," Box 10, Folders 15, 13.

119. Dobbins Papers, "Pen Pictures of Southern Seminary Personalities," Box 10, Folder 14.

Seminary in 1929, after the death of Mullins in 1928. He remained in that position through the Great Depression until his retirement in 1942.[120]

Dr. Sampey was most well-known as an Old Testament and Hebrew professor, even though his love was the English New Testament and Greek, but while grading for Broadus, Sampey realized the gifting of a student named A. T. Robertson in the language and preferred him to teach New Testament and Greek.[121] Sampey was then assigned to teach Hebrew and Old Testament. Dobbins said that at once, "Sampey threw himself into the task of mastering the Old Testament and especially the Hebrew language."[122]

The students affectionately referred to Dr. Sampey as Tiglath.[123] "Tiglath-pilesar," Dobbins recalled, "Somehow he reminded them of Pul, the Assyrian warrior-king who is reported to have conquered forty-two nations."[124] Sampey was not only a great master-teacher according to Dobbins, but, "almost everything he did had teaching value.[125]

Dr. Sampey endured several of the great trials in Southern Seminary's history. It is important to recall his position relative to the Whitsitt Controversy. Sampey supported Whitsitt, even after he offered his resignation, and he attempted "to start a circular letter among the trustees to nullify Dr. Whitsitt's resignation."[126] In a most ardent speech at Long Run Association he declared Whitsitt was justified in his right to freedom of research.[127] This speech is important, not simply to select sides for or against Whitsitt, but to place Sampey in proper relation to the dispute. Clyde Francisco hints at the impact of the controversy upon Sampey, "There is no question but that the Whitsitt controversy influenced Dr. Sampey in his decision to tread lightly on historical criticism, for he knew far more than he taught or wrote about."[128]

120. Sampey, *Memoirs*. Sampey records parts of his story in detail, as his memory allows, the experiences of his life. This work preserves much of the history of the seminary, both controversies and triumphs. Of interest to this work is Sampey's explanation of the seminary's involvement with the International Lessons Committee, including Broadus and his own participation.

121. Dobbins Papers, "Pen Pictures of Southern Seminary Personalities," Box 10, Folders 15, 13.

122. Dobbins, *Great Teachers*, 40.

123. Johnson, *Of Parsons and Profs*, 35–43. Dobbins, *Great Teachers*, 36. Francisco, "John R. Sampey," 460.

124. Dobbins, *Great Teachers*, 36.

125. Dobbins, *Great Teachers*, 48.

126. Mueller, *A History of Southern Baptist Theological Seminary*, 173.

127. See Wills, *Southern Baptist Theological Seminary*, 207–8 and Mueller, *A History of Southern Baptist Theological Seminary*, 169–70.

128. Francisco, "John R. Sampey," 467. Francisco presented another piece of interesting evidence relative to Sampey's position by quoting one of his works. "In a day

As Wills has argued the controversy that was set in motion regarding Whitsitt was less about Baptist history and Landmarkism than about traditional orthodoxy and the progressivism of "evangelical liberals."[129] Based on my knowledge and research, Sampey never openly declared a progressive position, but his stance in the Whitsitt Controversy positions him toward that polemic. He would demonstrate that sort of sway in his views regarding Sunday School curriculum as well.[130]

Dobbins respected Sampey for his work in the classroom, but also as a member of the International Lesson Committee. Dobbins recalled Sampey's response:

> When asked, "What do you consider your greatest life-work?" Dr. Sampey passed in review some of his accomplishments and honors. Then he said, "I count my greatest work to have been chairman of the Uniform Lessons Committee of the International Sunday School Association (later the International Council of Religious Education) for forty-six years."[131]

Sampey gave guidance to the lesson selection committee for nearly half of a century.[132]

---

when the theory of evolution is under violent attack, he wrote in his 'The Heart Of The Old Testament': 'It is interesting to note the general correspondence between Genesis and modern science in the order of creation. In both accounts there is progress from the lower forms of life to the higher, the series reaching its climax in the appearance of man on the earth. Those who are disturbed by minor discrepancies between the theories of scientists and the statements in Genesis should not overlook the fact that the author of Genesis did not seek after scientific precision. He uses the language of appearance and of every-day life. Had he used scientific terminology, the religious purposes of the narrative might have been obscured. Let the astronomer and the geologist and the biologist pursue their researches with perfect freedom. We must not forget the wise saying of Cardinal Baronius: 'The intention of Holy Scriptures is to teach us how to go to heaven, and not how the heavens go.'" The significance of this quote to Dobbins is the way in which science is viewed. Science is viewed as a separate arena of epistemological truth that may or may not coincide with Scripture, but should be viewed on par with Scripture. This is the same approach Dobbins took with the "social sciences." Dobbins used psychology to gain understanding of human nature in order to meet the needs of the parishioners. This needs driven approach began to dictate the duties of the pastorate, which eventually led to the clinical approach to pastoral counseling.

129. Wills, *Southern Baptist Theological Seminary*, 229.

130. Wills, *Southern Baptist Theological Seminary*, 326. Wills suggested that many of the trustees preferred Ellis Fuller to be hired after Sampey so that he could, "shore up the seminary's flagging reputation for orthodoxy."

131. Dobbins, *Great Teachers*, 47.

132. Sampey, *Memoirs*, 76 and 268. Sampey served the International Sunday School Lesson Committee for forty-six years, 1895–1941. Also see Dobbins, *Great Teachers*, 47.

The importance of Sampey's involvement with the Uniform and Graded Lessons Committee must not be overlooked. Dobbins would later be responsible for this division of the seminary's curriculum, and he was doubtlessly impacted by the work of his colleague. The fear among the preachers, Sunday School leaders, and teachers was that the curriculum committee had decided to use extra-biblical material. Sampey was not shy in recalling the criticisms that were laid against the lesson committee. The justification for the extra-biblical material was explained by saying, "The same divine agencies that shaped the biblical history of the Hebrews are still operative in the world, and on a larger scale than ever before."[133] Frank Glenn Lankard wrote *A History of the American Sunday School Curriculum* and reported the same motivation for using the extra-biblical material, "The Union regarded the Bible as the basis of religious instruction but felt that it should be supplemented by material drawn from other fields, believing that the divine agency which was at work in the Bible is still in the world today."[134]

The shift in source for Sunday School curriculum was indicative of the times. In the same way Mullins suggested a separate source of authority for truth, namely experience, the curriculum committee practiced a similar epistemology. Sampey highlighted the concern of the committee as he quoted one of the speakers in favor of the Uniform and Graded Lessons, "The old education regarded the body of truth, or the material first—then the child. The new education places the child first, studies his needs, and then seeks the material which will satisfy these needs. The old education placed the material first, the child second; the new education places the child before the material."[135] The curriculum committee decided to use psychology to identify human nature and needs in order to formulate Sunday School curriculum that would theoretically meet those needs.

Dr. Sampey could not plead ignorance in his approval of the Graded Lessons, because he was aware of the criticism, even from his own convention. Sampey recorded this criticism in his own book, *The International Lesson System*:

> One of the most vigorous attacks came from the pen of Rev. Harvey Beauchamp, a prominent Sunday-school worker among Southern Baptists. Mr. Beauchamp contended that the lessons were unsound in the matter of conversion; that extra-biblical lessons ought not to have been inserted in the Series;

133. Sampey, *The International Lesson System*, 159.
134. Lankard, *A History of the American Sunday School Curriculum*, 277.
135. Sampey, *The International Lesson System*, 178.

> that the Scriptures were wrested from their natural meaning, to provide texts for some of the lessons; that important topics found no place in the Series; and the Lesson Committee, contrary to all precedents, were now presuming, through the very structure of the Graded Systems, to interpret Scriptures for the Sunday-schools.[136]

In 1910, the criticism was causing questions at the SBC meeting in Baltimore, and J. M. Frost, Secretary of the Sunday School Board of the convention, led the SBC to protest the curriculum.[137]

The Southern Baptist Convention was not exempt from the cultural advances of liberal theological scholarship as demonstrated in the lessons committee. The new methods of education, driven by the theories of genetic psychology and educational psychology were being accepted by the International Lesson Committee.[138] What were the influences that motivated the committee in this new methodological approach to religious education? Lankard answers with the following insight:

> The closing years of the 19th century mark changes and advances in the study of the Bible and Religion. The scientific method was gaining such headway in education and psychology began to make itself felt in the field of religion. This spirit was first reflected in a number of books which appeared around 1900 dealing with investigations of a scientific nature in the field of religion. Among the pioneers of this period were Starbuck, Coe and Hall.[139]

Arlo Brown writing, in 1923 *A History of Religious Education in Recent Times,* concurred with Lankard. Both writers identified the prevailing cultural milieu in which education, specifically religious education, was enmeshed:

> Many brilliant psychologists made a great contribution to religious education in the years 1900 to 1910. In addition to the

136. Sampey, *The International Lesson System,* 205. Beauchamp's final statements should have concerned Baptists, especially since the committee was ecumenical, and Baptists would not always agree with the scriptural interpretations of the other denominations represented on the committee.

137. Sampey, *The International Lesson System,* 206–7.

138. These apprehensions were adjacent to the concern of ecumenism relative to the committee.

139. Lankard, *A History of the American Sunday School Curriculum,* 276–77. Lankard is referring to the work of Edwin Diller Starbuck, George A. Coe and G. Stanley Hall. Each of these men will be discussed in more detail in the following chapter.

two writers [Starbuck and Coe] previously mentioned, such men as William James, G. Stanley Hall, and others were especially stimulating and suggestive. The creators and writers of the International Graded Lessons in some of the series relied much upon the investigations of these men.[140]

As a result, the influence of scientific method, progressive education, and the psychology of religion continued to grow and affect the practice of the lesson planners. C. B. Eavey recognized this influence in retrospect.

Methodology and man-made ideas had so fascinated writers of Sunday School lessons that they practically eliminated the Bible in their planning of lessons. The experience-centered lessons turned out to be lessons with much of man's supposed knowledge and little of God's revealed truth in them.[141]

The importance of these revelations regarding the work of Sampey is in relation to Dobbins. Dobbins had great respect for Sampey as demonstrated by his panegyric chapter in *Great Teachers Make a Difference*. Dobbins worked closely with President Sampey during the years of the Depression and afterward in order to stabilize the financial situation of the seminary. There is little doubt that Sampey spoke of his passion and "greatest life-work" with Dobbins.[142] One should not find it surprising that the men from whom Dobbins would later solicit help in obtaining new methods as a teacher were the same men who influenced the International Lesson System, of which Sampey was a key participant, to shift its focus in curriculum to extra-biblical sources.[143]

THE NEED FOR EFFICIENCY

Mullins began a lecture series on Sunday School work at the seminary in February, 1902 in conjunction with the work and support of the Sunday School Board of the SBC.[144] Sunday School was viewed at that time as the

---

140. Brown, *A History of Religious Education in Recent Times*, 237. See Eavey, *History of Christian Education*, for a more detailed description of the development of Sunday School in America, both pedagogy and curriculum.

141. Eavey, *History of Christian Education*, 288.

142. Dobbins, *Great Teachers*, 47.

143. Dobbins would later study directly under George Albert Coe. Coe was a pioneer in religious education with Starbuck, and both were influenced deeply by G. S. Hall and William James. Later in this chapter Dobbins's introduction to Coe will be explained. A more detailed explanation will appear in the following chapter.

144. Mueller, *A History of Southern Baptist Theological Seminary*, 186–87.

responsibility of the laity and in the previous century it had operated independently from the church.[145] Broadus, Manly, and Sampey had supported the Sunday School movement because they believed it could benefit the teaching ministry of the church.[146] In 1863, Basil Manly, Jr., had impelled the Southern Baptist Convention to re-establish a Bible Board for publications.[147] A little more than forty years later, in 1906, Mullins introduced the department of Sunday School Pedagogy at Southern Seminary after the trustees had approved it in May of the same year.

Mullins selected B. H. Dement to lead the new department, and Dement introduced the course, Sunday School Pedagogy at Southern Seminary during the 1906–1907 session.[148] Dement was a key figure in the expansion of Sunday School pedagogy in Baptist theological education. Dobbins claimed that Dement, "laid the foundation on which were built the School of Religious Education of Southwestern Baptist Theological Seminary and later the Schools of Religious Education of New Orleans Baptist Theological Seminary and Southern Seminary."[149]

The argument here is not for or against the genesis of Sunday School pedagogy in the seminary curriculum; rather the content taught by Dement and his pedagogical style are of special concern. First, the content taught by Dement in the Sunday School Pedagogy course was laden with educational

145. Lankard, *A History of the American Sunday School Curriculum*, 61.

146. Dobbins Papers, "Pen Pictures of Southern Seminary Personalities," Box 10, Folder 15.

147. Mueller, *A History of Southern Baptist Theological Seminary*, 186–87. Mueller explained that Manly, Jr. proposed a Sunday Board in 1863. Due to the war, the old Bible Board that began in 1851 had to discontinue its distribution of tracts and Bibles. Dobbins did acknowledge that a separate Sunday School Board was created under the Home and Foreign Mission Board in 1863. Dobbins, *Can A Religious Democracy Survive?*, 64–66. Dobbins presented a short history of the Sunday school beginning with Robert Raikes and William Fox. He described the development of the Sunday school in the Southern Baptist Convention, mentioning the influence of Boyce, Broadus, Manly and J. M. Frost. He acknowledged that the Convention tried to organize a publication society, but it wasn't until 1891 that the Sunday School Board was established.

148. Southern Baptist Theological Seminary, *Catalogue of The Southern Baptist Theological Seminary, Forty-Eighth Session, 1906–1907*, 36. Dobbins Papers, "Pen Pictures of Southern Seminary Personalities," Box 10, Folder 15. This is the field that later became widely known as Religious Education.

149. Dobbins Papers, "Pen Pictures of Southern Seminary Personalities," Box 10, Folders 16. Dement left Southern Seminary in 1917 to become the president of the Baptist Bible Institute, which is now New Orleans Baptist Theological Seminary. J. M. Price, the pioneer in Religious Education at Southwestern Seminary, was a student of Dement. Dobbins implied that the influence of Dement upon Price directly resulted in the creation of the Religious Education department at Southwestern Seminary upon Price's arrival in 1915.

and genetic psychology. The course description from 1906, the inaugural year, accurately depicts the influence of the young science.

> This course was given for the first time during the session of 1906–7, and since this Seminary is pioneer in Sunday School instruction, such modifications will be made in the course as the progress of events may demand. The following lines of study are proposed for the session of 1907–8: During the fall term especial attention will be paid to Educational Psychology, or the message of genetic Psychology to religious teachers, embracing a scientific and practical study of child nature as well as of the adult mind; a brief history of educational schemes, a consideration of the Psychology of Religion, and a study of the Pedagogy of Jesus.[150]

Second, neither Dobbins nor Mullins were antagonistic to the content taught by Dement; their concern was that his pedagogical style was traditional and transmissive, intended simply to transmit information from professor to pupil. Dobbins said that Dement's courses "were pretty dull and dry," and that "He was a pretty good preacher, but not a teacher."[151] During his days as a student, Dobbins described many of the professors at Southern Seminary to be quality teachers, but not genuine educators. Dobbins was not so troubled by the content of the courses, but considered this style of pedagogy to be outdated.[152] Mullins and Dobbins were not satisfied with the traditional didactic style, which was the impetus regarding the evolution of religious education and the reason why Mullins called upon Dobbins, "to broaden the field" of practical studies.[153] They believed modern techniques were necessary to prepare preachers to lead churches in the current age.

In correspondence with Wayne Oates, Dobbins revealed his belief regarding the pedagogy of many of his predecessors. Dobbins had just finished proof-reading the chapter Oates wrote paying tribute to him as a great

---

150. Southern Baptist Theological Seminary, *Catalogue of The Southern Baptist Theological Seminary, Forty-Eighth Session, 1906–1907*, 36–37.

151. Dobbins, "Oral History Interviews," 25–26.

152. Dobbins did not seem to have a problem with the content taught by most of his professors. He demonstrated agreement with Mullins, Gardner, Sampey, and Dement. He did, however, express distaste for some of the material George Eager used. Dobbins was selected to teach Pastoral Theology as a part of Church Efficiency. Pastoral Theology had been taught by Eager. He used Washington Gladden's, *The Christian Pastor*, and Richard Baxter's, *The Reformed Pastor*. Dobbins said these works were, "literature of another day." Dobbins Papers, "Dobbinology," Box 9, Folders 21, 6. This document by Elmer Leslie Gray is an interview with Gaines Dobbins entitled, "Dobbinology." Subsequent citations will be as follows: Gray, "Dobbinology."

153. Dobbins, *Gaines S. Dobbins*, 59.

teacher.[154] In the first draft Oates had written a strong and negative contrast between Dobbins and many of the other professors at Southern Seminary. Oates's criticism included several of the men Dobbins wrote about in *Great Teachers* because, as Dobbins explained in a response letter, these are "the teachers I have praised!" Dobbins suggested that Oates omit the paragraph and explained to Oates his case, "We would not want to cast any reflection on these good men who did the best they know how in the matter of methodology without the help that came to us later from a depth study of teaching and learning."[155] It is clear Dobbins believed his forerunners to have less than desirable pedagogy, and part of his vision was to assimilate an intentional modern approach to teaching and learning, a style he would learn from his courses and mentors at Peabody, Columbia Teacher's College, Vanderbilt, and Chicago University.

INVITATION

Mullins stirred a vision to transform intentionally the "practical" courses introduced at Southern Seminary. The new department would expand upon the work of Dement, Gardner, and Landrum Leavell.[156] Rufus Weaver, from Mercer University, and J. B. Weatherspoon both were offered the professorship to lead the new department left by the vacancy of Landrum Leavell. Both men refused the offer.[157]

Determined to inaugurate this new department, Mullins called upon Gaines Dobbins. Dobbins was a former student of Mullins and after graduation had begun work as a Christian journalist with the Baptist Sunday School Board of the Southern Baptist Convention.[158] Mullins called Dobbins in April 1920 inviting him to lead the Department of Practical Studies and to become Professor of Church Efficiency and Sunday School Pedagogy.[159] Mullins believed there was, "a lack of preparation of Southern Seminary

154. Oates, "Gaines S. Dobbins," in Dobbins, *Great Teachers*. Oates sent Dobbins a rough draft copy for him to approve before sending to the publishers. See Dobbins Papers, Box 8, Folder 42.

155. Dobbins Papers, Box 6, Folders 1–3; Box 8, Folder 42.

156. Leavell taught Sunday School pedagogy at Southern Seminary from 1915–1920. He also worked at the Sunday School Board of the Southern Baptist Convention as the "first secretary of the Baptist Young People's Union in the Department of Student Work." See "Biographical Sketch," in Landrum Pinson Leavell Collection.

157. Dobbins, *Gaines S. Dobbins*, 56.

158. Dobbins, *Gaines S. Dobbins*, 40–54.

159. Dobbins, *Zest for Living*, 35. Dobbins, *Gaines S. Dobbins*, 55–56.

students in the 'practical' field."[160] Dobbins recounted the phone conversation that he said, "changed the course of my life."[161]

> It was a spring Saturday, my day off from the office, and I was busy in our backyard garden. The telephone rang and my wife announced, "Long distance call for you from Louisville."

"This is E. Y. Mullins of Southern Seminary," the voice declared. "The Executive Committee is prepared to nominate you to a seminary professorship to succeed Landrum Leavell, who, as you perhaps know, has had a break in health and must resign."

"Wait a minute," I interrupted, "you must have the wrong person. This is G. S. Dobbins of the Sunday School Board. Maybe you want E. C. Dargan, one of our featured writers."

> "No," he asserted. "You're the man we want. I've talked it over with Van Ness and he agrees to let you go. We want to continue the tie between the Seminary and the Sunday School Board and enlarge Leavell's service from part-time to a full-time department." Then, with characteristic decisiveness, "Good-bye. I'll see you in my office Tuesday morning," he hung up the receiver.[162]

In 1920, Dobbins began as Professor of Church Efficiency and Sunday School Pedagogy. During his thirty-six years at Southern Seminary, his titles would morph from Efficiency to Church Administration and from Sunday School Pedagogy to Religious Education. The new "Department of Practical Studies" was intended to aid pastors in gaining practical experience and to become more efficient administrators regarding modern problems facing churches. Soon after Dobbins arrived on campus as a new faculty member, President Mullins requested a meeting with him to reset the vision of the new department. "This school is too content-centered," Mullins said. "We want it to be more closely tied to the churches and we want to turn out men who have more practical experience."[163] As a part of this same conversation Dobbins explained:

> [Mullins] told me I was primarily to help create a department of religious education which was called Sunday School pedagogy

160. Dobbins, *Gaines S. Dobbins*, 59.

161. Dobbins, *Zest for Living*, 118.

162. Dobbins, *Zest for Living*, 118. Dobbins recounted this same story in an interview with Badgett Dillard. Dobbins, "Oral History Interviews," 32–36. Leavell had been used as an interim on loan from the Sunday School Board to teach about the Sunday School, but Mullins wanted to include Church Administration in the curriculum.

163. Dobbins, *Gaines S. Dobbins*, 64.

at that time and had not commanded much attention. I also was
to take over Dr. Eager's course in Practical Theology. Dr. Mullins
took off his glasses in characteristic fashion and looked at me
quizzically and said, "I don't like that title. I teach theology and
I think what I teach is practical." So I said, "Let's find a better
name for it; I don't like it either. It isn't theology in the real sense
of the word and it isn't just practicality." We hit on the idea of
calling it Church Efficiency and it went by that title for the first
few years.[164]

RESIGNATION

Dobbins had a miserable first year as a teacher and offered his resignation to
Mullins.[165] Dobbins wrote, "Throughout the world of theological education
there were stirrings of discontent because the curriculum was too content-
centered and inadequately oriented toward equipping the student for effectiveness in pastoral ministries."[166] Among Southern Baptists, J. M. Price was
experiencing the same reports and similar difficulty at SWBTS.[167] Mullins
refused the new professor's resignation, stating that he would help Dobbins
go elsewhere to learn from other schools what he needed to learn.[168] What
follows is the account Dobbins gave to Badgett Dillard in an interview:

> After commencement I went to Dr. Mullins and said, "Doctor, I
> am sorry, but I am in the wrong place. I would like for you to ac-
> cept my resignation and let me go back to Nashville." He shook
> his head and pondered and said, "No, I am not going to do it. I
> know you haven't set the woods afire, and I didn't expect you to.
> You were given a task that nobody has ever had before. You had
> no precedent. No," he said, "you go on. Give it another year. If
> we called somebody else he would be in the same situation you
> are. He wouldn't know what to do any more than you've known

164. Gray, "Dobbinology," 5. The term efficiency was being used among the business industry to describe the practices that would produce the greatest return. Dobbins
certainly relied upon business efficiency principles, but the name for this department
may have come from Mullins's involvement in the Efficiency Commission of the SBC.
From 1914–1922 Mullins served on the commission providing recommendations to
the SBC for ecumenical involvement and ways to improve missionary enterprise. See,
Wills, *Southern Baptist Theological Seminary*, 287–90.

165. Dobbins, "Oral History Interviews," 33. Dobbins, *Gaines S. Dobbins*, 58.

166. Dobbins, *Great Teachers*, 79.

167. Maguire, *J. M. Price: Portrait of a Pioneer*, 65–68. Dobbins, *Great Teachers*, 80.

168. Dobbins, *Gaines S. Dobbins*, 58.

what to do, and you have made a pretty good start. The students like you."[169]

Consequently, Mullins should be given partial credit for charting the course for Dobbins as he set out to redefine pastoral theology in the more practical terms of church administration and church efficiency.[170] Mullins and Gardner relied heavily upon pragmatism and psychology for the content of their courses—an expectation passed on to Dobbins. These influences and the need that appeared for Dobbins aggregated toward one solution. He would pursue study with the men who were considered the avant-garde of educational methodology, educational psychology, and psychology of religion.[171]

As a student at Southern Seminary, Dobbins appreciated the content of the classes, but believed the techniques used by his professors were "old-fashioned."[172] After returning as a professor and feeling defeated at the completion of his first year, Dobbins resolved to acquire a new pedagogical approach.[173] Only speculation could surround the conversations between Mullins and Dobbins during his troubles as a rookie professor. What cannot be disputed are the sources to which Dobbins was referred by Mullins. By the recommendation and help of Mullins, Dobbins ventured to New York to learn modern educational theories.[174]

Dobbins would be influenced and affected deeply by the men and their ideologies he encountered while studying during summer breaks and sabbaticals.[175] George Albert Coe was Dobbins's major professor, and he recommended classes with John Dewey, William H. Kilpatrick, Edward L. Thorndike and Harrison S. Elliot.[176] Dobbins recalled the advice of Coe, "I

169. Dobbins, "Oral History Interviews," 34–35.

170. Crouch, "The Influence of William James," 2. Crouch identifies the integral influence of Mullins upon Dobbins that encouraged the change in pastoral theology at Southern. "Faculty decreased the role of the Scriptures in determining the content and methodology used in pastoral ministry instruction as pragmatic and psychological considerations took center stage during Mullins's tenure at Southern Seminary."

171. The thesis also includes business efficiency as a major factor in professionalizing pastoral care. It was through personal study and the challenge Mullins gave him to write his first book, *The Efficient Church* that motivated Dobbins to pursue expertise in the field of business efficiency and administration. This would be a knowledge that helped him formulate the specialized aspects of the new pastoral theology he promoted later in his career.

172. Dobbins, *Gaines S. Dobbins*, 35.

173. Dobbins, *Great Teachers*, 79–81. Dobbins, *Gaines S. Dobbins*, 58.

174. Dobbins, *Gaines S. Dobbins*, 58. Edge, "Gaines S. Dobbins—The Teacher" 371–72.

175. Dobbins, "Oral History Interviews," 35. Dobbins, *Gaines S. Dobbins*, 58–59.

176. Dobbins, *Great Teachers*, 80–81. Dobbins, *Gaines S. Dobbins*, 58–62. The

don't care what they are teaching . . . I want you to expose yourself to some master teachers, to observe their methods and objectives, to study their personality and philosophy—not to imitate them but to find yourself and determine the course you will pursue in a lifetime of teaching."[177] Dobbins admitted, "I took his advice and a new world opened up to me as I studied not only books and subject matter but great teachers in action." He continued, "The winds of change blew on me from many directions."[178]

The influence of further education on Dobbins replaced the traditional epistemology of Scripture with psychology and efficiency as primary sources in the formation of religious education and pastoral care. The newfound methods of Dobbins formed into what would be affectionately referred to as, "Dobbinology."[179] These notes were compiled with extensive dependence upon men's theories of education, communication theory of journalism, and efficiency engineering.[180] Each of these distinguished categories had evolved from the new speed of life and demands of the culture. What did these men teach that so enlightened Dobbins? The following chapter will explore the progressive theories of education, mainly educational psychology and efficiency in order to demonstrate the impact of each upon Dobbins and his works.

CONCLUSION

This was the progressive philosophical and theological atmosphere that Dobbins entered as both a new student and a new faculty member. Comparatively, the influence of Mullins upon Dobbins seems greater than the other professors at Southern Seminary, but the culmination of these influences produced two specific motivations for his future study. First, Dobbins demonstrated frustration with the approach of several of his professors to the art of pedagogy. He did not believe their teaching style to be modern, but traditional, lacking in preparing ministers for the duties they would face in the pastorate. This drove him to search out new methods of pastoral leadership and education for the church.

---

impact of these men is evident by the use of reference in the first several books published by Dobbins. Dobbins, *Zest for Living*, 35. This book demonstrates the influence through his entire life, as *Zest for Living* was published toward the end of his life.

177. Dobbins, *Great Teachers*, 81.

178. Dobbins, *Great Teachers*, 81.

179. Oates, "Gaines S. Dobbins," in Dobbins, *Great Teachers*, 89.

180. Dobbins, *Gaines S. Dobbins*, 63–64.

Second, Mullins and Gardner highlighted what they believed to be authoritative theories of experience and the new science of psychology as means to understand human behaviors. The teaching and innovative theories of these two men seemingly gave Dobbins permission to pursue a source stream other than the Scriptures to guide him in creating different methods of pastoral duties.

Chapter 2

Tyranny of The Social Sciences in "Dobbinology"

INTRODUCTION

In order to gain understanding of the shaping influence of Dobbins on pastoral care in the Southern Baptist Convention, research must not be confined to his works on the subject. While his works regarding pastoral care are pointed,[1] a solitary focus will cause the inquirer to miss how pastoral care became specialized and the degree to which secular psychology contributed to its formation. His works were largely a result of the accumulation of his class notes.[2]

The aim of this chapter is to provide evidence that the theories of business efficiency, educational psychology, progressive education, psychology of

---

1. Dobbins, *Building Better Churches,* 27. Dobbins, "Pastor as Counselor," 421–29. Dobbins, "Capturing Psychology for Christ," 427–36. Dobbins, "Case Studies in Solution of Pastoral Problems," 434–43. Dobbins, "The Psychological Approach to Religion," 442–51. These are simply a sample of the articles Dobbins wrote regarding pastoral care and counseling.

2. Dobbins, *Gaines S. Dobbins,* 68–70. See Gray, "Dobbinology." Oates, "Gaines S. Dobbins," in Dobbins, *Great Teachers,* 89. Oates says, "My introduction to Dr. Dobbins, then, was in his classroom, I was impressed with the fact that he had already prepared his lecture material in his workbook. This had been mimeographed and served as the basis for class participation. We called this book 'Dobbinology.'"

religion and religious education within Dobbins's works were assembled as the foundation of his methodology.[3] This evidence provided is intended to draw a simple correlation; Dobbins's works were infused with the philosophy and methodology of the progressing social sciences of the early twentieth-century by direct influence. This chapter, along with the one following, will reveal that it was the culmination of several subjects in Dobbins's mind and practice that produced a professionalized view of pastoral counseling.

Each of the men discussed herein leveraged their ideologies for significant impact in the culture of the west. It should be no surprise that those same ideologies wielded significant influence upon the religious leaders of that same culture. To trace theological concepts alone may not reveal the compromise that this thesis suggests. One must track the cultural and ideological concepts that chipped away at orthodox theological practice in order to explain the current situation of pastoral care and counseling. Holifield explained this phenomenon within the broader spectrum of American religious memes:

> . . . this is not to suggest that the history of pastoral activity corresponded simply to changing theological conceptions. It is the interweaving of theology with other fields of learning, such as psychology and ethics, and the interconnection of pastoral activity with changes in culture and society that reveal the complexity of the cure of souls in the mainstream of the American churches. Pastoral theology was never a self-contained intellectual system, but rather a complex of inherited ideas and images subject to continued modification in changing social and intellectual settings.[4]

Dobbins was one of the interweavers within the Southern Baptist Convention to integrate other fields of learning with theology that caused a pivot in several Baptist theological conceptions.

Dobbins was determined to change the form of theological education, in an effort to add practicality to the training of pastors. Allen Graves, writing an essay in honor of Dobbins said, "Dr. Dobbins was sure of one thing—change. How to deal with a changing world, how to respond appropriately to changing circumstances, how to guide the processes of change that were both inevitable and often desirable were matters of great concern."[5] Dobbins responded to the modern changes with a progressive vision of organizational

---

3. Psychology of Religion will be highlighted in greater detail in subsequent chapters.

4. Holifield, *A History of Pastoral Care in America*, 30.

5. Graves, "Gaines S. Dobbins—Mr. Church Administrator," 384.

ecclesiology, person-centered religious education, and clinical pastoral training. The changes in pastoral theology, pastoral care, and pastoral counseling, from Dobbins's perspective, were not tacit. The following sections reveal the categories of thought from which Dobbins synthesized his views, which accumulated into the specialization of pastoral care and counseling.

BUSINESS EFFICIENCY

Dobbins was influenced by three major people or groups toward the ideas of efficiency. First, Arthur Flake, of the Baptist Sunday School Board utilized business methodology in growing Sunday School. Second, progressive educators also yielded to the principles of efficiency and, by so doing, these principles were reinforced as a part of Dobbins's training in religious education. Third, the works of Harrington Emerson, Frederick Taylor, and Roger Babson had tremendous impact on Dobbins's formulation of the "Efficient Church."

During the early twentieth century, the public pressure toward efficiency and economy grew not only for business but also in the arena of education.[6] The success of American businessmen like Carnegie, Rockefeller, and Vanderbilt pressured educators to "become more practical in order to serve the business society better."[7] The table was now prepared for, "the great preacher of the gospel of efficiency, Frederick W. Taylor, and his disciples."[8] The theories of the efficiency experts had expanded and were applied in several ways in churches and schools. Arthur Flake, head of the Sunday School Department of the SBC in 1920, utilized the principles from business experts in order to outline his five-fold formula for Sunday School growth.

Arthur Flake

When Dobbins began teaching church efficiency courses at Southern Seminary, he recalled that they did not have any literature available, with the exception of one volume: "We did have a little book, Flake's book, out of which grew the Flake doctrine of building standard Sunday School."[9] Dobbins was referring to Flake's Formula for Sunday School growth, which Arthur Flake modeled after the Sears, Roebuck, and Company's philosophy of business

6. Callahan, *Education and the Cult of Efficiency*, 222.
7. Callahan, *Education and the Cult of Efficiency*, 8–9 and 18.
8. Callahan, *Education and the Cult of Efficiency*, 18.
9. Dobbins, "Oral History Interviews," 34.

management and efficiency.[10] Dobbins's statement revealed that the new philosophy he sought to introduce to pastoral theology and practice was predicated largely upon business efficiency of the modern era rather than Scripture. Dobbins was convinced that Flake's Formula would advance educational ministries in the church, change the ecclesiological structure, and alter pastoral theology. He said,

> I suspect that the greatest single influence that turned us away from a pulpit centered ministry to more of an educational centered ministry the teaching church—was Arthur Flake's Building A Standard Sunday School [sic]. That caught on. That's what we want. We can do that. We can improve our Sunday Schools, we can reorganize, and we're going to do it, and you know the formula.[11]

Without adequate literature, where would Dobbins's search for material to provide for the pastoral trainees? Dobbins admitted that he "hadn't had any training in pastoral work." When asked whether or not he gained pastoral training as a seminarian, Dobbins replied, "No, only incidentally. Dr. Eager told about some of his experiences as a pastor. That was about as far as we went, and that didn't fit into the pattern for most of us."[12] He did not, however, want to teach in the same way as Eager since Dobbins did not believe that his pedagogical style was adequate. Dobbins claimed himself to be "ignorant of the techniques of the pastor" even though he had modest experience from pastorates in Mississippi.[13]

Dobbins was somewhat dejected due to the lack of teaching materials for the new department for which he was responsible. After refusing Dobbins's resignation, Mullins challenged him to create the seminary literature necessary to prepare the pastors for the modern era. Mullins gave Dobbins

10. Arthur Flake's, *Building a Standard Sunday School,* was originally published in 1919, and Dobbins was aware of his five-fold formula when he began as a professor in 1920. Dobbins, *Gaines S. Dobbins,* 67. Also see Dobbins, "50 Years of Church Administration," 4–14. Dobbins, "Oral History Interviews," 72. Dobbins said, "I did some research on that, and I discovered that the idea that Flake presented came from the experience of two Chicago merchants, Sears and Roebuck, and the manager whose name I don't remember." Dobbins referred to Flake's Formula as Flake's "laws." As will be seen throughout this chapter the use of the term laws in the social sciences was an attempt to make them more empirical. Dobbins approach to understanding human nature, especially for teaching and learning, was based upon the "laws" proposed by the educational psychologists and religious educators at the Teacher's College.

11. Dobbins, "Oral History Interviews," 72.

12. Dobbins, "Oral History Interviews," 33.

13. Dobbins, *Gaines S. Dobbins,* 40–43.

the course of action saying, "Now you go to work on a book and I will give you the title, 'The Efficient Church.'"[14]

The Efficient Church

The contribution Dobbins made to the field of administration often overshadows the contributions he made to religious education and pastoral counseling. Church administration became the new paradigm for ecclesiology, understood in terms of efficiency principles. The primary reasons he is most remembered as an administrator are his inaugural books in the field and his experience as an administrator through Southern Seminary's financial struggles.[15] The most appropriate explanation is that administration predominated Dobbins's thinking so that it became the impetus for specialization in other areas.

As mentioned previously, Dobbins's first book on administration came as much from necessity as it did from a desire to make a contribution to theological education. The dearth of literature, however, was in large part related to the new vision of pastoral theology proposed by Mullins and Dobbins. Dobbins had to look outside of the realm of theology, which had been the foundation of pastoral theology, for his inspiration in directing the new department of practical studies. His first two books relating to the

---

14. Dobbins, "Oral History Interviews," 36. This quote is from Dobbins's recollection of the conversation between him and Mullins after his first year as a professor in the new field. Incidentally, the book was named similar to the department they had just begun, they called it 'Church Efficiency.'

15. Dobbins, "Oral History Interviews," 46–52. Dobbins recounts the impact of the Depression upon the seminary and responsibilities he had in helping Dr. Sampey lead Southern Seminary out of debt and through many turbulent financial struggles. In a personal letter to Wayne Oates, Dr. Dobbins described his administrative role. "I carried very heavy administrative responsibilities throughout Dr. Sampey's administration as president. Dr. Mullins died in 1928, leaving the seminary with a million dollar debt. A year later the financial crash came, followed by a long depression, and Dr. Sampey and the trustees turned to me to be the seminary's financial agent and treasurer. (without pay). [sic] At first we could not even pay interest on the debt. I spent untold hours effecting economies, meeting with officials of the bank that held our notes, negotiating refinancing with an insurance company, finding money in various ways and helping keep students supplied with food, saving our downtown property as well as our credit, and never missing a payroll! All this I did so quietly that very few knew about it, for I was determined not to let this administrative responsibility interfer [sic] with my teaching. During this time we paid every dime of the debt, endowment was significantly increased, and our invested funds emerged worth more than we paid for them. Of course I do not claim credit for all this but responsibility was squarely on my shoulders. Dr. Sampey tells something of this story in his Memoirs." Dobbins Papers, Box 8, Folder 42.

topic of church efficiency, *The Efficient Church* and *The Churchbook*, made his reputation.[16]

The Efficient Church revealed that Dobbins was reliant upon business efficiency models in order to transform ecclesiology and pastoral theology. As Dobbins described his early days as a professor he remembered, "It was an age of emphasis in administration, on efficiency."[17] He seemed to gravitate toward the ideals of efficiency because he believed the church to be a business. "A church is a business enterprise," said Dobbins, "and must, therefore, meet ordinary requirements of a business institution. It handles money, holds property, assumes obligations, and through properly qualified representatives must possess legal standing in the community and in the sight of the law."[18] The efficient view of the church presented a paradigmatic shift in theoretical and functional ecclesiology. Dobbins seemed aware of this innovative perspective when he said, "[*The Efficient Church*] was revolutionary. It was the first book on administration on a seminary college graduate level to be printed that I know anything about."[19]

The monetary success of The American Industrial Revolution, enhanced by efforts of business efficiency, demanded attention. Dobbins noted, "There were men in industry, in production, in selling, who had been caught with the idea that there were laws governing efficient operation of an institution, of a business, of an industry. And so I got hold of one of those books and was intrigued by it."[20] The church, according to Dobbins, had been stymied by traditionalism and slouchy organization, because of "underdeveloped spiritual resources."[21] The effectiveness of church leaders

16. Dobbins, "Oral History Interviews," 38.

17. Dobbins, "Oral History Interviews," 36.

18. Dobbins, *The Efficient Church*, 92–93.

19. Dobbins, "Oral History Interviews," 38.

20. Dobbins, "Oral History Interviews," 36.

21. Dobbins, *The Efficient Church*, 19, 38–47. "One of the most difficult of these problems arises from the fact that our progress in methods of church work has not kept pace with the progress of material civilization . . . Families are constantly moving, home life is weakened, moral standards fluctuate, temptations are multiplied, class and social lines are sharply drawn. Lodges, clubs, business and social organizations, community welfare organizations, commercialized amusements, all tend to complicate the work of the church. Specialization in employment, the reduction of life to schedule and routine, the struggle for livelihood and to keep up appearances, the fact of unemployment, the extremes of wealth and poverty—these are not all new problems, but they present new phases and demand new effort at solution. What is bound to happen if church leaders and workers are incapable of meeting and coping with these difficult situations?"

was abated by the amount of duties expected of them. Dobbins said these men were, "under-paid and over-worked."[22]

One of the disciples of efficiency expert Frederick Taylor, was Harrington Emerson. Emerson was said to have given the movement of efficiency "a moral fervor that had all the earmarks of a religious revival."[23] Both Emerson and Taylor deeply impacted Dobbins's approach to church efficiency and administration.[24] Dobbins expounded:

> I found that approaching the subject of Administration from the standpoint of the efficiency engineer appealed to the students and held their attention. The efficiency experts were beginning to create a reputable literature in their field. I got hold of some of the literature, Emerson's famous Twelve Principles of Efficiency and other books. I saw at once the relationship between the scholarly work and the courses in business administration that were being developed at Harvard, Yale, Princeton, Columbia, and elsewhere. At Vanderbilt and Peabody I examined how a university teacher's college got students ready for their jobs. My assumption was that a minister has a vocation. Preaching is involved, but not only preaching. A minister is the pastor of a church, as administrator. Out of my study grew my first effort at a book, The Efficient Church.[25]

Harrington Emerson, according to Dobbins, was one of the most successful practical efficiency experts of his time.[26] Dobbins called Emerson's book, The Twelve Principles of Efficiency, "a classic in the commercial and industrial world."[27] Dobbins continued to justify his use of the secular resource by noting, "It is remarkable how effectively these principles apply in the realm of religious endeavor."[28]

Dobbins employed Jesus' explanation of the tree being known by its fruit as the New Testament test of modern efficiency.[29] James Ryan questioned whether Dobbins began with the efficiency principles and read them

22. Dobbins, The Efficient Church, 19.

23. Dobbins, The Efficient Church, 25.

24. Dobbins, The Efficient Church, 19–25. Dobbins summarized the Twelve Principles of Efficiency, written by Emerson as a basis for his own doctrine of efficiency.

25. Dobbins, Gaines S. Dobbins, 64.

26. Dobbins was also influenced by Roger Babson, Frederick Taylor and F. A. Agar in the area of efficiency. See Ryan, "Administrative Theory of Gaines Stanley Dobbins," and Dobbins, Gaines S. Dobbins, 64.

27. Dobbins, The Efficient Church, 19.

28. Dobbins, The Efficient Church, 19.

29. Dobbins, The Efficient Church, 25.

into the text of Scripture or if he truly was able to identify principles of efficiency from the inspired words.[30] Nonetheless, Dobbins listed all twelve of Emerson's principles in order to make his case for what he believed was a New Testament Doctrine of Efficiency.[31]

Two specific aspects of efficiency as promoted by Dobbins require special attention for this thesis. First, the pastor was considered the key administrator tasked with organizing the church to operate more efficiently. Dobbins explained the transition toward a pastoral theology that was based on his business background and not a theological foundation:

> I came to this work at Southern Seminary out of the business world, the field of journalism in the practical newspaper business, and so I didn't have the professor's viewpoint. I looked at it from the viewpoint of the man in the pew. I inaugurated changes in the curriculum which involved studying the pastorate in the light of the actual situation—the study of the community, the study of the church and the study of the various functions of the minister.[32]

This was a shift from the historical understanding and function of pastoral theology.[33] Dobbins believed, as a condition of success, that all labor should become increasingly more specialized.[34] According to Dobbins, pastors had been ill-equipped to face the modernized role of the pastorate. Men trained in business would expect more from their church now that they had an understanding of efficiency principles from the industrial world. "The

30. Ryan, "Administrative Theory of Gaines Stanley Dobbins," 61. Ryan says, "Dobbins freely used ideas he had gleaned here and there at any point that suited his purposes in writing. While he attributed germinal ideas of administration to business experts such as Emerson, he clearly based his personal assessment of these ideas on Christian principles." Citing chapter seven of Dobbins's, *The Efficient Church*, Ryan says efficiency was a "fetish" for Dobbins and he always based his conclusions upon "Biblical principles of Christian service."

31. Dobbins, *The Efficient Church*, 19–26.

32. Gray, "Dobbinology," 2–3. Dobbins elected to combine the study of community and the study of church into one, because both were focused on the study of the individuals that make up both community and church. He sought to identify needs scientifically utilizing modern methods of psychological tests and measurements. The primary instrument he used was the survey, which was first used by G. Stanley Hall in studying the religious experiences and needs of adolescents.

33. The training of pastors, in Dobbins opinion, had been lacking the experiential aspect and therefore, needed to be adjusted to fit modern challenges of the pastorate. See Dobbins, *The Efficient Church*, 27–47. Also see Crouch, "The Influence of William James."

34. Dobbins, *The Efficient Church*, 15.

church inevitably responded to the pressure for better business methods
. . . The preacher of necessity became an organizer and promoter as well as
pulpiteer."[35] Dobbins elaborated further on the nature of this change:

> *Public Leadership is Conditioned on efficiency.* Mere personality,
> power of oratory, social and financial standing, prestige of office,
> will no longer suffice to give a man a place of permanent leader-
> ship. The age of "divine right of kings" is gone forever. The need
> for leadership was never greater, but men will follow a man only
> as he achieves results.[36]

The burden of administration was so cumbersome for the pastor that
the need arose for a new office, the minister of education.[37] Specialization
became the method to manage the burden of efficiency for pastoral duties
and church operations. "We have recognized," said Dobbins, "that to meet
the complex demands of the modern world the Christian leader must at
least put himself in the way of becoming a practical efficiency expert in
church organization and administration."[38] The church, therefore, was im-
peded by the philosophy of pragmatism and its desire for results.

The second target was to discover the needs of the congregation and
community in order to be more efficient as leaders, and to enlist and equip
parishioners. Dobbins argued that, "Regular and systematic surveys of the
community afford accurate information as to needs and possibilities."[39] The
men and women that the pastor was to reach would have received specialized training and would expect the same type of efficient organization from
the church.[40] According to Dobbins, "Efficiency principles have been applied to producing a higher type of human beings."[41]

The behavioral sciences were the means by which Dobbins believed
the needs of modern humanity could be understood.[42] Therefore, the
church was required to adapt in order to reach and enlist this newly defined individual. The philosophies of business efficiency were employed to
create church management strategies that were laden with ideologies from

---

35. Dobbins, "50 Years of Church Administration," 5.

36. Dobbins, *The Efficient Church*, 16. Emphasis in original.

37. Dobbins, *The Efficient Church*, 16–19. Ryan, "Administrative Theory of Gaines
Stanley Dobbins," 3.

38. Dobbins, *The Efficient Church*, 47.

39. Dobbins, *The Efficient Church*, 18.

40. Ryan, "Gaines S. Dobbins—Author," 412.

41. Dobbins, *The Efficient Church*, 17.

42. Dobbins, *The Churchbook*, 28–50. See Section 2, "A Church Knowing Its Community and Itself."

the behavioral sciences. Allen Graves said, "With the development of the human relations movement in American business and industry, more attention was focused upon the satisfactions of the individual participant."[43]

Dobbins even acknowledged that prior to the 1920s this new role and methodology of efficiency would not have been accepted in the churches.[44] This assessment by Dobbins could be an admission to the use of secular techniques and sources outside of the Scripture to guide church methodology. Graves provided acuity relating to the dependence of church efficiency on the behavioral sciences:

> An effective church or denominational administrator will be able to use the insights of the behavioral scientists in integrating all of those areas or disciplines that can be useful to administrative practitioners as they seek to understand, predict, and direct the behavior of individuals and groups.[45]

Graves also recalled the impact of efficiency ideals upon Dobbins, "The emphasis upon efficiency that made such an impact on business and industry in America in the early decades of the twentieth century made a significant impact on the thinking of the young professor. His first book title reflects that impact."[46]

Dobbins did not seem to alter his approach to administration throughout his career. He followed the trends of business efficiency from scientific management to human resources to mental hygiene; each of which were dependent upon the behavioral sciences.[47] *The Churchbook* written in 1951, twenty-eight years after his first book, became the sequel to Dobbins's earlier work on efficiency and demonstrated his consistency in following the trends.[48] This work was a detailed manual for pastors and churches to

43. Graves, "Gaines S. Dobbins—Mr. Church Administration," 386. Graves's observations could be said to point to the precursor of Mullins's doctrine of soul competency, which Dobbins believed, that led him to accept business efficiency favorably.

44. Dobbins, "50 Years of Church Administration," 5.

45. Graves, "Gaines S. Dobbins–Mr. Church Administrator," 387.

46. Graves, "Gaines S. Dobbins–Mr. Church Administrator," 385.

47. Ryan, "Administrative Theory of Gaines Stanley Dobbins." Ryan demonstrates the progression of thought and dependence of Dobbins upon efficiency principles. He pays special attention to the dependence upon the behavioral sciences in the realm of administration. Based on Ryan's conclusion, Dobbins's works follow the trend of administration, including its dependence upon the behavioral sciences.

48. Dobbins, "Oral History Interviews," 38. Ryan, "Gaines S. Dobbins—Author," 412.

follow, including examples of surveys the congregation should utilize to get to know the community.[49]

The efficiency proposed by Dobbins should raise particular questions for the reader. First, is Scripture sufficient? Dobbins knew this was a critique of his practice and responded by affirming that, "The New Testament is, of course, the sole, sufficient, and authoritative rule of faith and practice for a church that rejects ecclesiastical rule."[50] His use of business efficiency and the behavioral sciences indicate at least a compromise of his stated position.

Second, should the pastorate be specialized? Regardless of how one may answer this question, it is evident that the principles of efficiency created an atmosphere and system in which specialization became necessary. To the contrary, the pastoral duties assigned in Scripture do not seem to carry any connotation of specialization or professionalization of the office.[51]

Third, are the behavioral sciences a reliable source for understanding human nature? The models of efficiency, as demonstrated by Ryan, utilize scientific management, human resources and mental hygiene to understand human needs.[52] Dobbins appreciated the relatively new science and became dependent upon its techniques, especially tests and measurements, which emerged from social scientists like G. Stanley Hall and E. L. Thorndike.

Finally, the individual became the epicenter of the ecclesiastical mission. This idea should properly be connected to Mullins's view of soul competency as seen in the previous chapter. Understanding and empowering the individual became the pursuit of the efficient pastor. Dobbins preferred the explanation of human nature that came from the behavioral and social sciences. Ecclesiology and pastoral theology were to be aligned, out of modern necessity and efficiency, with the needs of individuals as defined and revealed by psychologists and sociologists.

49. Dobbins, *The Churchbook*, 28–50.

50. Dobbins, *The Churchbook*, 1. Dobbins referred to ecclesiastical rule as the church polity of those who do not believe in the autonomous local church. A church governed by ecclesiastical rule deferred to church tradition as much or, at times, more than the Scripture for its authority.

51. Hammett, *Biblical Foundations for Baptist Churches*, 163–77. "The most important texts are Acts 20:28–31; Romans 12:8; Ephesians 4:11–16; 1 Thessalonians 5:12; 1 Timothy 3:1–7; 5:17; Titus 1:5–9; Hebrews 13:7, 17; and 1 Peter 5:1–4." The primary roles of the pastorate entail ministry of the Word and shepherding the flock of God. Pastors are to be overseers, but this seems to be more in relation to his role as a steward of God using the authority of the Word; to be a faithful servant for the master.

52. Ryan, "Administrative Theory of Gaines Stanley Dobbins."

Religious Education and the Cult of Efficiency

The efficiency movement, with which Dobbins was enamored, was not confined to the business model, but was also an intricate part of the education reform of Dewey, Thorndike, and company.[53] Dobbins's involvement as a religious educator also gained him exposure to efficiency concepts that were utilized in progressive education. The efficiency movement came largely from the influence of the Industrial Revolution and as some have suggested, the impact of social Darwinism would guide the desire for efficiency due to the development of "scientific management."[54] The application of scientific management to the world of business, and later to education, was compared to the "change from the use of hand tools to the use of machinery."[55]

The reign of science and business in America aided educational reform as educators sought to emulate both disciplines. Thorndike, who was influenced by the efficiency movement, promoted the science of tests and measurements that Dobbins utilized to achieve educational efficiency.[56] Joncich demonstrated the influence of efficiency upon Thorndike:

> What did Thorndike think science had to offer educators that was superior to philosophy, tradition, or opinion? For one thing, he contended that schools could be run more efficiently with the help of science. The efficiency motif was a timely argument around the turn of the century.[57]

Thorndike sought to improve upon certain mental functions in order to bring about a more efficient human being.[58]

---

53. Callahan, *Education and the Cult of Efficiency*. This claim is demonstrated throughout the book. See also, Dobbins, *The Efficient Church*. Dobbins, *The Church-Book*. Dobbins, *Building Better Churches*.

54. Gutek, *Historical and Philosophical Foundations of Education*, 294–328. Joncich, *Psychology and the Science of Education*, 6–11 and 46–47. Callahan, *Education and the Cult of Efficiency*, 19.

55. Callahan, *Education and the Cult of Efficiency*, 20.

56. Dobbins Papers, Box 7, Folders 9–18. The archive material contains church surveys and various correspondences between Dobbins and the various church representatives. Once the survey was completed, Dobbins provided assessment and recommendation based on the data. Dobbins, *The Improvement of Teaching in the Sunday School*, 150–69. In chapter 9, "Let Us Test Our Teaching," Dobbins explained how tests and measurements can aid teaching. He also provided sample surveys for measuring fruitfulness.

57. Joncich, *Psychology and the Science of Education*, 6.

58. Thorndike, "Education as Science," in Joncich, *Psychology and the Science of Education*, 48–54.

Dobbins, in turn, explained his use of tests and measurements as akin to Jesus' test: "by their fruits ye shall know them."[59] While this is a misrepresentation of the intent of the passage, Dobbins attempted to justify his use of tests that he categorized as objective and subjective. Mathematically calculated measurements were considered factual, while the subjective measurements required a "qualified observer" to interpret the use of the data.[60] It should be noted that subjective data was gathered by either surveys or questionnaires like those created by Hall and Thorndike.

GEORGE ALBERT COE

Dobbins relied upon the educational arm of the church as the engine to run the sacred corporation, "The pastor as administrator, building a church to meet human needs, turns first to the educational organizations of the church as furnishing chief resources for the enterprise."[61] As a result, Coe became the pivot around which Dobbins would turn in order to advance his methodology into the efficiency paradigm.

With a lack of literature and frustration with transmissive learning, Dobbins sought out Coe and other modern educationalists for answers. Dobbins explained, "Throughout the world of theological education there were stirrings of discontent because the curriculum was too content-centered and inadequately oriented toward equipping the student for effectiveness in pastoral ministries."[62] This discontent had led him to study at Columbia Teachers College, one of the foremost teacher's colleges of his day. He was in search of modern pedagogical techniques of the religious education movement that moved away from transmissive learning. Once his application had been approved, Dobbins requested to study with Dr. Coe.[63] It is understandable that Dobbins would seek Coe to satisfy his discontent,

59. Dobbins, *The ChurchBook*, 100–101. Dobbins was referring to Matthew 7:16.

60. Dobbins, *The ChurchBook*, 100–107. Page 102 describes the objective and subjective testing. Sample surveys are shown on other pages throughout the book.

61. Dobbins, *Building Better Churches*, 196.

62. Dobbins, *Great Teachers*, 79. Chapter 7 of Dobbins's book pays tribute to George Albert Coe as an educational revolutionary. Samuel R. Stone wrote Dobbins on August 9, 1965 after reading *Great Teachers Make a Difference*. Stone said, "As I read about Dr. Coe, I kept saying to myself, 'That's what Dr. Dobbins did.'" See Dobbins Papers, Box 9, Folder 3.

63. Dobbins, *Great Teachers*, 81. Dobbins recounts the first meeting he had with George Albert Coe. Coe recommended that Dobbins choose master teachers to observe their style and method of teaching, not in order to emulate them, but to be exposed to their personality and philosophy. So Coe introduced him to Dewey, Thorndike, Kilpatrick, Elliot, and others.

since Holifield reported, "The patriarch of the movement was a philosopher of religion named George Albert Coe."[64]

The practical courses that Dobbins was responsible for teaching at Southern Seminary lacked academic respectability, and during his first few years of teaching, several members of the faculty expressed concern with the direction of the practical studies.[65] "There began to be murmurs," Dobbins recalled, "that these students were taking more time than was justified from Greek, Hebrew, history and theology."[66] These sentiments were shared in faculty meeting as Dobbins recalled:

> . . . one very notable scholar of our faculty cleared his throat a few times when the matter came up . . . and said, "I don't go for this. A student has three years in which to get the fundamentals of a theological education. If I had my way, we would somehow endow these students. I could wish they would do nothing except their classwork, not even preaching on Sunday, in order to give their full attention to getting the framework of a scholarly theological education."[67]

According to Dobbins, the students also shared this view with the faculty, and it was not a localized phenomenon. Dobbins had learned that J. M. Price was experiencing similar difficulty at SWBTS and the same tensions were apparent at other theological institutions.[68]

The influence of Coe helped to squelch any perception that Dobbins's disciplines were insignificant. The new methods of teaching rooted in the scientific would help establish respectability. Dobbins recognized Coe's ascendency in a field otherwise cast aside in academia. "His was the formative influence," said Dobbins, "that did much to give direction and vitality to the concepts and processes which have led teaching and training in the churches, as well as in seminaries and Christian school, to academic respectability and spiritual fruitfulness."[69] What did George Albert Coe instill in Dobbins that gave him confidence to press forward in what he previously thought to be a discipline that lacked academic respectability?

Coe's views on religious education were transforming the young discipline led by his promotion of "creative learning" in opposition to the traditional practice of transmissive teaching. His new methods promoted a

64. Holifield, *A History of Pastoral Care in America*, 225.

65. Dobbins, *Great Teachers*, 80.

66. Gray, "Dobbinology," 3.

67. Gray, "Dobbinology," 3.

68. Dobbins, *Great Teachers*, 80.

69. Dobbins, *Great Teachers*, 86.

modern view of anthropology built from the scientific influence of psychology of religion and educational psychology. Each of these elements shaped the thought of Dobbins that reconstructed his view of religious education, the learning process and the anthropology of the student.

Religious Education

The ecclesiastical focus of religious education at the beginning of the twentieth century was composed of binary streams of philosophy that impacted orthodox theology.[70] Dobbins promoted both streams, which are viewed as contributory to his views of religious education and pastoral care. The first stream was the necessity of Christian education as the task of the church to promote moral character, which was intended to breed the democratic spirit among believers.[71]

A core function of the Christian church is to be an educational institution, according to Dobbins. "Periods of educational neglect," he said, "have been uniformly periods of weakness and corruption in Christian history, while all the great revival movements have been accompanied by renewed emphasis on education, both as cause and as effect."[72] While few would disagree that an important function of the church is to teach, Dobbins set up an argument for education in the church that mimicked the state system of education. The government school systems were set to provide secular education and the church would provide religious education. "The ideal of education," Dobbins explained, "for every individual through the state school and the church school as separate institutions was heartily accepted by most of the Protestants or evangelical bodies."[73] The demarcation between sacred and secular seemed to be a battle won for humanists who sought diligently to erase religious sectarianism from education because they believed religion to be harmful to democracy.[74]

The shift seemed innocent enough to religious educators who began to see their discipline as respectable and useful to teach religion and morality. The deception lay behind the bifurcation of education into compartments of secular and religious. In order to educate an individual from the secular perspective, a system that explained realities in the natural realm, devoid of

70. Holifield, *A History of Pastoral Care in America.*

71. More will be said on this in the following section on John Dewey, since democracy in education is a theme revealed in Dobbins due in large degree to his influence.

72. Dobbins, *Can A Religious Democracy Survive?*, 57.

73. Dobbins, *Can A Religious Democracy Survive?*, 75.

74. Hunter, *The Death of Character*, 60.

the supernatural, would suffice. This explains why progressives in education focused on the arbitrary experiences of the individual to produce truth and not upon absolutes that were established by an all-powerful and authoritative God.[75] Moreover, those experiences were intended to be imbedded within a naturalistic and humanistic framework.[76]

George Coe believed that ecclesiastical traditions had been binding upon the Christian. Christians should shed the cloak of "ecclesiastical machinery" in order to pursue Christian experience. In other words, the church and its doctrines should not be the starting point for Christian education. Coe described the leading role of Christian experience as:

> That which gives Christian education its true and proper life is an experience that is obviously worth repeating and developing. The worth thus found and developed in the present experience is that which first makes vital the problems of doctrine, and it is the same experienced worth that furnishes the true test of all our ecclesiastical machinery.[77]

The second is truly a corollary of the first; anthropology had to be modified. This modification necessitated new techniques in order to stimulate the newly defined man according to evolutionary principles that guided the scientific understanding of anthropology.[78] The church began accommodating a new vocabulary that was steeped in the psychological jargon of the day. This meant religious educators spoke in terms of science, human development, tests and measurements, and personal experience.[79] Dobbins recognized that, "Specialists emerged who put the child at the center and demanded that content and method be made subordinate to the learner's experience."[80] This was a dramatic contrast to traditional views of anthropology that called for inward conformity to God's design of man in order to keep from evil and do that which was considered good.[81] Consequently,

75. Dewey, *Democracy and Education*, 306–23.

76. Dewey, *Democracy and Education*, 324–39.

77. Coe, *What is Christian Education?*, vi.

78. The shift in anthropology is evidenced by the necessity of new techniques. This aspect will be discussed further within this chapter under the sub-title New Methods: Anthropological Shifts.

79. Holifield, *A History of Pastoral Care in America*, 164.

80. Dobbins, *Can A Religious Democracy Survive?*, 101. The specialists Dobbins is referring to are, Pestalozzi, Herbart, Froebel, Montessori, Binet and Simon, G. Stanley Hall, Preyer, Dewey, Thorndike, Shinn and Baldwin.

81. See Dagg, *Manual of Church Order*, 271. Dagg represents the traditional position as he described the minister's duty to preach the Word of God as the truth so that the congregation may "drink in the word with delight, that their souls be refreshed by

Christianity could now be validated by experiences and "truth" realized from within.

Dobbins welcomed the scientific explanation of man because it added some degree of academic standing to his discipline. "Genetic and educational psychology," said Dobbins, "began to open a new world of understanding of the child's nature and needs."[82] Dobbins admitted that by the turn of the century these ideas were adopted in "Sunday School circles."[83] Prior to this advent, the reason for Sunday School, in the minds of the masses, was for children. This had been demonstrated to Dobbins by his colleagues. The curriculum in Sunday School pedagogy could not distance itself from this stigma without extraneous aid. There needed to be a change and Dobbins explained his solution:

> Summer courses in education convinced me that something radical would be necessary if "Sunday School pedagogy" was to be replaced by courses with reputable standing in religious education. I saw clearly that there were not two sets of principles in education—secular principles, applicable to the teaching of public school subjects on the one hand and "spiritual" principles, applicable to the teaching of the Bible and religious subjects on the other.[84]

The pressure to achieve academic credibility made Dobbins susceptible and favorable to the tidal transformation that education was undergoing. Coe "erased the boundary between 'secular' and 'religious' learning," for Dobbins, "and never ceased to express regret that ministers and Sunday School teachers seemed to ascribe some sort of magical power to the Scriptures that made its teaching and learning different from the teaching and learning of other subjects."[85] The church school now followed the lead of

---

it, and that it greatly increases their fruitfulness in holiness; with this knowledge, he will be stimulated to go forward in his work with boldness, and to endure all his toils with the sustaining assurance that his labor is not in vain in the Lord." In John 14:15 Jesus said, "If you love me keep my commandments." Combined with Romans 8:29, that statement demonstrates that there should be inward transformation for those who follow Christ.

82. Dobbins, *Can A Religious Democracy Survive?*, 101.

83. Dobbins, *Can A Religious Democracy Survive?*, 101.

84. Dobbins, *Great Teachers*, 80. This line of reasoning seems to negate the role of the Holy Spirit in religious pedagogy. There is a rather distinct view of persons and goals when comparing the secular and the sacred approaches to education. One's view of personhood dictates his principles of pedagogy and will inevitably promote corresponding methods of teaching and learning.

85. Dobbins, *Great Teachers*, 84–85.

the progressives, who guided the public systems of education.[86] Dobbins was willing to embrace the anthropological assumptions embedded in the new methodologies so that religious education could keep pace with the educational techniques of the public system.

New Methods

Psychology of Religion

The birth of psychology of religion is due in part to the intellectual frenzy spilling over from the Enlightenment and Darwinian thought. The areas of the world that remained religious were pressured by the new intellectualism. In an effort to maintain the status quo within the academy, religion and supernaturalism would need a way to be expressed in scientific terms. The elites in the West struggled to avoid their religious convictions but did not want to disregard the new knowledge.[87] As Robert Crapps summarized, "The psychology of religion as a scientific discipline belongs largely to the Western world and to shifting emphasis during the nineteenth and twentieth centuries. It came as a spin-off from the development of the social sciences in general and particularly scientific psychology."[88] Drakeford, argued similarly that, "while there have been occasional contributions from Europe, the United States has been the source of most of the outstanding work."[89] The coalescence of psychology and religion has made a rather odd couple. As Drakeford said, "Psychology of religion represents a shotgun wedding of two unlike disciplines."[90]

There are historians who believe Williams James to be the father of psychology of religion, perhaps due to his label as Father of American Psychology.[91] James suggested in his work, *Varieties of Religious Experience* that much of the credit for beginning the new scientific study should be given to E. D. Starbuck and J. H. Leuba.[92] James tried to lean upon the tradition

86. Dobbins, *Can A Religious Democracy Survive?*, 72–76.

87. Drakeford, *Psychology in Search of a Soul*, 9–16. Drakeford gives several reasons why "psychology of religion came to birth on American soil."

88 Crapps, *An Introduction to Psychology of Religion*, 3.

89. Drakeford, *Psychology in Search of a Soul*, 9.

90. Drakeford, *Psychology in Search of a Soul*, 4.

91. Strunk, "Humanistic Religious Psychology," in Malony, *Current Perspectives*, 27–35.

92. James, *Varieties of Religious Experience*, 11. E. D. Starbuck is mentioned no less than fifty-two times by James in his lectures on religious experience. He describes that

of Jonathan Edwards to demonstrate that the psychology of religion was not all together new. However, Edwards understood religious experience as something man cannot fully comprehend, a work done supernaturally.[93] Edwards highlighted religious experience in order to understand the state of man's heart. He was using religion essentially to understand psychology.[94]

The new discipline of psychology of religion offered a contrary perspective regarding religious experiences to that of Edwards. Rather than using the Scriptures to illuminate the religious experiences and motives of men, the scientific version of psychology of religion sought to explain these experiences as natural phenomena related to evolutionary maturity. Scientific psychology was to measure and interpret religion and provide explanation as to why these religious experiences occur. The antithesis is found in Edwards and other Puritans as they sought to use religion, based upon the Scripture, to understand the soul of man.[95]

Coe described the new discipline as the, "Application of Empirical Methods to Present Religious Phenomena."[96] He continued to pronounce the origins of such a discipline, crediting men with whom he worked closely.

Starbuck's manuscripts were crucial to his explanation of religious experiences. James does mention Leuba's and Coe's works in the psychological and scientific study of religious experiences, but his lectures are dependent in a greater degree to Starbuck, who wrote the first book on the subject.

93. James, *Varieties of Religious Experience*, 22. Edwards believed good works were an evidence of faith for all those who had been awakened by saving grace. See Edwards, *The Religious Affections*, 27–53. Edwards said, "God has given to mankind affections, for the same purpose which he has given all the faculties and principles of the human soul for, viz., that they might be subservient to man's chief end, and the great business for which God has created him, that is, the business of religion."

94. Edwards, *The Religious Affections*, 22.

95. Watson, *The Doctrine of Repentance*, 15–58. Watson begins by describing false repentance and then proceeds to describe the nature of true repentance. In both he aligns repentance with the attitudes and actions of the Scriptures rather than with a person's experiences. He acknowledges that a person's feelings and experiences can be deceptive. True repentance must be measured by the Scripture. Beeke and Penderson, *Meet the Puritans*, 200. Edward's *Religious Affections* was his defense regarding the validity of the Great Awakening. He was trying to argue a distinction between true and false religious conversions, not with scientific language or paradigm in view, but religious and supernatural explanations. Edwards is focusing more on the inability of man to see and understand the immaterial of man rather than he is the behavior that accompanies a truly saved person. He does accent the behavioral change that occurs in those who have had a truly divine experience, but this is only because man cannot see the root change in the heart of man. Further, Edwards is focused on the responsive behavior due to supernatural change from outside the man. The psychology of religion focuses more upon the inward adjustments of the man to validate and encourage his religious experiences.

96. Coe, *The Spiritual Life*, 12.

The first comprehensive and organized impulse to a scientific study of the religious phenomena in the midst of which we are living made its appearance in the present decade. In 1891 President G. Stanley Hall, of Clark University, published an article on the moral and religious training of children based directly upon the psychology of childhood and adolescence. Several pupils of his followed with further observations and analyses. Especially worthy of mention for the range and patient impartiality of his work is E. D. Starbuck, now of Stanford University. It would be easy to over or under estimate the value of the results thus attained, but this is at least may be claimed: We have here the crude beginnings of an empirical psychology of religious experience.[97]

Psychologists, beginning with Wundt in 1879, attempted to make application of laboratory methods in an effort to brand the social sciences as more scientific. George A. Coe and Edwin D. Starbuck, who influenced many,[98] tried to apply the newly created "scientific" psychological methodology, "in the field of religious experience."[99] Brown even correlated the influence of psychology of religion to the morphing arena of religious education: "The cause of religious education owes much to the development of the new science of psychology and the directing of the psychological investigation to the field of religion. *The Psychology of Religion*, Starbuck (1899), and *The Spiritual Life*, Coe (1900), created a sensation in religious circles."[100] Brown explained the excitement, "Just as the application of scientific methods to the study of biblical literature aroused a great interest in Bible study in the universities in the last quarter century—an interest in the psychology of religion in the first quarter of the new century has proved to be a great asset to religion."[101] However, as Anthony and Benson point out, it is a great asset only if one rejects doctrines of evangelical theology while embracing social Darwinism, Protestant liberal theology, and progressive education.[102]

97. Coe, *The Spiritual Life*, 12–13.

98. Drakeford, *Psychology in Search of a Soul*, 18–23. Kemp, *Physicians of the Soul*. Anthony and Benson, *History and Philosophy of Christian Education*. Gutek, *Historical and Philosophical Foundations of Education*. Each of these writers attributes influence of psychology of religion to James, Hall, Coe, Starbuck, and Dewey.

99. Brown, *A History of Religious Education in Recent Times*, 236–37.

100. Brown, *A History of Religious Education in Recent Times*, 236.

101. Brown, *A History of Religious Education in Recent Times*, 237.

102. Anthony and Benson, *History and Philosophy of Christian Education*, 346.

Nonetheless, psychology of religion, dissimulated as empiricism, began to reshape religious education and the church.[103]

Starbuck, the first man to write a book on the subject, was influenced heavily by G. Stanley Hall and Darwin's natural selection.[104] Starbuck's use of the phrase "storm and stress," coined by Hall, illustrated with clarity how an individual realizes truth through experience:

> The prevalence of religious doubt and storm and stress seems to be the result of natural selection. Those persons have been chosen out as most fit to exist who do not take things simply on authority, but who gain for themselves a rational hold on truth. Nothing is really understood at first hand until it has been called up into consciousness, and then worked over into experience.[105]

Dr. Wayne Oates summarized Starbuck's work by saying that he, "insists that religious experience is an intensification of the process of maturation . . . the teen-ager [sic] undergoes a rapid growth process which telescopes and intensifies these encounters in his developing selfhood."[106]

Starbuck further explained how he believed the instinct of religion arises from a conglomerate of impulses:

> It should be constantly borne in mind that religion has not been nourished from a single root, but that, on the contrary, it has many sources. Among the facts in the preceding chapters there are evidences that other deep-rooted instincts besides that of sex have been operative in religious development. Out of the instinct of self-preservation and the desire for fullness of life in the physiological plane, there seems to have arisen, by progressive refinement and irradiation, the religious impulse toward spiritual self-enlargement. Again, physiological hunger—an instinct even more primal than that of sex—widens into appropriativeness, delight in intellectual conquest, and finally into a craving for spiritual knowledge. That is, the religious feeling of

103. This is a point of primary importance to the thesis of this work. Religious Education first accepted psychology of religion in order to understand human nature, human needs, and desirable religious experiences. The framework created by psychology of religion within religious education opened the door for the necessity of specialized counseling within the church. As the cultural terrain bred a necessity within the church for training specialized counselors, Dobbins turned to psychology of religion as the means to validate such a position.

104. More will be explained relating to the connection between Starbuck, Hall and Darwinian principles in the section on Genetic Psychology later in this chapter.

105. Starbuck, *Psychology of Religion*, 399.

106. Oates, *Psychology of Religion*, 73.

hungering after righteousness may be in some sense an irradia-
tion of the crude instinct of food-getting. Pleasure in activity,
growing out of an overflow of nervous energy, seems also to
have been lifted to the plane of the spiritual life, and, in part to
underlie self-expression and joy in service as religious impulses.
In the beginnings of religion these instincts existed side by side,
and, in the functioning, brought into activity the lower nervous
centres. The process of religious development has consisted in
arousing discharges from these through the higher psychic centres, and in working them into higher synthesis.[107]

Based on Starbuck's explanation, religion is merely a part of an evolutionary
process of human development, and he is not alone in his thinking. Oates
said that, "Starbuck's view can be found also in Coe, Ames and others and
has made an enduring contribution to religious education."[108]

George Albert Coe built upon the pioneering work of Starbuck, G.
Stanley Hall, William James, and John Dewey.[109] Coe and James, along with
others, "made visible an approach that was to dominate discussion until
psychoanalysis made its impact on the American study of psychology of
religion in the 1920s and 1930s and was to influence the phenomenological
and humanistic studies of religion."[110] Anthony and Benson refer to Coe
and other early religious educators when they say: "These liberals tended
to provide humanistic or social interpretations to Christianity's doctrines
about God, mankind, salvation, redemption, Jesus Christ, the role of the
church, the authority of Scriptures, and the future of mankind."[111] The modern methods applied by Coe tended to diminish the authority of Scripture
and exalt man as creator of values.[112] According to Dobbins, "[Coe] believed
that man could increasingly come to an understanding of this growth process in the areas of moral and religious living, and that man had a responsibility to exercise a creative force in development of meaning, values, and
progressive achievements."[113]

107. Starbuck, *Psychology of Religion*, 403.

108. Oates, *Psychology of Religion*, 46.

109. Crapps, *An Introduction to Psychology of Religion*, 5. Anthony and Benson, *History and Philosophy of Christian Education*, 349.

110. Crapps, *An Introduction to Psychology of Religion*, 132.

111. Anthony and Benson, *History and Philosophy of Christian Education*, 347.

112. Anthony and Benson, *History and Philosophy of Christian Education*, 347.
These writers give highlights of Coe's influence upon religious education. They also argue that Dewey's influence upon Coe demonstrates why Christian Education has many
of the same methods and language utilized in public school education.

113. Dobbins, *Great Teachers*, 87.

Anthropological Shift

The psychology of religion was merely an attempt to apply the scientific method to religious experiences.[114] An empirical elucidation of man's most sacred experiences required a natural explanation of what was previously believed to be supernatural. Darwinian thought gave credence to an empirically persuaded commentary on religious experiences, which required an evolutionary framework for anthropology. The new methods promoted by Coe were in part a response to the new definition of man as proposed by the theory of evolution and, at times, promoted elements of the innately good man espoused by Rousseau. Dewey explained that modern educationalists align themselves with the thinking of Rousseau:

> [Rousseau] insists that existing education is bad because parents and teachers are always thinking of the accomplishments of adults, and that all reform depends upon centering attention upon the powers and weaknesses of children. Rousseau said, as well as did, many foolish things. But his insistence that education be based upon the native capacities of those to be taught and upon the need of studying the children in order to discover what these native powers are, sounded the key-note of all modern efforts for educational progress. It meant that education is not something to be forced upon children from without, but is the growth of capacities with which human beings are endowed at birth. From this conception flow the various considerations which educational reformers since his day have most emphasized.[115]

Coe adopted the new framework to justify his methodology of education and suggested that others do the same. "Everybody who has an articulate desire to be modern," said Coe, "is thinking about human nature in terms that he supposes to be those of the psychologist."[116] Coe is suggesting that a modern view of anthropology should come from the psychologist rather than the theologian. Coe explained how he believed the fundamentalist theologian promoted an anthropology that was binding on modern man.

> The more one looks into the course of religious thought, and of popular thought in general, since Darwin, the more certain becomes this conclusion. Biologists and biological psychologists, as far as I am aware, never claimed to add a single item to the

114. Coe, *The Spiritual Life*, 15–16.
115. Dewey and Dewey, *Schools of Tomorrow*, 1–2.
116. Coe, *Motives of Men*, 45.

already recognized list of beast-like qualities in men, and theologians never attacked evolution upon any such ground. Rather, what the new view of us added was an explanation of "how we got that way," and the explanation—mark this—constituted a partial excuse (not justification, but excuse) for much of our bad contact. It actually lifted from us a part of the condemnation that was inherent in the theological view of special creation.[117]

It cannot be assumed that Dobbins agreed with Coe on all points, but he is unashamed to declare his appreciation for his professor.[118] Dobbins's acceptance of these modern educationalists' ideals necessitated his agreement with their concept of anthropology as endowed with goodness and ability to discover truth. These concepts were accepted despite lack of reconciliation with the biblical account of man's innate nature and propensity towards sinfulness and wickedness.[119]

The new methods would not make sense nor be effective upon the noble man created "from the dust of the ground." Rather, the techniques implemented were due to an altered metaphysical belief that led inconspicuously to the necessity of new practices of education and care for modern man. If man is not like his savage ancestors, in the way Coe suggested, there was a need to produce new methods of learning that could be applied to the ever evolving modern man.[120] The sentiments of Coe were not subliminal. Coe understood the theological implications of such an anthropological position. He rebelled against the traditionally orthodox view of depravity and the redemption found in Christ alone:

> The sophistic that turned this into an alleged depletion of our moral vim is not far to seek. The reason why certain persons did not rejoice at excuses that evolution provides for much of our faultiness is that they did not want us to be excused, but condemned. They wanted this, not because they were vicious, but because they held a theology that required them to think so. And because this authoritative theology had settled upon one way as the only one whereby man could be released from the sins that beset him, it could not rejoice to discover that there are other openers of prison doors.
>
> If many of the dogmatically faithful did not think their way into quite all this detail, they realized at least that to accept at the

117. Coe, *Motives of Men*, 25.
118. Dobbins, *Great Teachers*, 79–88.
119. Romans 5:12–21.
120. Coe, *The Motives of Men*, 73–79.

hand of evolution an ennobled view of man or of God would involve admitting inadequacy and lack of true authority in the dogmatic system. The dogmas never were complimentary to human nature, but—O droll self-delusion—when science offered us a real compliment, dogma insisted that it was an insult to our exalted dignity![121]

He believed that the contrarieties of nature in man were to be remedied by stimulus and response in order to overcome wants that *may* lead to evil.[122] Coe understood clearly that his educational methodology was fixed upon a foundation contrary to theological orthodoxy, "The tradition of official Christianity has run to the effect that the heart of man is desperately wicked; that it is selfish, sensual, and self-deceived; and that it is incapable of improving itself until an infusion of divine power has made possible, first repentance, then new life."[123] Later in the same work, he alluded to the fact that the traditional fundamentalists were responsible for placing modern man in proverbial prison.[124] Each individual has adequate amiability for self-discovery and self-realization that would theoretically produce freedom for the person and improve his own self.[125] Coe described man's innate ability in contrast to the need for a regenerate work of the divine:

> We now have the groundwork for an explanation of the decay of belief in depravity even among those who have regarded themselves as faithful to the traditions of the elders. The doctrine, taken by itself, unrelieved by a counterbalancing doctrine of regeneration through the intervention of a merciful God, is too dreadful, too accusing of the Creator, to be endured. Therefore, when the doctrine of regeneration fails to be convincing in practice, the conviction grows that men are not so bad, after all. Natural amiability becomes more impressive, more suggestive of the hand of God in the creation of man, and natural unamiability actually gets overlooked or slurred over! The preaching of repentance naturally loses its bite, too. An odd swing of the pendulum, this. For, whereas the thunders of the law broke forth against the natural depravity of man, which he couldn't help, the bad conduct of naturally good men is not found particularly exciting![126]

121. Coe, *The Motives of Men*, 26.
122. Coe, *The Motives of Men*, 71–72.
123. Coe, *The Motives of Men*, 56.
124. Coe, *The Motives of Men*, 76–79.
125. Coe, *The Motives of Men*, 209–15 and 252–59.
126. Coe, *The Motives of Men*, 60.

Coe was at least honest enough to admit that his view of methodology is predicated upon a view of anthropology that is antithetical to that of conservative orthodoxy.

In his writings, Dobbins never gave specific indication regarding his position on evolution theory. However, in an interview with Badgett Dillard, Dobbins expressed favorable sentiments toward the theory.

> The evolution controversy was a handle for the ultra-fundamentalists. You can scarcely be an educated person and not recognize that there always has been an element of natural selection, natural evolution. Otherwise, you just have to deny the facts. And we had professors who were wise and well read, who didn't teach evolution in its radical sense, but who tried to get it across that God's creatorship was not invalidated by Darwin. And that is true. If you haven't read Darwin's Origin of Species [sic]. I hope you have looked at it . . .
>
> You know that he was wise enough not to take any theological view of the creation of man. In fact, he acknowledged that there has never been discovered the missing link. But his view was a [sic] red flag to the fundamentalists and all those then attacked the Seminary because it took a modified view of creation.[127]

His adoption of the "new methods" and belief in their effectiveness raises questions. According to Wayne Oates, "Dr. Dobbins had a way of taking hold of such rebellions and putting them to work."[128] It could be said that Dobbins tried to redeem the methods of the modern educationalists; but can the techniques of the progressives be used without residual effects upon an orthodox theology? The way one practices education unveils their core belief about anthropology.

---

127. Dobbins, "Oral History Interview," 39. Dobbins continued in his response to Dillard to use William Louis Poteat, President of Wake Forest University from 1905–1927, as an example of a Christian evolutionist. "And there were educated men, like Poteat of Wake Forest, who came out and out for the evolutionary theory. I've asked the question, 'Why did North Carolina insist on keeping Poteat as president when he was an out and out evolutionist?' The answer is, because he was such a great Christian. The students admired him. But he was an evolutionist. Now, he was a Christian evolutionist. He took his stand where most of us who have sense are taking it, that there is a creator, back of creation; there is a designer back of a design. Scientifically, when we study the universe, vast and vaster as the telescopes get bigger and reveal more, we are just bound to realize that there had to be a creator-designer back of the design. Now call him by whatever name, the Biblical name for him is diverse, you still have too many unanswerable questions as to how it all began without an omnipotent, omniscient creator."

128. Oates, "Gaines S. Dobbins," in Dobbins, *Great Teachers*, 94.

In his writings, Dobbins maintained an orthodox view of the depravity of man and the necessity of the redemption found in Christ. He was not as extreme in his stated anthropology as Coe. However, his methodologies were built upon the assumptions of the new anthropology. Dobbins touted the same creative learning as Coe, believing that education through experience, self-discovery, and self-realization would lead to a strong view of self as the way to growth and maturity.[129] This practice appeared to be an attempt to educate a redefined man according to an anthropology not expressed in Scripture. Therefore, the source of wisdom and instruction in order to effectively educate humanity came from a sourcebook other than Scripture.

As Mullins before him, and now his teacher Coe, Dobbins believed experience to be the highest goal of religious education. "It is experience," Coe said, "that teaches us what we want, but it does it by pricking us awake so that we ask questions and compare satisfaction with satisfaction, desire with desire."[130] Dobbins simply tried to link this philosophical shift of experience to the Scripture. "Jesus," he said, "lifted education to its highest level, that of *creative experience*. He utilized all other conceptions and methods, but brought them all to the service of his revelation of teaching not as formal transmission but as a mutual process of sharing whereby *life is given stimulation and guidance*."[131]

The use of stimulation in this manner is more akin to Thorndike's view of learning theory as read into Scripture rather than emanating from it.[132] Coe explained that this same type of stimulation, discovered by the scientific method, intended to help man find proper wants and desires in life through his experience, which leads to freedom. "An experience like this is an experience of freedom—an *experience* of freedom, not proof except in the sense that 'the proof of the pudding is in the eating.' Such experience would, however, become datum for any metaphysics that fully takes in man."[133] Therefore, Coe believed man should search for experiences to enjoy the good that gains freedom, but he is unsure how to define that which is good.[134] This is the logical position when man becomes the arbiter of good and evil. A result of sin in the garden was that man would know good and

---

129. Dobbins, *Can A Religious Democracy Survive?*, 100–101.

130. Coe, *Motives of Men*, 252.

131. Dobbins, *Can A Religious Democracy Survive?*, 17. Emphasis in original.

132. The final section of this chapter will explain Dobbins's connection with Thorndike's educational psychology.

133. Coe, *Motives of Men*, 72. Emphasis in original.

134. Coe, *Motives of Men*, 258.

evil, no longer as God saw it, but from the perspective of man bound to the naturalistic world.[135]

Transmissive vs. Person-Centered

Since his days at Mississippi College, Gaines Dobbins had been bothered by a certain pedagogical approach known as *transmission*. The transmissive method was established as the dominant style of teaching and referenced teaching as the transmitting of information. Dobbins believed this method was too content-centered:[136]

> In the thought of the earlier day teaching demanded just three prime essentials—Bible truths to be transmitted, a Christian through whom the transmissive process was carried on, and "scholars" to whom the Bible's truths, interpreted and applied, were transmitted. All else was more or less incidental.[137]

Young Dobbins saw a different approach to education from two of his college professors, Professor Patterson and Dr. Aven. They viewed education to be more person-centered than content-centered. Austin Dobbins, Gaines's son, would describe the unrest his father experienced while a senior at Mississippi College:

> Gaines was confronted with the conflicting claims of two differing types of education. According to the "transmissive" theory, the traditional theory of education, education is primarily concerned with content. According to the "person-centered" or "creative" theory, the primary concern of education is its effect upon individuals.[138]

Dobbins's struggle continued while a student at Southern Seminary. Most of his professors, with the exception of Mullins and Gardner, taught with the traditional methods. Mullins was fully convinced that the seminary had been too content-centered, and that the transition toward experiential

---

135. Genesis 2:15–17 and 3:4–7. This idea is a culmination of Erickson, *Christian Theology*, Plantinga, *Not the Way It's Supposed to Be*, 28–30, and Geisler, *Systematic Theology*, 771–72. All wisdom is found in God, but sin and its resulting spiritual separation has removed man from knowing God and his wisdom intimately without regeneration.

136. Dobbins, *The Improvement in Teaching the Sunday School*, 26. Dobbins, *Gaines S. Dobbins*, 63.

137. Dobbins *Can a Religious Democracy Survive?*, 100.

138. Dobbins, *Gaines S. Dobbins*, 30.

learning was an, "essential aspect of modern theological education."[139] The encouragement and permission given by Mullins seemed to be exactly what Dobbins needed to transform pastoral theology into practical courses that were person-centered. Gardner deserved partial responsibility as one who encouraged Dobbins's views on the transmissive method of learning. Dobbins said, "[Gardner] contributed to me the ideal of teaching as stimulating rather than transmitting thought."[140]

The curiosity and turmoil Dobbins had experienced since college was finally satisfied as he learned of the "creative learning" popularized in religious education by George Albert Coe. In addition, Coe considered the transmissive style of learning to be outdated. He believed biblical history, dogmas, and ecclesiastical forms to be entanglements upon any learner in the modern age.[141] Dobbins agreed by quoting Coe:

> As Doctor Coe puts it, "Transmissive education is . . . a short name for policies and practices that are based upon the assumption that the primary purpose of education, by which its particular processes are to be controlled and judged is the perpetuation of an already existing culture or some part of it." Applied to the Christian teacher, the assumption that prevailed is that his task is "to transmit a religion, and that the contribution of the teacher's personality is simply and solely that of reinforcement of the transmission-process."[142]

The proposed solution given by Coe was the concept of "Creative Education."[143] Coe believed there were certain aspects of modern life that Jesus or the Scripture never addressed. "How our modern mass-life can become Christian we simply do not know and cannot know except by experimentation; we must create the good life or we shall miss it."[144] Undoubtedly, this inferred that truth was to be created with each Christian experience. Creative learning was intended to express the creative act of the individual through their experience as a result of the learning process. Coe said, "*we cannot be Christian unless we take upon ourselves the burdens and the risks of re-creating in some measure our Christianity itself.*"[145]

139. Gray, "Dobbinology," 3. Dobbins, *Gaines S. Dobbins*, 64.

140. Dobbins Papers, "Pen Pictures of Southern Seminary Personalities," Box 10, Folders 14–15.

141. Coe, *What is Christian Education?*, 44.

142. Dobbins *Can a Religious Democracy Survive?*, 100–101.

143. Coe, *What is Christian Education?*, 31.

144. Coe, *What is Christian Education?*, 32.

145. Coe, *What is Christian Education?*, 32.

Dobbins praised Coe for his view of "creative experience."[146] Dobbins agreed with Coe and quoted him extemporaneously, "When people discover truth for themselves, they will revolt against error and wrong."[147] Dobbins bemoaned the way teachers had been trained in the past:

> These first schools for teachers were very little concerned with methods of teaching, and scarcely at all with the nature and needs of the child. Their object was to give the prospective teacher a working mastery of the subject matter to be taught, and practical help in "keeping order" and otherwise administering the school, which was generally a one-teacher affair.[148]

He expressed appreciation toward the International Council's choice to write curriculum that reflected the person-centered method. The new style of curriculum would suit the improvement in teaching he proposed, "It is insisted that the method shall be creative rather than transmissive, the leader's function of being defined as that of 'helping the student discover solutions for himself in light of his own particular leadership situations.'"[149] Dobbins was affirming the creation of truth as discoverable within the learner. Creative learning was the incitement behind Dobbins's new methods in teaching religious education. The techniques and the psychology that produced them became the practical guides by which Dobbins began to transform pastoral theology and ecclesiology at Southern Seminary.

The accoutrements that accompanied creative learning must not be forgotten. Anthropology found its explanations in psychology. Scripture was not considered a sufficient record of truth, while experience of the learner created truth for the Christian. The improvements of science are credited with the progress of modern man and religious education. Modern man must continually evolve his methods because conditions are always changing. The thoughts of Dobbins were reflective of his desire to stay ahead of the wave of modernism relative to methodology, "We dare not stand still, since to do so, relative to the swiftly moving procession of ideas, would be to go backward."[150]

---

146. Dobbins, *Great Teachers*, 84. Emphasis in original.
147. Dobbins, *Great Teachers*, 84.
148. Dobbins, *Can A Religious Democracy Survive?*, 72.
149. Dobbins, *Can A Religious Democracy Survive?*, 123.
150. Dobbins, *The Improvement of Teaching in the Sunday School*, 12.

GREAT TEACHERS

Dobbins believed that methods promoted by early religious educators freed theological education from its stale style of teaching. Dobbins was grateful for the men who taught before him and demonstrated his appreciation in a small book titled, *Great Teachers Make a Difference*, which he wrote in 1965. The dialogue that Dobbins had with William Fallis and Wayne Oates regarding this work provided insight as to why Dobbins became so enthralled with the religious education and the new methods birthed from key thinkers like Coe, Dewey, and Thorndike.[151]

The first correspondence letter of interest came from Dr. Fallis on September 17, 1964. Fallis confirmed his receipt of the manuscript for *Great Teachers* and after expressing his delight he explained, "The major problem is its length—or rather its brevity."[152] Fallis suggested two ways to raise the word count for publication. First, he requested that Dobbins write another personality sketch, since the book is a collection of tributes to teachers who impacted him in the art of teaching.[153] The second suggestion made by Fallis was, "to ask one of [Dobbins] former students to write a 5,000 word 'profile' of Gaines S. Dobbins."[154] Dobbins was not keen on the idea of someone writing a chapter on him, but in the final manuscript it was decided that Wayne Oates should write this chapter.[155]

Dobbins was given the opportunity to edit the chapter that was to highlight him as a great teacher. Oates sent a copy of the manuscript to Dobbins on November 4, 1964.[156] In an attempt to contrast Dobbins's new methodology of teaching to those of the previous generation, Oates was rather harsh. He wrote to Dobbins, "I have been somewhat candid, to put it mildly. I have directed my candor at the ghastly system in which you had

---

151. William Fallis was the Book Editor at Broadman Press, a man with whom Dobbins worked many times to publish several of his books. Wayne Oates is Dobbins's protégé in the field of psychology of religion and at the time of writing *Great Teachers* could be considered his most famous former student. Based on correspondence letters between Dobbins and Oates there was a strong relationship between the two until Dobbins's death.

152. Dobbins Papers, Box 8, Folder 22. Fallis letter to Dobbins, September 17, 1964.

153. Dobbins Papers, Box 8, Folder 22. Dobbins, *Great Teachers*, 7. This book grew out of a series of lectures Dobbins delivered at Golden Gate Baptist Theological Seminary. Chapter 7 is written in honor of George Albert Coe, the only non-Southern Baptist to be included.

154. Dobbins Papers, Box 8, Folder 22. Dobbins letter to Fallis, September 24, 1964.

155. Dobbins Papers, Box 8, Folder 22. Oates was suggested by Dobbins to write the chapter that Fallis recommended in order to achieve the word count.

156. Dobbins Papers, Box 8, Folder 42. Oates letter to Dobbins, November 4, 1964.

to work and the masterly way in which you went about changing it. I want you, however, to modulate my thoughts and language in any way you want it changed."[157] Dobbins responded on November 23 of the same year:

> First, let me tell you that I am both glad and humbled that you have written so frankly and yet so appreciative of my career as a teacher. Somehow you have disclosed to me what I myself had never quite put into words my philosophy of education and my concept of educational practice. Perhaps you have looked through glasses colored by your own creative views and methods. Anyhow, what you have written is what I wish might be true even though it is prejudiced in my favor.[158]

After expressing his appreciation to Oates and confirming his use of new and creative techniques, Dobbins provided an interesting editorial. The reader should pay special attention to Dobbins's acknowledgment of Oates's critique relative to the teaching techniques of men from the previous generation.

> In the second paragraph of page six you write with brutal frankness of your rebelliousness. *While all this is true,* I wonder if the paragraph might not well be omitted. Those against whom you rebelled are dead, in my sketches of them *I have tried to accentuate their positive virtues,* and it may appear to readers as incongruous that you should have so rebelled against the teachers I have praised! I suggest that the paragraph be omitted or modified. We would not want to cast any reflection on these *good men who did the best they knew how* in the matter of methodology *without the help that came to us later from a depth study of teaching and learning.*[159]

Dobbins reflected this same sentiment to Fallis, stressing that the reason he asked Oates to revise his chapter was due to his presentation of the teaching methods that Dobbins had written about favorably. "In Wayne's first draft," reported Dobbins, "he was rather costic [sic] about the teaching methods of some of the older seminary professors under whom he studied. I felt that this would be incongruous and suggested that these references be omitted. This he has done, to the improvement of the chapter, in my opinion."[160]

157. Dobbins Papers, Box 8, Folder 42. Oates letter to Dobbins, November 4, 1964.

158. Dobbins Papers, Box 8, Folder 42. Dobbins letter to Oates, November 23, 1964. To my knowledge, there is not a copy of the original manuscript of Oates's chapter. It would be interesting to see how sharply Oates contrasted Dobbins and the other men.

159. Dobbins Papers, Box 8, Folder 42. Emphasis added.

160. Dobbins Papers, Box 8, Folder 22. Dobbins letter to Fallis, December 29, 1964.

The interactions via correspondence between Fallis, Dobbins, and Oates offer clarity to anyone who questions Dobbins's views regarding the teaching methodology of the previous generation. He agreed with Oates's criticism of the teaching methodology and credited the new methods of modern education with the improvement of teaching. The chapter, as revised, was accepted and the book completed.

Although it never came to fruition, Dobbins responded to Fallis's first suggestion, to write another personality sketch. Dobbins was willing to add a chapter and his response is enlightening. Further, Dobbins's response to Fallis's suggestion demonstrated the effect Dewey had upon him:

> Originally I had in mind a chapter on John Dewey. I had a course with him in the last year that he taught at Columbia. He became controversial and in my opinion was widely misunderstood. I decided against including him because of his obvious agnosticism. He indeed made a difference but not of the kind that I have emphasized in the manuscript. My interpretation of this very fact might be useful.[161]

Austin Dobbins, his father's biographer, claimed that Dobbins believed Dewey's educational system to be, "too pragmatic," but a cursory view of Dobbins's early writings and course notes revealed a significant reliance upon the progressive educator's works.[162] Dobbins may have wanted to include Dewey, but he knew he would have to incorporate caveats. These may have prevented him from including Dewey in his volume *Great Teachers*, but it did not negate the influence Dewey had upon Dobbins.

JOHN DEWEY

Pragmatism[163]

Along with the growth of psychology of religion, America birthed a philosophy known as Pragmatism, which became the dominant force in education.[164] Charles Sanders Peirce coined the term "pragmaticism" and William

---

161. Dobbins Papers, Box 8, Folder 22. Dobbins letter to Fallis, September 24, 1964.

162. Dobbins, *Gaines S. Dobbins*, 62. Dobbins, "Oral History Interviews," 40. Dobbins Papers, Box 9, Folders 10, 11, 13, 14, 15, 16; Box 10, Folders 14–15.

163. Reed and Prevost, *A History of Christian Education*, 312. "John Dewey has probably influenced the direction of American education more than any other individual." Dewey's influence was not limited to public, secular education, but also extended into religious or Christian education.

164. Anthony and Benson, *History and Philosophy of Christian Education*, 327.

James credited him with "the principle of pragmatism."[165] Moreover, it was the influence of William James and John Dewey that made pragmatism a functional philosophy, especially in the realm of education. James became inclined to the pragmatic philosophy during a mental crisis in 1870.[166] In subsequent years, he would formulate his ideas about pragmatism. James described the problem with absolutes as being that they lead to what he called, "metaphysical paradoxes."[167] James described his solution to the supposed paradoxes:

> [As] I have enough trouble in life already without adding the trouble of carrying these intellectual inconsistencies, I personally just give up the Absolute. I just take my moral holidays; or else as a professional philosopher, I try to Justify them by some other principle.[168]

The quandary presented by James as intellectual inconsistencies led him to defend a thesis that proposed varied truth rather than absolutes. He explained:

> The truth of an idea is not a stagnant property inherent in it. Truth happens to an idea. It becomes true, is made true by events. Its verity is in fact an event, a process: the process namely of its verifying itself, its veri-fication. Its validity is in the process of its valid-ation.[169]

Dewey was not impacted by pragmatism as a young student, as he preferred an absolute idealism that had been promoted by Hegel.[170] After taking a course with Sanders and reading James's *Principles of Psychology*, Dewey's philosophy began to shift.[171] G. Stanley Hall, the pioneer of adolescent psychology, factored as a major influence upon Dewey while he studied at John's Hopkins University.[172]

165. Menand, *Pragmatism*, xv.

166. Menand, *Pragmatism*, xxxiv.

167. James, "What Pragmatism Means," in Menand, *Pragmatism*, 110.

168. James, "What Pragmatism Means," in Menand, *Pragmatism*, 110.

169. James, "Pragmatism's Conception of Truth," 114.

170. Menand, *Pragmatism*, xxii.

171. Gutek, *Historical and Philosophical Foundations of Education*, 339. Anthony and Benson, *History and Philosophy of Christian Education*, 330. Menand, *Pragmatism*, xxiii. Towns, *A History of Religious Education*, 310.

172. Anthony and Benson, *History and Philosophy of Christian Education*, 330–31. Gutek, *Historical and Philosophical Foundations of Education*, 339.

"For Dewey," Gutek stated, "life was a series of connected and related interactive episodes between the human organism and its environment."[173] Once Dewey became a professor at the University of Chicago, he tried to employ these pragmatic ideals within education in the Laboratory School.[174] Walter Athearn described how, "Dewey combined [pragmatism] with his social psychology and formed one of the most influential educational and philosophical schools of modern times."[175] He formed the school as a social experiment to establish the progressive education ideals such as "learning by doing."[176] Dewey described experiential knowledge, "If the living, experiencing being is an intimate participant in the activities of the world to which it belongs, then knowledge is a mode of participation valuable to the degree in which it is effective. [Knowledge] cannot be the idle view of an unconcerned spectator."[177] Dewey utilized this experimental method as a primary means of knowledge. He intended to replace religion as an authoritative source of knowledge in favor of the new "scientific" experimental method:

> The experimental method is new as a scientific resource—as a systematized means of making knowledge, though as old as life as a practical device. Hence it is not surprising that men have not recognized its full scope. For the most part, its significance is regarded as belonging to certain technical and merely physical matters. It will doubtless take a long time to secure the perception that it holds equally as to the forming and testing of ideas in social and moral matters. Men still want the crutch of dogma, of beliefs fixed by authority, to relieve them of the trouble of thinking and the responsibility of directing their activity by thought. They tend to confine their own thinking to a consideration of which one among the rival systems of dogma they will accept. Hence the schools are better adapted, as John Stuart Mill said, to make disciples than inquirers. But every advance in the influence of the experimental method is sure to aid in outlawing the literary, dialectic and authoritative methods of forming beliefs which have governed the schools of the past, and to transfer their prestige to the methods which will procure an active concern with things and persons, directed by aims of increasing

173. Gutek, *Historical and Philosophical Foundations of Education*, 344.

174. Menand, *Pragmatism*, xxiii.

175. Athearn, *The Minister and the Teacher*, 87. For help understanding Dewey's ideas of functional psychology see Athearn, 87–91, Menand's introductory chapter in *Pragmatism*, Benson and Anthony or Gutek's chapter dedicated to Dewey. Holifield, *A History of Pastoral Care in America*, 223.

176. Menand, *Pragmatism*, xxiii.

177. Dewey, "Theories of Knowledge," in Menand, *Pragmatism*, 210.

temporal reach and developing greater range of things in space. In time the theory of knowing must be derived from the practice which is most successful in making knowledge; and then that theory will be employed to improve the methods which are less successful.[178]

This lengthy excerpt serves several purposes. First, it demonstrates Dewey's view of knowledge. Dewey believed knowledge was only obtained by experience, because knowledge was a mode of participation. Second, Dewey's view of absolute truth and religion are uncovered. He believed that religion had hindered generations of the past from obtaining a better knowledge. This view was similar to Coe, but Coe was not willing to completely discard the religious element. The experimental method, according to Dewey, was sure to unlock a new insight that religion could not attain. One goal for Dewey was to replace the religious ideals because, in his mind, they were less successful with the experimental methods. Third, Dewey revealed his intention with the promotion of the new methods to obtain knowledge. Dewey utilized the system of education to promote this new theory of knowledge and the methods that would help each individual and the collective social groups obtain this knowledge.

The result of Dewey's beliefs became known as functionalism, instrumentalism or, the most widely used phrase, experimentalism.[179] As Gutek stated, "Learning, thus, became an activity by which a person adapted to the environment in a unified way instead of in a series of disconnected reactions. By this kind of unified, purposeful action, learning took place."[180] Education would no longer be content-centered but child-centered with focus on the needs of the pupil.[181] The methodology shifted so that the child would experience the act of learning. This alteration in methodology was reflected in curricular changes that now included: learning by doing, activity method, problem solving, group projects, and children's interest and needs.[182]

The progressive education of Dewey had a profound impact upon religious educators, even though he was an antagonist to supernaturalism.[183]

178. Dewey, "Theories of Knowledge," in Menand, *Pragmatism*, 211.

179. Towns, *A History of Religious Education*, 311. Gutek, *Historical and Philosophical Foundations of Education*, 345. Holifield, *A History of Pastoral Care in America*, 223.

180. Gutek, *Historical and Philosophical Foundations of Education*, 344.

181. Anthony and Benson, *History and Philosophy of Christian Education*, 332–33.

182. Gutek, *Historical and Philosophical Foundations of Education*, 348. Towns, *A History of Religious Education*, 319–26.

183. Anthony and Benson, *History and Philosophy of Christian Education*, 334. Gangel and Benson, *Christian Education: Its History and Philosophy*, 292–304. Gangel and Benson argue that Dewey was influenced most by behaviorism and Darwinian

Holifield revealed, "Dewey's ideas found initial expression in the churches within the religious education movement, which also helped secure a firm footing for psychology in religious communities."[184] He continued, "The launching of the Religious Education Association in 1903 signaled the beginning of an effort to reorganize the Protestant Sunday School in accord with the ideas of reformers like Dewey."[185] The fruit of Dewey's influence was seen in the International Graded Lessons from the International Council of Religious Education.[186] Eavey made this connection:

> The factor that bore the most definitely upon the thinking of these members of the lesson committee was the popular vogue of the pragmatic philosophy of which John Dewey was the leading exponent. This philosophy, spun out of the thought of man exalting an unfounded sense of human sufficiency, had tremendous effect on education, including religious education."[187]

This proposal was driven by the desire to adapt education to the stages of human development. The shift encouraged pastors to learn the "intricacies—or at least the rudiments—of developmental psychology."[188] It was during this time that theology was being divorced from religious education and the nomenclature became sociological and psychological rather than theological.[189] Due to the influence of psychology and pragmatism, Dewey was committed to the ideal of self-realization, which Coe believed was the task of religious education to accomplish.[190]

---

evolution. These foundations for Dewey forced him to redefine man as having an anthropology "dependent upon himself and his own methods to achieve whatever needs achieving in this universe." It must be noted that this anthropology is in direct opposition to a biblical anthropology. Any methods that attempt to address this anthropology cannot be utilized to approach a different view of man because methods are for the purpose of outcomes. If man is different according to the Bible, then the pragmatic and humanistic methods of Dewey will not achieve the biblically desired result.

184. Holifield, *A History of Pastoral Care in America*, 224.

185. Holifield, *A History of Pastoral Care in America*, 224. One of the reasons for Dewey's influence was George Albert Coe. Coe was one of the founders of the Religious Education Association and Coe was deeply indebted to the philosophy and methods of Dewey. See Reed and Prevost, *A History of Christian Education*, 333–34.

186. As mentioned in the previous chapter, Mullins and Sampey played a role in promoting International Council and the Graded Lessons.

187. Eavey, *History of Christian Education*, 287. Brown, *A History of Religious Education in Recent Times*, 237. Brown, also includes James and Hall as particularly influential in regard to graded lessons.

188. Holifield, *A History of Pastoral Care in America*, 224–25.

189. Person, *An Introduction to Christian Education*, 43.

190. Person, *An Introduction to Christian Education*, 225. Holifield, *A History of*

Democracy and Moral Education

The concept of democracy from Dewey cannot easily be separated from moral education. According to Hunter, "Democracy, for Dewey was inherently moral . . . In his naturalist frame of reference, moral values were nothing more than civic values; moral virtue was democratic virtue."[191] Society and the individual's interpretation of societal expectations becomes the arbitrary ruler of morality; therefore, Dewey theorized that morality would emerge from the democratic social objective and the new educative methodology centralized upon the child and society, which highlighted the naturalistic metaphysic.

> The procedure in the "new" education is thus reversed. One must start with the child, not the subject matter. Dewey's democratic conception of education begins at this point. "To begin with the child and help him build himself into an even more adequate personality, respecting himself and considering others—this is democracy."[192]

The shift in authority is not a surprise considering that, "the heart of Dewey's innovation was a rejection of revealed religion and foundation of educational practices."[193] The alternate focus should be deemed intentional. Above all else, Dewey is first and foremost a philosopher. He should be considered secondarily as a psychologist and educator while education became the arena by which he could implement his philosophy.[194]

Dewey's philosophy cannot be divorced from his methodology, although this is exactly what Dobbins attempted to accomplish. Dobbins ratified the church as an educational institution that was intended to continue the spirit of democracy within the church thus paralleling Dewey's conception of the public school system within democratic government. Dobbins argued democracy as the New Testament ideal and that education within the church is to perpetuate that ideal among its people.[195] Dewey was the main impetus for Dobbins's arguments and structure for democracy in education, but Mullins's soul competency is also present. The problem is that Dewey's concepts bear epistemological foundations contrary to those of Christianity. Hunter explained:

Pastoral Care in America, 225.

191. Hunter, *Death of Character,* 61.

192. Young, *The Influence of John Dewey in Religious Education,* 27.

193. Hunter, *Death of Character,* 60.

194. Young, *The Influence of John Dewey in Religious Education,* 25.

195. Dobbins, *Can A Religious Democracy Survive?,* 198–99.

> The *content of moral instruction* changed—from the "objective" moral truths of divine scriptures and the laws of Nature, to the conventions of a democratic society, to the subjective values of the individual person. The *sources of moral authority* shifted— from a transcendent God, to the institutions of the natural order and the scientific paradigms that sustain them, the choices of the subject.[196]

Dobbins adjoined democracy and education and these ideas clearly found their roots in Dewey. Dobbins said, "I didn't admire him too much as a teacher, but his books were tremendous. His Democracy in Education [sic] came to be one of my favorite books."[197] In Dobbins's argumentation for democracy as a basic Christian notion, Dewey's views were the primary concepts developed.[198] Dobbins quoted Dewey saying, "A democracy is more than a form of government; it is primarily a mode of associated living, of conjoint communicated experience."[199] Dobbins's views regarding democracy were subsumed in Dewey and his desire to eradicate authoritarianism from the puritanically dominated tradition of religion and education:

> Authoritarianism in government tends to produce slaves, for a slave, according to Plato, is "one who accepts from another the purposes which control his conduct." Freedom and democracy are thus correlatives. "Since a democratic society repudiates the principle of external authority," Professor Dewey continued, "it must find a substitute in voluntary disposition and interest. These," he concludes, "can be created only by education."[200]

The formation of the state and church schools brought an increased demand for teachers. These needed to be not just any teachers, but those who had specialized training in the new methods of education in order to facilitate child-centered and experience-based learning. Dobbins said, "The idea of training teachers in the Sunday School is closely associated with the development of teacher-training in the public school."[201] The Graded Lessons that had been formed around the theories of Hall, Dewey, and Coe demanded specialized teachers and "churches began the employment of

---

196. Hunter, *Death of Character*, 146.

197. Dobbins, "Oral History Interviews," 40.

198. Dobbins, "Oral History Interviews," 29.

199. Dewey, *Democracy and Education*, 101, in Dobbins, *Can A Religious Democracy Survive?*, 29.

200. Dobbins, *Can A Religious Democracy Survive?*, 29.

201. Dobbins, *Can A Religious Democracy Survive?*, 72.

directors of religious education."[202] Dobbins expressed the strain placed on churches due to jettisoning of the old programs and methods in favor of the new methods. "The demand now was for specialists who could produce materials and evolve plans that would give to the churches specialists in teaching and administration, and lift the school of the church to a higher education level."[203]

EDWARD THORNDIKE

Genetic Psychology[204]

Darwin's theory of evolution was not confined to biology. Grinder opined, "Darwin had assumed in the *Origin of the Species* that the theory of evolution would explain both organic and psychical evolution, but he left unanswered the critical issue of evolutionary relations among physical, mental and emotional aspects of development."[205] Edward Thorndike described Darwin's contribution to psychology:

> Darwin gave psychology the evolutionary point of view. Psychology had studied the human mind by itself alone and had taught that our minds were all made after one pattern mind, which worked as it did for no intelligible reason, but just because it did. Darwin showed psychologists that the mind not only is, but has grown, that it has a history as well as a character, that this history is one of hundreds of thousands of years, and

202. Dobbins, *Can A Religious Democracy Survive?*, 105.

203. Dobbins, *Can A Religious Democracy Survive?*, 106.

204. Thorndike was not a genetic psychologist because he refuted recapitulation. Grinder (*History of Genetic Psychology*) believes that Thorndike delivered the final blow to the Biogenic Law. However, this section is included here, not because Thorndike was a genetic psychologist, but because he supplied the alternate theory of educational psychology in order to present stages of development in growth and maturation. He also provided the framework that was dependent upon the heritage of Darwinian psychologists to interpret the nature of man and the means of growth and adjustment. Thorndike's educational psychology would provide the dominant means of tests and measurements in order to determine the laws of human nature and learning that infused both public and religious education. The importance of understanding genetic psychology as demonstrated in chapter 1 is because this was the subject taught within the inaugural course on Sunday School Pedagogy at Southern Seminary by B. H. Dement. Dobbins continued to teach the elements of genetic psychology as proof for stage development when he took over professor of Sunday School Pedagogy.

205. Grinder, *A History of Genetic Psychology*, 133.

that the mind's present can be fully understood only in the light
of its total past.[206]

Darwin could not develop the specifics of his theory, especially in the realm
of heredity or the incorporeal. Many theorists came to his aid in order to
champion the tenets of Darwinian biology across the disciplines, and no
one applied the implications of Darwin's theory more broadly than Ernst
Haeckel.[207] Haeckel used remnants of Lamarckian recapitulation to develop
a Darwinian-based theory of development that became known as Biogenic
Law.[208] It was proposed that man not only evolved biologically, but also the
conscience, or the soul of man, went through a similar process of development. While Haeckel was considered Darwin's chief European apostle, the
first echelon of genetic psychological theorists included more than him.[209]
Sigmund Freud based much of his theories, including the psychosexual
stages of development and the unconscious mind, on the works of Darwin
and Haeckel.[210] Fritz Mueller, Edward Cope, and Herbert Spencer were also
contributors to the Darwinian application of conscience development that
influenced education and developmental theories in America.[211]

206. Joncich, *Psychology and the Science of Education*, 37.

207. Grinder, *A History of Genetic Psychology*, 89. "Alfred Russell Wallace lent com-
patible insights and fresh, independent data. Charles Lyell strengthened Darwinism
from the viewpoint of geology, and Thomas H. Huxley mustered skeptical philosophers and beat back theological uprisings. None of Darwin's support however, proved
as indispensable as that furnished by a band of paleontologists and biologists who
recognized that in the genealogy of embryological forms they might verify Darwin's
hypothesis of species descent and simultaneously inaugurate a science of individual
development." Almy, *How Christian is Christian Counseling?*, 97.

208. Gould, *Ontogeny and Phylogeny*. Gould provided the most complete explanation of Lamarckian theory, Haeckel's Biogenic Law, ontogeny, and phylogeny. Grinder,
History of Genetic Psychology, 89–96. Almy, *How Christian is Christian Counseling?*, 97.
The terminology of law was akin to the natural sciences, believing that psychological
development was similar to physiological development and that man was governed
by laws like the natural universe. Edward Thorndike, although he did not believe in
recapitulation, used "law" to describe differing aspects of the psychological science
of education that he developed. See Joncich, *Psychology and the Science of Education*,
Thorndike, *Educational Psychology*, and Thorndike, *The Principles of Teaching*.

209. Almy, *How Christian is Christian Counseling?*, 97.

210. Almy, *How Christian is Christian Counseling?*, 89–112. Webster, *Why Freud
Was Wrong*, 228–40. Boa, *From Augustine to Freud*, 83. Boa says, "An underlying theme
in all of Freud's work is his commitment to a deterministic view of the individual as a
complex system that functions on every level in accordance with the laws of nature."
Almy, *How Christian is Christian Counseling?*, 89–112. Webster and Almy give primary
credit to Frank Sulloway in, *Freud, Biologist of the Mind*, for his connection between
Darwin, Haeckel, Fleiss, and Freud.

211. Eavey, *History of Christian Education*, 211. Grinder, *A History of Genetic*

The first tier of theorists would be soon replaced with a second wave of evolutionists, headed by G. Stanley Hall. Hall was deeply affected by Haeckel's theory of recapitulation and used it to explain his theory of adolescence. As Grinder said, "Hall revered [recapitulation] as the first principle of genetic psychology."[212] Hall's work as a developmental theorist had strong influence upon educationalists, especially his two-volume book *Adolescence*.[213] William H. Kilpatrick said of Hall, who was president of Clark University, "America believes, as does no other country, that education must be based on a study of psychology. That this is due in no small degree to the influence of President Hall."[214]

Hall fused several disciplines that had an impact on the arena of religious education. First, Thorndike recognized the influence of Hall in genetic psychology, which would later be called educational psychology: "each decade since the *Origin of the Species* appeared has shown a well marked increase in comparative genetic psychology. Of our own countryman, for instance William James, Stanley Hall, and John Dewey have consistently worked at psychology on a genetic basis."[215] The deep roots of genetic psychology, born from the seed of Darwinism, can be verified in 1932 by the Dean of Boston University School of Religious Education and Social Services, Walter Athearn:

> This doctrine of natural selection has had profound influence on education practice. Most of us are evolutionists to-day, but few of us would attempt to account for the progress of the human species on the basis of accidental adjustment to a shifting environment . . . We are coming to see that human consciousness, by whatever process it entered the evolutionary series, presents facts which cannot be explained by any preceding level of racial development. When consciousness came, organic adaptation to environment was supplanted by conscious control of the environment, and men came to have dominion over all the earth.[216]

Psychology, 90.

212. Grinder, *History of Genetic Psychology*, 90. Gutek, *Historical and Philosophical Foundations of Education*, 339. Gutek describes Hall as a pioneer in child and adolescent psychology.

213. Grinder, *History of Genetic Psychology*, 207. Drakeford, *Psychology in Search of a Soul*, 18. Drakeford was a distinguished professor of psychology and counseling at Southwestern Baptist Theological Seminary from 1956–1967. Oates, *Psychology of Religion*, 46, 72–73. Oates was professor of psychology of religion at Southern Baptist Theological Seminary from 1947–1974.

214. Curti, *Social Ideas of American Educators*, 396.

215. Joncich, *Psychology and the Science of Education*, 38.

216. Athearn, *The Minister and the Teacher*, 5–6.

While Athearn did not believe in recapitulation, a legacy of evolution promoted by Hall is evident in his educational psychology. Second, Hall's impact on the synthesis of major disciplines is reported as unequalled:

> The cloistered years at American and European universities
> enabled Hall to become conversant in theology, philosophy,
> anthropology, biology, physiology, anatomy, psychology, and
> neurology. Moreover, his immense capacity for absorbing and
> integrating information surpassed that of most of the noted
> scholars with whom he studied.[217]

Third, Hall developed and utilized the questionnaire in his study
of adolescence, which became "one of the most widely used instruments
in the investigation of psychology of religion."[218] Fourth, G. Stanley Hall
was responsible for Sigmund Freud's only visit to the U.S. in 1909, which
introduced psychoanalysis to American psychologists.[219] Fifth, as Kemp
described:

> No one can rightfully be called the founder of the psychology of
> religion, but as much credit is due to G. Stanley Hall as to any
> one individual, not only for his own efforts, but also for the fact
> that he was the type of personality that inspired others to take
> an interest in the field.[220]

Finally, Hall influenced the next tier of men who would carry the torch
of educational psychology and psychology of religion, many of whom were
his contemporaries. Edwin D. Starbuck, George Albert Coe, and Edward L.
Thorndike were among the beneficiaries of the work of William James and
Hall. All of these men would have profound impact on religious education
in general and on Southern Baptist education specifically.[221] One profound
impact of Hall on the work of Southern Baptists was his indirect influence
on graded lessons for Sunday School curriculum:

> Many brilliant psychologists made a great contribution to re-
> ligious education in the years 1900 to 1910. In addition to the
> two writers [Starbuck and Coe] previously mentioned, such
> men as William James, G. Stanley Hall, and others were espe-
> cially stimulating and suggestive. The creators and writers of the

217. Grinder, *History of Genetic Psychology*, 203.

218. Drakeford, *Psychology of Religion*, 18.

219. Drakeford, *Psychology of Religion*, 17.

220. Kemp, *Physicians of the Soul*, 100.

221. Oates, *Psychology of Religion*, 73. Anthony and Benson, *History and Philosophy of Christian Education*, 343–77.

International Graded Lessons in some of the series relied much upon the investigations of these men.[222]

This is an important subject to understand since the curriculum of Southern Seminary included genetic psychology as a part of their course work in Sunday School Pedagogy.[223] As Dobbins led the department of Church Efficiency and Sunday School Pedagogy, genetic psychology remained an intricate part.[224] Holifield recognized the reliance upon genetic psychology for Sunday School educators and Sunday School curriculum:

> Proposing that education be adapted to the stages of human development, they prepared "Sunday School material and teaching guides for infants, toddlers, primary education pupils, older elementary children, junior high school youngsters, senior highs, older youths, young married adults, mature adults, and senior adults. Agreeing that education was a process in which the total personality passed through predictable stages of growth, they urged pastors to learn the intricacies—or at least the rudiments—of a developmental psychology.[225]

Dobbins was one of these men who followed in the footsteps of John Sampey and others who had worked with the International Lesson Committee to develop the curriculum to which Holifield referred. This explains why the theories of Thorndike in educational psychology were exceedingly valuable to Dobbins. Upon the transition away from the belief in recapitulation, Thorndike proposed the tenets of educational psychology. Nonetheless, the reader is able to see the influence of genetic psychology upon educational psychology and the psychology of religion.

Educational Psychology

The work of Edward Thorndike made a significant impact on Gaines Dobbins.[226] One may find it curious that Thorndike had such an effect on

222. Brown, *A History of Religious Education in Modern Times*, 237.

223. See discussion of B. H. Dement in chapter 1.

224. Southern Baptist Theological Seminary, *Catalogue of The Southern Baptist Theological Seminary, Sixty-Ninth Session, 1920–1921*, 43.

225. Holifield, *A History of Pastoral Care in America*, 225.

226. Dobbins, *Gaines S. Dobbins*, 62. Dobbins, *Great Teachers*, 96. In his course notes for Educational Principles 123, Dobbins asked, "What principle values have been derived from the study of animal behavior? From the psychological laboratory? What brought about the shift from fragmentary study of personality as a whole? What is the most helpful aspect of scientifically oriented psychological studies for improvement of

Dobbins since "Darwinism represents one main stream flowing through Thorndike's work; another is experimentalism."[227] Thorndike built upon G. Stanley Hall's ideas of development, but vehemently opposed his recapitulation ideas.[228] While he may have rejected recapitulation, "The imprint of evolutionary thesis is manifest in every line of Thorndike's endeavors."[229]

Dobbins remembered that, "Thorndike, with massive frame and head and massive intellect to match, led us through labyrinths of educational psychology to a better understanding of the teaching-learning processes and to understanding the different levels of intelligence and individual differences."[230] Thorndike described the stimulus and response as the job of the teacher, "to produce desirable and prevent undesirable changes in human beings by producing and preventing certain responses." It has been reported that Dobbins's "fundamental law of education, produces stimulation which leads to satisfaction and response."[231] Again, the reader may notice the streams of experimentalism and laws of learning from Thorndike in Dobbins: "According to educational theorists, inadequate methods block satisfaction and response."[232] Dobbins clearly demonstrated the influence of Coe and Thorndike when he said, "in the new concept of curriculum, the teacher is no less important, but the role is different. No longer is the teacher's part thought of as primarily that of transmission of information and inspiration but much more importantly that of stimulation to inquiry and participation.[233]

To Thorndike, the ability to measure behavioral responses made learning scientific. Dobbins demonstrated agreement with Thorndike's value of tests and measurements, "In every field of modern endeavor tests and measurements have played an important part."[234] Dobbins continued his applause for the scientific view of anthropology by stating, "No movement in modern education has been productive of richer fruitage than that of scientific tests and measurements. Never has the world, more than now, demanded adequate results from the expenditure of time and money."[235] Both

education?" See Dobbins Papers, Box 9, Folder 15.

227. Joncich, *Psychology and the Science of Education*, 5.
228. Grinder, *Genetic Psychology*, 237.
229. Joncich, *Psychology and the Science of Education*, 36.
230. Dobbins, *Great Teachers*, 82.
231. Dobbins, *Gaines S. Dobbins*, 76.
232. Dobbins, *Gaines S. Dobbins*, 66.
233. Dobbins, *The Improvement of Teaching in the Sunday School*, 118.
234. Dobbins, *The Improvement of Teaching in the Sunday School*, 121.
235. Dobbins, *The Improvement of Teaching in the Sunday School*, 121.

Dobbins and Thorndike wanted their efforts to make education more effective and more efficient.[236] In the end, Dobbins affirmed, "Modern progress is largely the result of scientific improvement."[237]

Stages of Development

Thorndike refuted recapitulation theory, but he did not eradicate the view that learning followed the physiological pattern of evolutionary development. In an attempt to ameliorate this view, Thorndike argued that learning was based upon neurological connectivity at varying stages of human development. These stages coincided with the chronological development of man and education was intended to aid man's growth at the various stages by presenting proper environment and stimuli that would "produce desirable and prevent undesirable changes in human beings."[238]

Thorndike's theories of educational psychology asserted that different stages of physiological development afforded varying levels of connectivity that created a fluctuating ability for plasticity in man which resulted in learning.[239] These definable stages included variables such as environment, heredity, and mental functions.[240] Thorndike asserted, "The need of education arises from the fact that what is, is not what ought to be."[241] Therefore, the teacher must understand these stages of mental functioning that are a part of the original nature and tendencies of man, because, "in order to control human nature, the teacher needs to know it."[242] Thorndike concluded by expressing the value of psychology in understanding the laws of human nature in man's original tendencies:

> The science of psychology gives the laws of changes in intellect and character. The teacher studies and learns to apply psychology to teaching for the same reason that the progressive farmer studies and learns to apply botany; the architect, mechanics; or the physician, physiology and pathology.[243]

236. Dobbins, *The Improvement of Teaching in the Sunday School.* Dobbins, *The Efficient Church.* Joncich, *Psychology and the Science of Education,* 55.

237. Dobbins, *The Improvement of Teaching in the Sunday School,* 12.

238. Joncich, *Psychology and the Science of Education,* 61.

239. Thorndike, *Educational Psychology,* 141–52. Also see, Thorndike, *Original Nature,* 11–15.

240. Thorndike, *Original Nature,* 209–44.

241. Thorndike, *The Principles of Teaching,* 1.

242. Thorndike, *The Principles of Teaching,* 7.

243. Thorndike, *The Principles of Teaching,* 7.

Holifield identified this view in both Thorndike and Coe as the impetus for encouraging pastors to seek understanding of secular psychology. Education was believed to be the "process in which the total personality passed through predictable stages of growth." Therefore, pastors were urged, "to learn the intricacies—or at least the rudiments—of a developmental psychology."[244] The importance of this cannot be understated as an aid to developing pastoral dependence upon psychology. The educational theories of Thorndike and Dewey, with their predecessors, James and Hall, provided the template for religious educators like Coe to follow. The developmental theories were utilized in religious education to cultivate an age-graded structure for student learning and teacher training corresponding to every stage of development.

Dobbins is part of this lineage as a primary promoter of these ideas of stage development and education within Southern Baptist life.

> Human growth obeys the laws of growth in other realms. Physically, man grows by renewal of the cells that constitute his body. The health of the body depends upon light, heat, food, exercise, protection, and care. Our chief concern, however, is not for the growth of the body but for the growth of the mind and soul. Here we find a striking similarity between the requirements of physical growth and requisites to growth in the intellectual and spiritual realm.[245]

He employed the logical results of these theories in his methodology for training teachers. He encouraged teachers to understand their pupils.[246] Teachers were responsible for managing graded classes that corresponded to varied stages of development. Dobbins explained that "Life itself *grades* people, and we follow nature's leading by arranging them in groups according to age, sex, and interests."[247] Since life is marked by these age periods, teachers must be trained for each stage of development within the corresponding department of the Sunday School.[248] Teaching, according to Dob-

---

244. Holifield, *A History of Pastoral Care in America*, 225. Holifield continued by crediting George Albert Coe as the patriarch of this movement. Holifield demonstrated that the theories of religious education and the religious educators are the catalysts who caused psychology to flourish within theological education. This connection is vital to the thesis of this work, since Dobbins is identified as the religious educator within the Southern Baptist denomination who was the catalysts for the submerging of pastoral care into the secular psychologies.

245. Dobbins, *Deepening the Spiritual Life*, 25.

246. Dobbins, *The Improvement of Teaching in the Sunday School*, 54.

247. Dobbins, *The Improvement of Teaching in the Sunday School*, 66.

248. Dobbins, *The Improvement of Teaching in the Sunday School*, 66–69.

bins, was to seek the fulfillment of the needs of the pupil by guiding them into experiences to discovery of truth. Bible knowledge and Bible truths come through experiences in the learner and the teacher is to *stimulate* the learner in order to achieve the learning outcome consistent with the proper stage of the student.[249]

Law of Effect

Thorndike centered upon child-development theories, using science to measure intelligence and growth. Moreover, Thorndike was best known for his application of the stimulus-response theory to education.[250] Human learning, similar to that of animals, is achieved by a series of connection-forming experiences.[251] The varieties of learning proposed by Thorndike are termed as laws in an attempt to equate them with the science of nature. The law of effect can be defined as a modifiable connection being made between a stimulus and response and being accompanied or followed by a satisfying state of affairs. In Thorndike's words, the law of effect is defined as "the greater the satisfyingness of the state of affairs which accompanies or follows a given response to a certain situation, the more likely that response is to be made to that situation in the future."[252] When the response is "satis-fying" the connection is strengthened, but it is weakened when the response is "annoying."[253] He used the stimulus-response theory to propose laws of human development that had a major impact on the field of education.[254]

The law of effect demonstrates the stimulus response theory that is incorporated into Dobbins's methods.[255] Satisfying needs reinforces results, according to Dobbins, and those needs change with varying circumstances.[256]

---

249. Dobbins, *Guiding Adults in Bible Study*, 16–63. Dobbins, *The Improvement of Teaching in the Sunday School*, 54–107. Dobbins, *Deepening the Spiritual Life*,17–43.

250. Anthony and Benson, *History and Philosophy of Christian Education*, 329.

251. Thorndike, *Educational Psychology*, 138.

252. Joncich, *Psychology and the Science of Education*, 79.

253. Joncich, *Psychology and the Science of Education*, 71

254. Kilpatrick, "The Project Method," in Athearn, *The Minister and the Teacher*, 136.

255. Dobbins, *The Improvement of Teaching in the Sunday School*. This ideology can be seen in multiple chapters of this book as Dobbins proposes child-centered learning and emphasizes the importance of the environment of the teaching and learning. For better understanding of the impact of the law of effect on Christian Education see Price, et al., *A Survey of Religious Education*, 91–94.

256. Dobbins, *Guiding Adults in Bible Study*, 59–60.

Teaching toward needs is a concept utilized by Dobbins as another way of expressing the law of effect in terms of experience.[257]

William Hacker has written a fascinating dissertation connecting the ideas of Thorndike as reflected in the curriculum of Southern Baptists.[258] In it he asserted that, "Dobbins presents a point of view similar to Thorndike's, that man is different from other animals in his ability to learn and change."[259] The plasticity of human learning in adults was attributed, in both Thorndike and Dobbins, to presenting stimuli based on the psychologically identified needs of man.[260] Both men view man's needs as the key motivator in connection-forming stimuli that leads to learning and adjustment by experience.[261] "Each response," said Dobbins, "results in a certain amount of learning, which is then used for the guidance of future responses."[262] Thorndike expressed this idea best and sounds similar to Coe's explanation of man's motives:[263]

> The original basis of the wants which so truly do and should rule the world is the original satisfyingness of some states of affairs and annoyingness of others. Out of such original satisfiers and annoyers grow all desires and aversions; and in such are found the first guides of learning.[264]

CONCLUSION

James Ryan observed an interesting trait in Dobbins that followed the pragmatic mode Mullins instilled in him. Ryan said, "Dobbins freely used ideas that he had gleaned here and there at any point that suited his purposes for

257. Dobbins, *Guiding Adults in Bible Study*, 57.

258. Hacker, "Learning Theories of E. L. Thorndike," 128–49. Hacker draws his conclusions presenting the parallels in prior chapters by statistical analysis of the curriculum against markers identified as key aspects of Thorndike's theories. In the final chapter he presents several authors who utilize Thorndike's concepts in their writings. He quotes Dobbins many times to demonstrate the theories of Thorndike that Dobbins uses.

259. Hacker, "Learning Theories of E. L. Thorndike," 124.

260. Thorndike, *Educational Psychology*, 73. Dobbins, *Guiding Adults in Bible Study*, 17.

261. Thorndike, *The Original Nature of Man*, 123–34. Dobbins, *Guiding Adults in Bible Study*, 19–30 and 49–62. In chapter 2, Dobbins addresses experiences as the key to learning and in chapter 4 presents needs as the key to satisfying experiences.

262. Dobbins, *Guiding Adults in Bible Study*, 17–18.

263. Coe, *Motives of Men*.

264. Thorndike, *The Original Nature of Man*, 123.

writing."[265] This certainly seems to be true as Dobbins piecemealed varying techniques, methodology, and ideology from many individuals. There is a sense in which his eclecticism is to be understood as following the same influences that have been demonstrated to impact mainline Protestants in regard to religious education and pastoral care.[266] One must take into account Dobbins's eclecticism before he may be truly understood.[267] The accumulation of business efficiency, progressive education, psychology of religion, and educational psychology, provides clarity for specific creations within Dobbins's system of pastoral theology and ecclesiology.

Without business efficiency one would be hard pressed to grasp Dobbins's concept of ecclesiology. Efficiency gave the framework for specialization within the different functions of the church. The pastoral function was more akin to a manager or administrator of a company than aligned with the biblical roles of a pastor. As the pastor is engaged in managerial tasks, other staff would be needed who are specialized in areas of ministry. The laity were being specialized in their employment and expected the church to operate upon similar tenets.

Without progressive education, the church school has little mission other than to train children with transmissive methods that are binding and not conducive to true learning, according to Dobbins. The concepts of religious education promoted by Coe combined the methods of the naturalists based on a corresponding anthropology. The demand for teacher training also necessitated specialization of ministers of education, which paralleled the specialization demanded from the template of efficiency. In the mind of Dobbins, the educational ministry of the church is to operate as the chief resource for the enterprise of the church as a business. The chief resources of the educational ministry, however, were educational psychology and the progressive education of Dewey.

Without educational psychology, there would be no framework for graded systems of curriculum or schemes to further understand human nature and provide explanation as to how man learns. The roots of educational psychology, namely genetic psychology, also proposed anthropology contrary to traditional biblical understanding. Without psychology of religion, man cannot be measured according to the scientific method. Therefore, teaching principles reliant upon the stimulus and response method of the law of effect would not be adequate. Dobbins would not have a reason to implement tests and measurements, if the scientific view of man were not prevalent.

265. Ryan, "Administrative Theory of Gaines Stanley Dobbins," 61.

266. See Holifield, *A History of Pastoral Care in America*.

267. Dobbins, *Gaines S. Dobbins*, 62.

This chapter demonstrates that the educational ministry of the church became the pipeline that ushered in the psychological. Upon the convergence of the specialization of efficiency, the theorized man of psychology of religion, and learning methods of progressive education, one will find the role of the professionalized counselor. The combination of these factors under Dobbins naturally produced the specialization of counseling in the pastorate. As the next chapter will demonstrate, the pastor as counselor follows the techniques and methods produced by psychology of religion and the secular practitioners.

Chapter 3

The Professional Pastoral Care in "Dobbinology"

DOBBINOLOGY

"Dobbinology" was born partially from discontent with the previous generation and partially out of necessity. The transition in pastoral theology is evident due to the lack of literature as a basis for the discipline. Therefore, Dobbins made it his task to begin writing books pertaining to the evolving role of the church and its pastor. For Dobbins to contribute to the fields of ecclesiology and pastoral theology was a daunting task since Southern Seminary was noted for its academic scholarship.[1]

Once E. Y. Mullins, President of Southern Seminary, challenged him to continue as a professor, Dobbins accepted it with vigor and determination. His students acted as a proper sounding board, and with trial and error Dobbins produced material to suit the roles of the church and pastor within the modernizing world. He described the progress and process of the material production in retrospect after his second retirement:

> Grimly I knuckled down to curriculum making, summer study, observation, experimentation, and by the Grace of God and the students, created courses and a literature that seem to have

1. Dobbins, "My Sixty Years of Involvement," 137.

stood the test of time. Anyhow, my mimeograph machine and I survived, as I added course to course and the "practical field" became a fixture not only at Southern but in almost all accredited seminaries.[2]

Findley Edge, a student of Dobbins and his successor as the Basil Manly, Jr. Chair of Religious Education, provided a description of the student notes known as "Dobbinology:"

> Another innovation of Dr. Dobbins was the workbooks which he provided for his students in church administration and religious education. Each of these areas bridged two major fields of study. On the one hand, there was the field of the theory of management or philosophy of administration and, on the other hand, there was the field of religion and the church. Often those who had serious knowledge of management and administration did not relate this knowledge to the church. And those who knew about the church often had no serious knowledge of management and religion. To bridge the gap, Dr. Dobbins, who was one of the few who was knowledgeable both in the field of administrative theory as well as the field of religion and in the area of education as well as the organized life of the church, sifted from his extensive reading excerpts from the best books and articles in the respective fields and brought these together into a workbook which was mimeographed and provided for the student.[3]

In the same article, Edge indicated that the primary influences upon his professor's notes were Dewey, Kilpatrick, and Coe.[4] The workbooks described by Edge were not bound to the realms of administration or religious education. Each of Dobbins's courses were developed in similar fashion with comparable workbooks.[5] His biographer said, "[Dobbins] was sometimes accused of writing a book for each course he taught."[6]

Dobbins became distinguished as "Mr. Mimeograph" around campus for his use of the machine in the development of his workbooks. As a "young professor with nothing but a fertile mind and a mimeograph machine," Dobbins worked through material in an attempt to provide literature in his

2. Dobbins, "My Sixty Years of Involvement," 137.

3. Edge, "Gaines S. Dobbins—The Teacher," 375.

4. Edge, "Gaines S. Dobbins—The Teacher," 372.

5. Samples of his workbooks may be viewed in the Dobbins Papers, Box 9, Folders 10–17, or Findley B. Edge Papers. As a student of Dobbins, Edge's collection contains some of the original sourcebooks, syllabi, and study guides.

6. Dobbins, Gaines S. Dobbins, 340.

assigned fields.[7] He briefly explained how he obtained such a title during an interview, appropriately titled "Dobbinology," with Elmer Gray:

> I had to go to various sources, to experience, and to students who helped me and with the aid of a mimeograph machine, for which I became rather famous—or infamous, I had to provide the literature as we went along. We made the curriculum for the first five or six years.[8]

Dobbins affirmed his use of the mimeograph to produce the new literature, but greater issues surfaced in his comments. First, the source from which the literature was produced should not be overlooked. This is the importance of the previous chapter, detailing the influence of Coe, Dewey, and Thorndike. It was a new day for pastoral theology and church administration—in the Southern Baptist denomination, Dobbins was setting the pace. The milieu created regarding ecclesiology, pastoral theology, and religious education pressed Dobbins to cull from the progressive and psychological ideologies a consistent methodology for pastoral training. Since the social sciences dominated Dobbins's approach to every other area of ministry, it should be no surprise to learn that his views of pastoral care and counseling were acquired from the same.

Second, the lack of literature in the fields to which Dobbins was assigned demonstrates the axiomatic shift from traditional pastoral theology to a modernized version predicated upon a paradigm of administration as the primary pastoral duty. Elmer Gray asked Dobbins about the development of literature on church administration, and he immediately responded by saying, "That was the problem. There was some literature from another day."[9] Washington Gladden's, *The Christian Pastor,*[10] and Richard Baxter's, *The Reformed Pastor,*[11] were two of the volumes to which Dobbins referred.

---

7. Dobbins, "Gaines S. Dobbins: Journalist, Teacher, Administrator," 340.

8. Gray, "Dobbinology," 7. Dobbins reported the same process in "Oral History Interview" with Dillard, 34. Dobbins also described more specifically how his first book, *The Efficient Church*, was written. This seemed to be similar to the process he used to produce his other works as well. "It took me two or three summers to write it. My process was, I would write a chapter, mimeograph it, and give it to the students to get their reaction. And we would discuss it. I didn't have them memorizing any of it or outlining it. We would just discuss it. Will it work, is it valid, is it too radical? The book was largely dictated there in a little room in the old Seminary building where we kept the mummy. And I would go in there and lock myself in and talk to the mummy." Dobbins, "Oral History Interview," 37–38.

9. Gray, "Dobbinology," 6

10. Gladden, *The Christian Pastor*.

11. Baxter, *The Reformed Pastor*. Baxter's work was originally published in 1656.

Interestingly, he demonstrated his belief that the role of administrator was the primary work of the pastor.[12] It was not unusual for him to consider works related to pastoral care and pastoral psychology under the general umbrella of administration.[13] Dobbins endeavored to alter the established approach to pastoral theology into a disparate direction, and as a matter of course there was need for inventive literature.

This literature, in book form or as course notes, reflected the influence of the social sciences.[14] Church efficiency and administration were subsumed by the movements of scientific management and mental hygiene— both of which were directed by sociologists.[15] The foundation of religious education was the psychological explanation of man and his behavior. Since learning theories were the product of psychological testing and assessment, consequently the psychological worldview invaded the theological. Dobbins's works reflect that influence.

Dobbinology was thoroughly infused with the new sciences that were being validated as academically respectable. This does not mean that he left theology out altogether. Rather, Dobbins wanted to adapt theology to fit the new science in order to supply the tidal wave of demand for practical pastoral experience in the changing world.[16] Dobbins attempted to apply the progressive ideas of pastoral theology in specific directions. It is reported that, "Dr. Dobbins led Southern Seminary and Southern Baptists in fashioning an adequate concept and practice of ministry in a surprising number of areas: education, journalism, administration, pastoral care, worship, evangelism and many more."[17] In each of these areas, Dobbins wrote with the consistent and vigorous paradigm of ecclesiology he had adapted from efficiency principles and the social sciences. The use of these secular sources, however, was overlooked because, "'Dobbinology' produced results!"[18]

---

12. Gray, "Dobbinology," 6–7. Oates, "Organizational Development and Pastoral Care," 352.

13. Oates, "Organizational Development and Pastoral Care," 6. Demonstrated Dobbins's view of pastoral care and counseling as under the auspice of church administration; so his title as "Mr. Administrator" includes his work regarding pastoral care.

14. Dobbins Papers, Box 9, Folders 10–17; Box 10, Folder 14.

15. Ryan, "Administrative Theory of Gaines Stanley Dobbins," 8–10, 124–36.

16. It is not my intention to cover every aspect of "Dobbinology," but to familiarize the reader with this term and to raise the point that most all of his works were referred to in this way. The discussion of "Dobbinology" is meant to serve as a precursor to focus on his work in the area of pastoral care.

17. McCall, "Editorial Introduction," 335.

18. Dobbins, *Gaines S. Dobbins*, 341.

PASTORAL CARE

The Religious Educator and Pastoral Care

While Dobbins was certainly recognized as an innovator for his work in ad-ministration and religious education within the Southern Baptist Conven-tion, he is seldom acknowledged for his contributive work in pastoral care. Curiosity may lead one to ask why the task of pastoral care and counseling fell to Dobbins at Southern Seminary. Dobbins's primary duty was within the disciplines of ecclesiology and religious education. These tasks involved the role of the pastor within the local church and, therefore, within pastoral theology.[19] His view of religious education was merely a product of his view of ecclesiology. The first specialization created to aid the pastor with his duties was minister of education, but others soon followed.[20] If he believed the pastor to be an administrator of a business, then the enterprise model would demand also specialization of pastoral care.

Specialization within the pastorate did not cease with the addition of the minister of education or the minister of music. The specialization of other pastoral duties expanded into the role of the pastor as counselor. "The religious educators," Holifield explained, "quickly became cast as the 'psy-chologists' within the seminaries and churches. Even friendly critics sug-gested that they talked too much about stimuli and inferiority complexes. But they set the stage for the appearance of 'modern pastoral psychology.'"[21] The progressing development of pastoral counseling mirrored the contours of social changes and the altered paradigm of the religious educator. The SBC emulated the progressing development of pastoral care and counsel-ing. In addition to religious education, another product of his ecclesiology was pastoral care and since his ecclesiological paradigm was dictated by administration, he regarded pastoral care as one of its branches.[22] There-fore, as a religious educator, it was natural for Dobbins to ferry the ideas of pastoral care and counseling, as a specialization, into the seminaries and the churches of the convention.

19. Dobbins believed that the role of preaching was akin to corporate counseling. He described the way to maintain unbroken fellowship within the church as "we-psy-chology." See Findley B. Edge Papers, Psychology of Religion, Third Term, Agenda 2.

20. Dobbins, *A Ministering Church*, 78–81.

21. Holifield, *A History of Pastoral Care in America*, 226.

22. Dobbins, *Gaines S. Dobbins*, 87.

Pastoral Care Literature

Dobbins did not intentionally neglect pastoral care as a function of the pastor in his early writings. His focus, rather, was certainly on adjusting the paradigms relating to the pastor as administrator and the specialization of religious education. Once these two paradigms became established in the Southern Seminary curricula, Dobbins could devote attention to other elements related to pastoral duties.

The pioneering books of Anton Boisen, Richard Cabot, and Russell Dicks were not available until 1936.[23] Therefore, when Dobbins assumed his position on faculty at Southern Seminary in 1920, Clinical Pastoral Education had not been created. Consistent with Dobbins's vision for ecclesiology and pastoral theology was the development of practical experience for pastors. It would take some time, however, for clinical pastoral training to evolve. For the decade spanning 1925 until around 1935, a new paradigm was advancing for pastoral care that aligned itself with the social sciences, liberal theology, and progressivism of the day.[24] Richard Cabot and Anton Boisen were largely responsible for the creation of Clinical Pastoral Education, which became an odd conglomerate of the ministry of pastoral care, social work, and the care of a physician in an attempt to aid those with mental illness.[25]

Dobbins began to follow their paradigm for pastoral care, but literature to support the system remained meager. Wayne Oates remarked on the leadership Dobbins provided to bolster a body of literature in pastoral care, "Therefore, the task at hand was to develop literature that would stand the test of classical biblical, historical, ethical, and historical scrutiny and at the same time implement the findings of contemporary psychology, psychiatry, psychotherapy, and social work."[26] Through the new techniques of religious education, Dobbins had become captivated by the productions of psychology:

> The marvels of science, whether or not one be a qualified scientist, disclose areas of amazing interest. Psychology, once thought akin to the "black arts," has now been popularized as the study

23. Oates, "Organizational Development and Pastoral Care," 352. Boisen, *Exploration of the Inner World*. Cabot and Dicks, *Art of Ministering to the Sick*.

24. Thornton, *Professional Education for Ministry*, 23–71, 151–58. An entire section is dedicated to Clinical Pastoral Education, because of its impact on the development of pastoral training at Southern Seminary under the leadership of Gaines Dobbins.

25. Thornton, *Professional Education for Ministry*, 28–71.

26. Oates, "Organizational Development and Pastoral Care," 352.

of mind and behavior of the characteristics of individuals or groups. And thus has brought within reach and interest of the many. In an age of technology, the trial-and-error method of learning a trade or developing needed skills has given way to on-the-job training, which becomes a matter of absorbing interest to those who would become competent technicians.[27]

In producing the new literature, he sought scholarly excellence through the use of the scientific method embedded in psychology and sociology. Oates recalled that, "Dr. Dobbins often cautioned graduate students in the program not to be superficial and given to gimmickry. He insisted that the primary resources of the great psychologists, sociologists, and educational philosophers be read. He decried secondary and tertiary sources."[28] One reason that the therapeutic model of pastoral care began to take form at Southern is because Dobbins was encouraging the students in the program to study psychologists and sociologists as prime authorities.[29] The goal was to develop a broad database for pastoral care. However, the obvious source of this database was not Scripture. The social scientists would be the guide under the new paradigm for pastoral care.[30]

THE NECESSITY FOR SPECIALIZED TRAINING

Wayne Oates acknowledged in 1978 that he was dealing with a "fork in the road" as to whether or not pastoral counseling should become more specialized.[31] When Oates referred to becoming more specialized, he meant that the pastor ought to seek more specialized training in the psychotherapeutic model. However, at this time, the pastoral counselor was already specially trained in the psychotherapeutic model in the Southern Seminary curriculum, including psychological explanations of religious experiences. The problem that ensued was a distinct bifurcation in counseling.[32]

The "fork" to which Oates referred demonstrated at least two things. First, the trajectory toward specialized counseling in the pastorate had already been set during Dobbins's tenure. Second, there was a need to clarify that the work of the pastor was not to be a specialized field of counseling. These two points inevitably meant that prior to Oates's leadership in this

27. Dobbins, *Zest for Living*, 26.

28. Oates, "Organizational Development and Pastoral Care," 352.

29. Dobbins, *Zest for Living*, 63–65.

30. Oates, "Organizational Development and Pastoral Care," 352.

31. Oates, "Organizational Development and Pastoral Care," 356.

32. Dobbins, "Capturing Psychology for Christ," 434–36.

department the trajectory had already been set by Dobbins at Southern Seminary toward specialization.[33]

The roots of specialization at that point were too deep. Edward Thornton reported that pastoral counseling had become specialized, prodded by the professional development of the psychiatrist and social worker that were considered more competent and successful than those in ministry.[34] Thornton clearly demonstrated that the trend of specialization in the 1920s and 1930s had been set. Anyone who demonstrated a desire to care for the *soulish* problems of persons would need more specialized or professional equipping: "the times," he said, "require more education."[35] The training, whether secular or theological, was undergirded with the psychological model of man as the basis for anthropological understanding and counseling techniques. Dobbins sought out this type of training in pastoral care under the influence of Anton Boisen, Karl Stolz, Seward Hiltner, and others leading the pastoral care movement.[36] The following will explain a portion of how that professional trend developed in Dobbins's estimation.

Decade of Standardization[37]

Dobbins seemed somewhat reactionary in his approach to pastoral theology, which created a tendency toward specialization: "The pastor I have magnified in his New Testament function as bishop, *episcopus*, 'overseer.' He is not only preacher but also teacher and teacher of teachers."[38] During Dobbins's days as a student and as professor, there was a deep-seated belief in training pastors to preach. "In the main," said Dobbins, "pastoral care and church administration were subordinated to the preparation and delivery of

33. It could be said here, that Dobbins was following the intellectual trend of the pastoral care movement, which pragmatically appealed to his efficiency driven model of ecclesiology and pastoral theology.

34. Thornton, *Professional Education for Ministry*, 29.

35. Thornton, *Professional Education for Ministry*, 29.

36. The influence of Boisen and Hiltner are explained later in this chapter. Karl Stolz's works were primary texts for Dobbins's courses psychology of religion. The second term in his course one psychology of religion Dobbins used Stolz, *The Psychology of Religious Living*, as a primary text. In the third term Dobbins used, Stolz, *Pastoral Psychology*, as the primary text. See Findley B. Edge Papers, Psychology of Religion Notes.

37. Dobbins, "The Contribution." Dobbins designated the decades as follows: 1920–1930 (Decade of Standardization), 1930–1940 (Decade of Organizational Complexity), and 1940–1950 (Decade of Specialization).

38. Dobbins, "The Contribution," 185.

sermons."[39] While the aspect of preaching may need to have been expanded, Dobbins chose to swing the pendulum of focus in the direction of the pastor as an overseer.[40] This was due in part to Dobbins's belief that the churches and seminaries "were caught in a cultural lag."[41] The change was so dramatic that Dobbins said:

> The title of the course long known as pastoral theology was changed to church efficiency . . . Soon church efficiency was changed to church administration, and other courses in the practical field were introduced—evangelism, worship, pastoral counseling, clinical training. The shift was steadily toward the preparation of the minster as pastor and church administrator.[42]

Dobbins explained in retrospect how administration unfolded and impacted each area of pastoral theology in an article entitled, "50 Years of Church Administration as I have Seen It." Dobbins stated, "Administration thus gets back to the meaning of the original word—*ad,* in order, *ministrae,* to serve. The New Testament word for administrator is *episcopos,* 'one charged with responsibility to see that what needs to be done is done right.'"[43] Allen Graves said, "The books, articles and lectures of Dobbins probed every sphere of church administration, helping the minister to *administer* programs of evangelism, pastoral care, worship, Bible teaching, and Christian training, the enlistment and training of church leaders."[44]

Decade of Organizational Complexity

During Dobbins's time, the church began attempts to meet the needs of individuals through programmatic structures, often with homogeneous

---

39. Dobbins, "50 Years of Church Administration," 4.

40. Dobbins, "Oral History Interviews," 62–66. Dobbins explained the discontent of the faculty upon the hiring of Duke McCall as the President of Southern Seminary. Part of the discontent was with McCall's background as an administrator and not as a theologian. Dobbins said that the faculty wanted a "body of divinity" and that the school of music and school of religious education did not belong in the curriculum. Dobbins even said he was, "ousted" by their efforts, which led eventually to his retirement and move to Golden Gate Baptist Theological Seminary.

41. Dobbins, "50 Years of Church Administration," 4.

42. Dobbins, "50 Years of Church Administration," 4.

43. Dobbins, "50 Years of Church Administration," 7. Emphasis in original.

44. Allen, "Gaines S. Dobbins—Mr. Church Administration," 384. Emphasis in original.

divisions.[45] The complexities of the business-like structure of the church required better organizational structure. As programs of the church grew, each one developed a separate pattern of organization. The pastor was, then, responsible as the administrator of the ever-increasing complexities of the organization. Dobbins recognized this pattern when he said, "As the church grew in numbers, the burden became too heavy for the pastor to bear."[46] Following the increase in demand for efficiency and specialization in the secular world, the church mirrored this trend. "Out of this need," Dobbins explained, "arose the office of educational director."[47] The addition of the minister of education exemplified the specializing tendency created by the complexity of church programs. The position then became the first among others as the structure grew.

Decade of Specialization

In *A Ministering Church*, Dobbins explained that the organizational structures of a church are dependent upon size. "The problem," Dobbins recognized, "is that of maintaining the original church pattern established by the New Testament and yet changing the methods of its operation to meet new needs."[48] The needs shifted because manpower was replaced by machinery, the scientific method replaced trial and error, and the population increased explosively. The programs of the church were pressured to meet the changes of modern demands. Dobbins, therefore, concluded, "Unchanged churches in a changed and changing environment would meet the fate of any other organism—they would perish."[49]

Complexity, therefore, derived from the efficiency model, and the modern pace of life demanded specialization. The pastor was recognized as the "chief of staff" or the "*primus inter pares*—first among equals," according to Dobbins.[50] The pastor was to set the spiritual standards of the staff and be administratively responsible for each of the delegated duties.

---

45. Dobbins used Women's Missionary Union and Brotherhood as examples of these programs.

46. Dobbins, "50 Years of Church Administration," 5.

47. Dobbins, "50 Years of Church Administration," 5.

48. Dobbins, *A Ministering Church*, 27.

49. Dobbins, *A Ministering Church*, 27.

50. Dobbins, "50 Years of Church Administration," 7. Dobbins, *A Ministering Church*, 84.

The evolution of the church staff began with the ministers of education and music.[51] Additional specialists were required based on the growing demands of the churches—and the more complex the organizational structure, the greater the variety of specialists.[52] "As our churches have grown in size and complexity, I have seen clearly that pastors must have alongside them specialists in the organization and administration of the varied program of worship, teaching, training, service."[53] Therefore, church administrators, age-graded directors, recreation directors, and associate pastors or assistants for pastoral counseling would be required.[54] "Through the staff, the pastor multiplied himself; and the staff members in turn multiplied themselves by increased leadership, growth, and fruitfulness of the church organizations."[55]

A normative in Dobbins's modern world was professionalization of various pastoral duties. Church members in their various occupations had become known as "professionals" in their respective fields of study. The pressure of organization and needs for the pastor, Dobbins believed, inescapably demanded professionalization, "All of this was in line with the trend in public demand for professional competency."[56] Dobbins acknowledged the tension between the traditional views of the pastor and this modern phenomenon of professionalization; however, he acquiesced to what he believed was modernity's requirement:

> Neither does the minister like to think of himself as a professional specialist. He does not want to narrow his interests to one aspect of the work of the church or one aspect of the kingdom of God. Yet in a day of specialism he is bound to admit that he cannot carry on all phases of modern church's manifold activities equally well. Like other men, he must find his vein, develop his aptitudes, and give his major attention to that which he can do best. As a church grows in size, it grows in complexity of organization, and this complexity inevitably calls for specialization.[57]

---

51. Dobbins, *A Ministering Church*, 82.

52. Dobbins, "The Contribution," 185. Dobbins, *A Ministering Church*, 82.

53. Dobbins, *A Ministering Church*, 185.

54. Dobbins, *A Ministering Church*, 79–84.

55. Dobbins, "50 Years of Church Administration," 7.

56. See Dobbins, *A Ministering Church*, 76–78. Dobbins, "50 Years of Church Administration," 7.

57. Dobbins, *A Ministering Church*, 76.

PASTOR AS COUNSELOR

As the professionalization among church staffs grew, counseling became one of the final additions to be specialized. Dobbins correctly believed counseling to be intrinsic to the pastoral duty, "The heart of pastoral care is thus seen to be contained in the concept of the minister as shepherd."[58] Elsewhere, Dobbins would add, "As a matter of fact, counseling is the original pastoral function."[59] Dobbins seemed to rebut the thesis of this work in his assertion, "I cannot insist too strongly that counseling is not a pastoral specialty."[60] Upon further investigation, however, this statement is meant to say that the specialized skills of active listening will help the pastor be a better administrator, better teacher, and better evangelist. He is duplicating the sentiment of Seward Hiltner. Pastoral care encompassed every act of the church and the pastor, in that way, according to Dobbins and Hiltner; it was not a "specialty." The shepherding perspective of the pastor is to influence all the other operations of the church and functions of the pastor.[61]

During Dobbins's time, there were two ways in which the function of pastoral care and counseling were viewed in pastoral theology. "Pastoral care," Hiltner explained, "was generally divided into a general branch and a special branch. The special branch dealt with types of individual cases. The general branch dealt with the whole group or subgroups."[62] Dobbins's comments, contextually, were referring to the general branch of pastoral care, since discussion that followed highlighted the benefits of pastoral care to other pastoral functions. The *special branch* of pastoral care was certainly driven toward specialization in Dobbins's practice.

Dobbins's custom was to describe the pastoral role of counseling in terms of the classic tradition, but he acquired ideologies and terminologies from the psychological model to enhance the demand for specialized skills.[63] The imagery of pastor as shepherd and physician of the soul is what is meant by the classic tradition.[64] The psychological model was dependent

---

58. Dobbins, *A Ministering Church,* 155.

59. Dobbins, "The Pastor as Counselor," 421.

60. Dobbins, "The Pastor as Counselor," 426.

61. Hiltner, *Preface to Pastoral Theology,* 19–20. As Dobbins argues that counseling is not a specialty, because counseling enhances all of the duties of the pastor. Hiltner makes the same argument, but this is what he refers to as "general pastoral care." Special pastoral care is what Hiltner sought to make professional. See n127 and n128 and J. I. McCord's explanation of Hiltner's mission to professionalize pastoral care.

62. Hiltner, *Preface to Pastoral Theology,* 19.

63. Dobbins, "The Pastor as Counselor," 422–25.

64. See Oden, *Care of Souls in the Classic Tradition,* 11–42, for an explanation of

upon the clinical method of experience and the psychological explanation of mental disturbances. Dobbins wanted to maintain continuity with the classic tradition, but the theological training he adopted, rooted in the psychological model, required specialized training to acquire specialized skills for counseling. In the end, pastoral counseling succumbed to the prevailing tendency of professionalism. Dobbins expressed the heart of the counseling process by appealing to those he considered leaders in the field:

> Seward Hiltner says that "the special aim of pastoral counseling may be stated as the attempt by a pastor to help people help themselves through the process of gaining understanding of their inner conflicts." . . . Otis Rice declares that pastoral counseling takes place when "the parishioner is permitted to present his problem, to marshal his own resources for solving that problem." . . . Russell Dicks says "pastoral counseling consists of directive listening, supportive listening, interpretation, reassurance."[65]

Capture Psychology for Christ

Dobbins's reliance upon Hiltner, Rice, Dicks, and others demonstrated his mission to capture psychology for Christ. The complexities of modern life were to blame for the increased menacing of the mental and spiritual welfare. "Today," Dobbins said, "we are realizing as never before that psychology may be one of the most valuable means for dealing with the everyday problems of life."[66] The use of psychology was intended to explore and understand human nature, and in so doing, provide remedies to quiet the souls of men. Referring to spiritual and mental illness, Dobbins explained:

> Illness growing out of such conditions cannot be treated with the usual assortment of medicine from the laboratory and the drug store. There is deep and imperative need for another kind of treatment, and it is in this field that psychology is beginning to make its greatest contributions.[67]

The explanation of mental illness, at this point, was broken into two distinct arenas. First, the physio-genic causes of mental anguish deserved

---

the classical tradition of pastoral care. See also Purves, *Pastoral Theology in the Classic Tradition*.

65. Dobbins, "The Pastor as Counselor," 425.

66. Dobbins, "Capturing Psychology for Christ," 427.

67. Dobbins, "Capturing Psychology for Christ," 429.

the attention of the psychiatrists. Secondarily, those with mental and spiritual disturbances—the causality seen as psycho-genic—should seek the pastoral counselor in order to provide something to live for and a purpose of life.[68] This simple bifurcation sounds convincing until one grasps the foundation for expertise in understanding human nature for the pastor lies in the discoveries of psychology. "In all this," Dobbins explained, "psychology will help to an understanding of the individual himself, of the nature and the cause of his trouble, of his deep moral and spiritual needs."[69] The pastor, in order to be a skilled counselor, must become specialized in the field of psychology, or more particularly in the psychology of religion. Naturally, these fields of study became a staple within the curriculum at Southern Seminary.[70]

Psychological Model

The psychological approach to counseling demanded specialization and professionalized training for pastors. In the psychological model, the psychologists helped to explain human nature, the sociologists help categorize differing personalities within various environments, and psychologists from assorted theories proposed therapeutic prevention and cure.[71] The psychological model had morphed over time from the laboratory of Wundt,[72] to behaviorism, to dynamic psychology, and finally, to what Dobbins called "true functional psychology of religion." The value of religion came to aid mental and physical health through the "psychological process of the unification of a discordant self which takes religious form."[73] Oates later reported that this model would require a, "highly specialized person in pastoral counseling."[74]

---

68. Dobbins, "Capturing Psychology for Christ," 434–36.

69. Dobbins, "Capturing Psychology for Christ," 436.

70. Wayne E. Oates Papers, Box 9, Folder 37. Fuller and Oates, "An Official Statement of Policy," in Fuller et al., *A Tenth-Year Report*, 6. The full document appears in the appendix.

71. See Dobbins, *Zest for Living*, 60–64. Dobbins, "Capturing Psychology for Christ," 433–36.

72. Lionni, *The Leipzig Connection*. This volume explains the Wundtian influence upon the leaders in American education and psychology during the early twentieth century. Included are men like G. S. Hall, Dewey, Thorndike, and others who were influential in Dobbins's ideas, progressive education (both religious and secular), and psychology (including the new pastoral care movement).

73. Dobbins, "Capturing Psychology for Christ," 433.

74. Oates, "Organizational Development and Pastoral Care," 356.

Specialized Counselors

The influence of psychology has been demonstrated as the basis for efficiency and religious education. Adaptation to the psychological model demanded specialization throughout the church schematic due to the complexities offered by modern life. The solution for Dobbins was that "A growing church needs not one, but a team of administrators."[75] Dobbins also argued, "Since no man can be a many-sided specialist, equally adept in meeting the varied demands of a modern church, planning began to take the place of haphazardness in securing for the pastor adequate assistance."[76]

In order for church staff members to carry on specialized operations, professional development would be necessary in the form of education, experience, or both. For pastors, training in Clinical Pastoral Education became a mainstay in the curriculum at Southern Seminary. Dobbins was convinced CPE would provide the practical experience necessary to properly equip young ministers for their pastoral duties.[77]

The size of the church would dictate the level of specialization needed for any given staff. Dobbins prescribed the necessary professionals for each level of growth. At the final stage of growth, the church would need to employ a staff counselor dedicated to this task of professional pastoral counseling. Dobbins described the staff addition as, "the assistant or associate pastor, serving alongside the pastor in all his ministries often with special responsibilities for pastoral counseling."[78]

The role of the professional counselor with specialized training would grow more influential over time. Categories were devised identifying those with spiritual, psychological, and physiological problems. Specialists were required for each of these categories and the pastoral counselor needed further specialization in order to remain competent according to the psychological model.[79]

75. Dobbins, "50 Years of Church Administration," 7.

76. Dobbins, A Ministering Church, 79.

77. Dobbins, A Ministering Church, 163–66.

78. Dobbins, A Ministering Church, 84.

79. Stolz, Pastoral Psychology, 23–28. The original version was printed in 1932. This book was the primary text for Dobbins's courses in psychology of religion as a professor at Southern Seminary. As will be discussed in the following chapter, the categorization is what led to Oates's proposal of the "ministry of referral" for pastors. If a pastor or pastoral counselor was in a situation in which they felt ill-equipped, they would refer to the specialist they believed was trained to best aid the counselee.

Specialized Skills

The pastor is always a counselor. Dobbins agreed by proclaiming, "Today the imperative call is for pastors who are skilled and effective counselors."[80] In a similar way Dobbins said, "The question is not whether the pastor will or will not be a counselor. The question is whether he will be skilled or unskilled, a master of the art or a bungler, a helper or a hinderer as he deals with people and their problems."[81] Dobbins was acknowledging a special skill set necessary for the pastor to become a quality counselor. "Counseling," said Dobbins, "requires more than professional skills."[82] This statement reveals that the skills of counseling must not be less than professional, but supersede professionalized skills. He would add that, "The pastor is not a psychiatrist nor a consulting psychologist, but not less than these men of science he needs to know *the techniques of the counseling procedure.*"[83]

The essential skills to which Dobbins referred were rooted in what would become known as humanistic psychology, led by Abraham Maslow and Carl Rogers. Dobbins utilized many primary resources to better understand pastoral counseling. A few leading scholars in this field, who added to his view of pastoral theology in general, and pastoral counseling in particular, were Seward Hiltner, Russell Dicks, Gordon Allport, and Carroll Wise.[84] The skills these men promoted often took the shape of the humanistic psychologists Carl Rogers and his post-Freudian psychotherapeutic mentor Otto Rank. It should be mentioned that Rank was also a common source for Dobbins in his understanding of pastoral care.[85]

The client-centered approach to counseling appealed to Dobbins. He had been convinced of the educational theory that promoted creative learning or "person-centered learning" from Coe. The person-centered approach to counseling was consistent with the way he believed a person learned; therefore, the compatibility seemed fitting.[86] Maslow's humanism was

---

80. Dobbins, "The Pastor as Counselor," 422.

81. Dobbins, *A Ministering Church*, 161.

82. Dobbins, *A Ministering Church*, 161.

83. Dobbins, *Building Better Churches*, 334. Emphasis in original.

84. Dobbins, *Zest for Living*, 65. Dobbins, *Building Better Churches*, 456–57.

85. Dobbins, *Building Better Churches*, 455–57. Dobbins listed a Classified Bibliography that included Pastoral Service and Psychology and Counseling. The bibliography is evidence for his primary sources, Otto Rank is included. See also Dobbins Papers, Box 9, Folders 10–16; Box 10, Folder 14.

86. The reader may reference Rogers, *On Becoming a Person*, 279–313. Rogers here asserts the same influence as Dobbins in the arena of education, namely, Dewey and Kilpatrick. Rogers also promotes nondirective teaching and counseling as methods conducive to learning, along with unconditional positive regard from teacher to

formed as the hierarchy of basic needs. He theorized that a person becomes fully human or achieved a true sense of being through self-discovery.[87] Creativity enhanced the path to self-discovery and self-actualization[88] which, from an existential perspective, aided the discovery of identity. Ironically, all of this is rather consistent with the educational theories that Dobbins adopted from Coe. The learner created new truth through experiences that originated from within.

The person-centered approach to counseling was driven by active listening. This technique of counseling was brought to mainstream by Carl Rogers,[89] but was used in the new pastoral theology as a primary method of pastoral counseling.[90] As a leader in the field, Hiltner, affirmed this trend:

> Does this mean that pastoral guiding is nondirective and client-centered? In the sense of the purpose for which those terms were coined by Carl R. Rogers, the answer is Yes. "Nondirective" was intended to show that the imposition of externals on internals, however subtle, would not finally be therapeutic in result. "Client-centered" was intended to show that one begins and proceeds from the best possible grasp of internals—that is, the inner frame of reference of the other person so far as it can be grasped. With these intentions we are wholly in accord.[91]

Dobbins reflected the client-centered approach of Rogers as well. The influence was directly from Rogers's works, as well as from Hiltner and other writers in the pastoral care movement. Dobbins left little doubt regarding his association to client-centered counseling, especially regarding the technique of active listening:

---

student. Ironically, the years Rogers and Dobbins were students at Teacher's College and Union overlapped.

87. See Maslow, *A Theory of Human Motivation*, 370–96. Maslow, *Toward a Psychology of Being*, 14–18, 6691, 117–26.

88. Maslow, *Toward a Psychology of Being*, 118–19.

89. Hiltner credited Rogers use of "nondirective" in Rogers, *Counseling and Psychotherapy*. Rogers and Hiltner were contemporaries on faculty at the University of Chicago.

90. Hiltner, *Preface to Pastoral Theology*, n25 from Chapter 6. Hiltner demonstrates the rapid growth of literature in the pastoral care movement, naming Wise, Charles F. Kemp, Carl J. Scherzer, Paul B. Maves, A. Graham Ikin, Russell Dicks, and Richard Cabot as primary contributors. Dobbins turned to many of these men to further his views on pastoral care. For a clear understanding of the new pastoral theology also see, Oglesby, *The New Shape of Pastoral Theology*.

91. Hiltner, *Preface to Pastoral Theology*, 154.

In every aspect of pastoral care and counseling stress is laid on the high importance of being a good listener . . . In the counseling philosophy selective listening is more important than talking. Trained to speak, the minister may talk too much. Every phase of ministry would be enriched if he could learn to practice the art of listening. Perhaps on occasions the greater part of his service to others will be to listen.[92]

The greater humanistic approach to psychology can be detected as well in Dobbins's summation of the heart of the counseling process:

1. Personal, face-to face-relationship

2. between person or persons needing help and one skilled in the art of providing help

3. in which the person needing help is stimulated and guided to self-expression, self-revelation, and self-understanding

4. in which the one seeking to provide the help enters intelligently and sympathetically into the other's difficulty and furnishes a screen upon which it may be freely projected

5. as a result of which the troubled friend discovers the real root of the difficulty, finds resources for dealing with it, and undertakes constructively a solution of his own choosing

6. in all of which Christ and the Gospel are given maximum opportunity to demonstrate their adequacy for every need in every area of life

7. with conscious dependence upon the Holy Spirit for illumination and guidance and with quiet confidence in the fulfillment of Christ's prayer promises when the conditions are met.[93]

The humanistic goals of counseling should be immediately recognizable to the reader. Stimulation should be employed to encourage the needy person toward self-guided expression and discovery.[94] The congruence of Rogers is apparent in the counselor's attempt to be a screen upon which the counselee may freely project himself.[95] The solution is of the counselee's own choosing because the pastoral counselor is nondirective in his approach and

---

92. Dobbins, *A Ministering Church*, 166. See also Dobbins, *Building Better Churches*, 334.

93. Dobbins, "The Pastor as Counselor," 426.

94. Maslow, *Toward a Psychology of Being*, 26–44, 118–26.

95. Rogers, *On Becoming a Person*, 282–85.

the person must fully realize themselves from within.[96] The final two sum-mations seem to be an addendum necessary for any clergy claiming Christ. Core skills of the counseling process were embedded in the nondirective, client-centered, and self-actualizing of humanistic psychology—made pos-sible by the acceptance of psychological methodology and techniques in edu-cation and the scientific view of man promoted in the psychology of religion.

These types of requirements necessitate professional and specialized training in multiple disciplines. Dobbins expressed, "The psychiatrist or medical psychologist may or may not believe in a personal God but makes use of the concept as having therapeutic value if it aids in the recovery of mental health."[97] The philosophical assumption of pragmatism can be seen in Dobbins, as methodologies may be used from irreligious sources so long as it aids recovery. The pastor, also, must be proficient in the science of religion and religious experiences, otherwise known as the psychology of religion. He must know in detail the professional work of the psychologists:

> In the main, the psychologist and the religionist have come to count each other as allies rather than as antagonists. Studying the patient's needs and seeking his restoration to health, the psy-chiatrist recognizes the therapeutic value of worship. Seeking to supply his parishioner's needs, the minister finds guidance from the understanding of persons supplied by the psychologist. Russell J. Becker thus stated it:
>
> When the psychologist takes his methods of empirical investigation (be they questionnaire, experimental situation, epidemiological survey, participant observation, or whatever) to the data of religious life, the result is a welcome increase in the body of human knowledge . . . [sic] Both the psychologist and the informed religious person have felt satisfied with the growth of psychology of religion. To the psychologist it is an extension of a science of psychology. To the informed religious person it is an increase in our knowledge of the truth.[98]

CLINICAL PASTORAL EDUCATION

Dobbins was brought on faculty by Mullins with the intention to teach prac-tical courses. The vision given by Mullins sustained him in his search for

96. Maslow, *Toward a Psychology of Being*, 93. "As he gets to be more purely and singly himself he is more able to fuse with the world, with what was formerly non-self."

97. Dobbins, *The Church at Worship*, 105.

98. Dobbins, *The Church at Worship*, 114.

practical training to aid pastors in their care for their congregations. Dobbins articulated that the demands upon the modern pastor were predominantly different than in prior days. Additional motivation to bolster pastoral training was supplied by what Dobbins believed to be inadequate pastoral training. "In my student days," Dobbins recalled, "nearly half a century ago the course in Pastoral Theology dealt helpfully with many practical matters which then confronted the pastor."[99] However, his experience during his first pastorate left him feeling ill-prepared for pastoral duties.

> I went out into my first pastorate wholly ignorant of the psychological approach to the work of the pastor, and had to stumble through the solution of problems which I had never dreamed I would face. Called soon thereafter to teach in Southern Seminary, I determined to introduce my students to the developing field of psychology of religion.[100]

Dobbins's initial solution was the utilization of the experiential techniques and methods of the modern educational theorists to make his courses more practical. The continuation of this model into pastoral theology naturally adapted to fit the practical training goals of Dobbins. He was merely fostering among Southern Baptists this same trend that was occurring within theological education in the United States.[101]

How would the seminary student deal with the modern problems of the parishioners? The answer Dobbins provided set the course of pastoral theology at Southern Seminary toward the psychological model:

> A course had been introduced at the Seminary labeled "Psychology of Religion." It proposed to bring the newly developed "science of mind and behavior" to the service of theology and sociology. I inherited this course. Quickly I realized that psychology had a far greater than academic contribution to make to the equipment of the minister for personal and group ministries."[102]

The expressions of discontentment with traditional theological education by Dobbins were akin to those that established CPE. Thornton reported, "Clinical training began as a reaction against traditional theological

---

99. Wayne E. Oates Papers, Box 9, Folder 37. Dobbins, "An Historical Description," in Fuller et al., *A Tenth-Year Report*, 4.

100. Dobbins, "An Historical Description," in Fuller et al., *A Tenth-Year Report*, 4.

101. Holifield, *A History of Pastoral Care in America*, 221–29.

102. Dobbins, *Zest for Living*, 63. Charles Spurgeon Gardner taught this course at Southern Seminary prior to Dobbins.

education, but it was a reaction at the periphery of seminary life."[103] The periphery could be identified as religious educators. E. Brooks Holifield noticed this trend when he said, "Dewey's ideas found initial expression in the churches within the religious education movement, which also helped to secure a firm footing for psychology in the religious communities."[104] George A. Coe, Dobbins's professor, was not ignorant of the same connection between religious education and the influence of psychological method based on his explanation from *The Spiritual Life*:

> Why should not the care of souls become an art—a system of organized and proportioned methods based upon definite knowledge of the material to be wrought upon, the ends to be attained, and the means and instruments for attaining them? Such an art would require scientific insight into the general organization of the mind, and especially into the particular characteristics of the child mind, the youth, and the mature mind.[105]

Coe's words from 1900 could be considered somewhat prophetic. The discontent within theological education, secular psychology's invasion into religious education, and theological liberalism conjoined to form a reactionary proposal known as clinical theological education. "Theological liberalism," Thornton recognized, "prepared the way for the initial acceptance of clinical pastoral education in seminaries such as Chicago Theological Seminary, The University of Chicago Divinity School, Union, Yale, and the major schools of Boston."[106] The same discontent, the same psychology and remnants of theological liberalism, paved the way for acceptance of the professional model of Clinical Pastoral Education at Southern Seminary.[107]

---

103. Thornton, *Professional Education for Ministry*, 24.

104. Holifield, *A History of Pastoral Care in America*, 224.

105. Coe, *The Spiritual Life*, 21.

106. Thornton, *Professional Education for Ministry*, 27.

107. Fuller et al., *A Tenth-Year Report*. The first chapter of this book is important for this point. The acceptance of pragmatism, sociology, psychology, and the science of religious experience by Dobbins's predecessors helps to understand the influence of theological liberalism at Southern Seminary. Many of the faculty in the School of Theology at Southern Seminary seemed to recognize the divergence at differing points in the development of religious education and clinical training for pastoral students. See Dobbins, "Oral History Interviews," 62–67. See also Gray, "Dobbinology," 2–3. Dobbins explained discontent with the curriculum changes during his first five years and then again at the end of his career. He even says he was "ousted"; meaning he was happy to retire early from Southern Seminary and begin teaching at Golden Gate Baptist Theological Seminary due to these discontents.

Clinical Pastoral Education at Southern Seminary

Several reasons may be identified as to why Southern Seminary, under Dobbins's leadership, took such an interest in Clinical Pastoral Education. First, former pastoral students expressed discontent with the inadequacies of their training in counseling. Oates explained that present and former students "reported the need for more equipment during their seminary years in the direct pastoral ministry to persons in the context of their daily pastoral office."[108]

It was this same discontent that led Dobbins to further study at various colleges and universities with Coe and other modern educationalists:

> It was my early good fortune to have some courses with John Dewey of Columbia and Harrison Sackett Elliot of Union. About this time I came to know Anton Boisen, father of the movement for clinical training of theological students, and Karl Stolz, who was attracting graduate students in psychology of education to Hartford. Increasingly I became more committed to this experiential and person-centered philosophy of education and practice of pastoral care.[109]

Dobbins introduced the reader to several main sources who satisfied his discontent with traditional theological education. It is not necessary that the influence of Dewey be revisited, but H. S. Elliot deserves brief attention as a significant figure in this process.

Elliot's influence became a common thread between religious education and pastoral counseling. Elliot taught Carl Rogers as a student at Union and also Seward Hiltner.[110] Rogers influenced the CPE movement with active-listening, unconditional positive regard, congruence, and incongruence. Holifield called Rogers "a virtual guru for the pastoral counseling movement."[111] Hiltner became the primary writer associated with the pastoral care movement and the new pastoral theology that employed the CPE model for clinical theological training.[112]

Early in Dobbins's career, Dewey, Coe, and Kilpatrick were the main influencers on his educational methodology, but others soon became significant. Harrison S. Elliot furthered Dobbins thinking, "with [Elliot's] concept

108. Oates, "Organizational Development and Pastoral Care," 349.

109. Dobbins, "An Historical Description," in Fuller et al., *A Tenth-Year Report*, 4.

110. Rogers, *On Becoming a Person*, 8. See Holifield, *A History of Pastoral Care in America*, 226–27.

111. Holifield, *A History of Pastoral Care in America*, 227.

112. See Hiltner, *Preface to Pastoral Theology*.

of teaching through discussion method, in which he insisted that teaching is stimulation to discussion and learning is participation in a group."[113] Religious educators during this time were known as "psychologists" within the churches.[114] Like Elliot, religious educators began to teach theories of personality, pastoral counseling, and psychology. His group methodology also had a profound impact upon Dobbins.[115] Elliot's influence on Dobbins continued indirectly in the area of pastoral care, because Elliot brought Seward Hiltner to Union Theological Seminary, "where they developed pedagogical methods that became standard in the pastoral care courses of Protestant seminaries."[116] Dobbins's books and course materials reflect the impact of Hiltner.[117]

Second, the advent of World War II demanded attention from theological students and their supervisors. The war created the opportunity out of which Dobbins moved to discover his approach to pastoral counseling. Dobbins explained how the war appropriated his approach to clinical training:

> When World War II broke upon us, I was teaching a well-attended course in psychology of religion, with major emphasis on counseling. One day a call of distress came from the superintendent of the Louisville General Hospital. He explained the shortage of orderlies and attendants, due to the war conditions, and asked if some arrangement could be made to source the services of theological students on a part-time basis. A call for volunteers brought hearty response from the class.[118]

The students were vitalized, and their study and viewpoint of the ministry were enhanced by the practical experience in the hospital.[119] The demand

---

113. Dobbins, *Great Teachers*, 82.

114. Holifield, *A History of Pastoral Care in America*, 226.

115. Dobbins, *Great Teachers*, 96.

116. Holifield, *A History of Pastoral Care in America*, 227. Dobbins, *Gaines S. Dobbins*, 85. Dobbins use of such terms as "depth psychology," "interpersonal relations," "pastoral care," "social activism," and "theology of hope" demonstrate the mixture of influence from religious educators and psychology. Hiltner was one of many influential figures upon Dobbins's understanding of pastoral care. See his biography (86) for a more full bibliography. One can easily recognize the influence by perusing Dr. Dobbins's recommended resources for psychology, pastoral care, and education at the end of many of his books.

117. Fuller et al., *A Tenth-Year Report*. See Dobbins, *A Ministering Church*, Dobbins, *Building Better Churches* and Dobbins, *The ChurchBook*.

118. Dobbins, "An Historical Description," in Fuller et al., *A Tenth-Year Report*, 4. See also Dobbins, *Zest for Living*, 64.

119. Dobbins, "An Historical Description," in Fuller et al., *A Tenth-Year Report*, 4

remained throughout the war and Oates acknowledged the special need that arose once it had passed, "At the end of World War II, large numbers of men who had been combat soldiers and chaplains did not wait to be asked. They demanded a serious response to their need for thorough equipment in pastoral care."[120]

Third, there was a desire to be missional. According to Oates, the endeavor toward clinical training in pastoral care, from the beginning, was perceived by Dobbins as mission.[121] The untouchables of the day were those who had been diagnosed as mentally ill, and Dobbins saw an opportunity for theological students to minister to those who had been cast aside. Dobbins turned to Boisen's model of CPE after learning of his bout with mental illness, "[Dobbins] was at the University of Chicago for summer study. Anton Boisen was bringing a series of lectures growing out his personal experience and subsequent ministries for the mentally ill."[122] As the program grew, Oates kept in mind that "the central motive of this sort of training is to strengthen and enlarge, and make more effective the missionary interest and enthusiasm of the student."[123]

Fourth, CPE provided a more practical approach to theological education, particularly pastoral training. Dobbins wanted to see theological training become more clinical, in part because, this maintained a standard of academic quality. Scholarly excellence was necessary within the progressive world of professionals; therefore, the minister should have similar professional training. The students cooperated with other professionals at the hospital such as doctors, nurses, psychiatrists, and social workers. According to this model, the pastor should also be professionally trained so as not to be at a deficit when interacting with these other professions. In the *Tenth-Year Report* of the clinical training program at Southern Seminary it is explained that, "Clinical training is aimed to equip the minister with such insights and skill that he may not 'be ashamed of the gospel' in the presence of the people of these other professions also dedicated to the service of mankind."

120. Oates, "Organizational Development and Pastoral Care," 349.

121. Oates, "Organizational Development and Pastoral Care," 351.

122. Dobbins, *Zest for Living*, 63–64. Dobbins invited Boisen to Southern Seminary for a conference and a series of lectures to classes. "This visit [by Boisen] was followed with ones by consultants in this field, including a notable lecture series by Luther Weigle of Yale Divinity School, who gave scholarly recognition to what I [Dobbins] was trying to do."

123. Wayne E. Oates Papers, Box 9, Folder 37. Fuller and Oates, "An Official Statement of Policy," in Fuller et al., *A Tenth-Year Report*, 3. A similar argument is made today that calls for theological students to pursue missional living molding professional licensure with theological education. See Williams, "Counselors as Missionaries," 28–40.

Thornton confirmed that this type of training came into theological education via religious educators:

> Clinical pastoral educators have been the allies, sometimes wittingly but often unwittingly, of those educational statesmen who have decided that the ministry ought to be a profession as well as a calling, that theological education must become professional education incorporating the sciences, just as centuries ago it expanded to include the humanities.[124]

For Southern Baptists, this flow of professional training was identical. Holifield recognized that "[Dobbins's] courses in religious education introduced the new pastoral theology into southern conservatism. By 1927, the theological seminaries were offering a number of courses on 'personality,' but most of the instruction in counseling took place in the religious education classes."[125]

Living Human Documents

Dobbins's focus on experience in the Christian life gave greater credence to Boisen's ideology. Boisen believed in studying "living human documents" as a source of truth. In CPE the center point is to understand a person in a similar way as one would understand the Bible as a living document.[126] The Bible is intended to be read and understood based on its source as being inspired truths or reality. In much the same way, to view someone as a living document is to understand their experiences as truth and reality that may supersede any other form of truth and inspiration.[127]

As pastoral care was being developed from the pattern of psychology, Dobbins began to interact with the prime thinkers and architects of Clinical Pastoral Education.[128]

124. Thornton, *Professional Education for Ministry*, 28.

125. Holifield, *A History of Pastoral Care in America*, 227.

126. Hiltner, *Preface to Pastoral Theology*, 51. "The person who has done more than any other in our century to prepare the soil for a new pastoral theology is Anton Boisen. He was not only one of the founders of clinical training for the clergy; a quarter century ago he set for the thesis that there was a similarity in process between some forms of religious experience and some forms of mental disorder. In studying 'living human documents,' even those in deep disturbance, one was not, he held, merely studying psychology or psychiatry, but also theology. For it is out of just such experiences, he contended, that great religious insights have emerged in prophets and mystics of the past."

127. Dobbins, *Deepening the Spiritual Life*, 31–43. Dobbins's explanation of the value of human experience was on par with the revelation of Scripture.

128. See Dobbins, *Zest for Living*, 65. Karl Menninger, Lawrence Frank, Seward

Hiltner was key and, in a tribute written about him in *Pastoral Psychology*, James I. McCord declared that Hiltner sought to professionalize pastoral theology.[129] Dobbins used precisely the same techniques with his students and encouraged his successors to follow. After being influenced by Boisen's "living human documents," Hiltner also tested his theology with Paul Tillich and Erich Fromm. McCord said,

> A different Seward Hiltner returned to Chicago after World War II and a different *Geist* began to appear in the nation and the churches. In a sense, theological education was now ready to become professional, and Seward Hiltner was prepared to lead it in this pilgrimage . . .
>
> His work in integration is seen, first of all in his *Preface to Pastoral Theology,* where Pastoral Theology is defined as "that branch or field of theological knowledge and inquiry that brings the shepherding perspective to bear upon all the operations and functions of the church and the minister, and then draws the conclusions of a theological order from reflection on these observations."[130]

The attempt to make pastoral training professional was realized in the adoption of Boisen's CPE model and the modifications made in the new pastoral theology of Hiltner. Ellis Fuller, president of The Southern Baptist Theological Seminary in 1943, requested Dobbins and Oates to write a report on the progress of the Department of Psychology of Religion and Pastoral Care. The *Tenth-Year Report* includes brief historical remarks that recount the significance and creation of the program, and outlines a plan for moving forward. Oates identified and described the importance of clinical training:

> This type of training is called "the clinical pastoral training of theological students." The training is based upon the conviction that the reason for pastoral failure and disillusionment is that the student's theoretical learning overbalances his emotional development and maturity which comes only from experience and the acceptance of responsibility for the care of people. Furthermore, this sort of training is based upon the conviction that the

---

Hiltner, Carrol Wise, Carl Rogers, Karen Horney, Gordon Allport, Russell Dicks, and Richard Cabot as books he recommended to his students. There was a special shelf in the library that contained these particular works and others like them that promoted the new pastoral theology of clinical theological training.

129. McCord, "Seward Hiltner's Contributions," 13–16. For a more extensive explanation of Hiltner's impact on pastoral theology, see Oglesby, *The New Shape of Pastoral Theology.*

130. McCord, "Seward Hiltner's Contributions," 15.

most reliable way of learning is the study of *"living human documents"* of people who are in acute personal need of the gospel of Christ. In this way the student's ideals are harmonized with reality, and he more readily becomes a servant of Christ who can see the world as it is without despair, and who can see the possibilities of his people in Christ without too much optimism.[131]

Dobbins resolved any questions that may remain as to his intent or desire for the clinical training of pastors. The foundation of the pastoral care model at Southern Seminary had been established clearly as a psychological approach driven by the desire to understand religious experiences of others as "living human documents." Professionalized training for pastoral care was thriving at Southern Seminary, and based on Dobbins's estimation, would remain the template for theological training of pastors for years to come.

It will thus be seen that in the course of ten years the psychological approach to pastoral care, religious education, theological and Biblical interpretation, and religious experience has moved out into a secure place in the curriculum of Southern Baptist Theological Seminary. The way ahead challenges to new adventures and to creative thought and experience. Theological education can never be the same in the light of these progressive developments.[132]

CONCLUSION

Dobbins was the man responsible for adopting the professional psychological model. His veneration of the modern educationalists, with their theories and techniques, eventually shaped his practice of pastoral care. This modification to pastoral theology imported the professional model of pastoral training into Southern Seminary.

Dobbins did not seek to eliminate the responsibility of care and counseling from the pastor, "By virtue of his calling as an undershepherd of Christ, the pastor is to be a counselor, one who gives guidance to persons who have troublesome problems."[133] Instead, he sought to help the pastor gain the professional skills of a counselor in order to aid every aspect of his ministry.

131. Fuller and Oates, "An Official Statement of Policy," in Fuller et al., *A Tenth-Year Report*, 2.

132. Dobbins, "An Historical Description," in Fuller et al., *A Tenth-Year Report*, 6.

133. Dobbins, *Zest for Living*, 61.

The trend toward specialization in religious education eventually led to professional training for pastoral care. Theological education at that time seemed to bear the mark of specialized counseling designed to be commensurate with other professions such as doctors, lawyers, psychologists, psychiatrists, and social workers. Dobbins outlined the inclination toward specialization within theological education and the pastoral duties. The pressure arose from the modern demands placed upon the pastorate within the efficiency model of ecclesiology proposed by Dobbins. As the church members became specialized in their vocations, the expectation was projected onto the pastor to professionalize his training accordingly.

Dobbins sought the model that was produced by the scientifically inclined community in order to re-shape theological training for pastors. The psychological model in the form of Clinical Pastoral Education was aligned with his previously adopted educational methodologies. In order to maintain academic credibility within the seminary community, Dobbins preferred clinical training.

Clinical Pastoral Education created by Boisen, especially his concept of "living human documents," offered the practical training that Dobbins believed met the theological training need of the moment. CPE was modified by Hiltner after the influence of Elliot and the liberal theology of Paul Tillich, into what was called the new pastoral theology. The template of the new pastoral theology of Hiltner incited the movement of pastoral care. One of Hiltner's goals, which Dobbins followed, was to prepare pastoral care providers with professional training proportionate to conventional vocations. By his own admission, Dobbins had succeeded and rejoiced that clinical training would remain as a guarded portion of the curriculum at Southern Seminary.

Chapter 4

The New Department of Psychology of Religion

INTRODUCTION

What began as a new department in practical studies in the vision of E. Y. Mullins had produced a multiplicity of specializations for the pastorate. Dobbins assumed the custodial duty associated with the practical studies and with it formed a new ecclesiology and pastoral theology. A result of the new pastoral theology was specialized training for the pastoral counselor. The training began by hand-selecting certain students to volunteer in local medical facilities. It was not long before the new clinical training for pastors made its way into the curriculum at Southern Seminary.

Dobbins was responsible for the creation of another new department that was consistent with his adjusted ecclesiology and pastoral theology. Since pastoral counseling had become a specialty, there needed to be a department in which the pastors could receive even more professional training. Current students and alumni voiced their opinion in favor of more professionalized training for the pastor, and Dobbins responded.

As the new department was being developed, Dobbins remained primarily responsible for Church Efficiency, Religious Education, and Psychology of Religion. As these departments grew Dobbins maintained his commitment to specialization, and in that commitment, he chose men to assume leadership in the departments that were too large for him to manage. He appointed Findley Edge as Assistant Professor of Religious Education at Southern Seminary and Wayne Oates as Assistant Professor of Psychology of Religion and Pastoral Care.

This chapter will demonstrate that Dobbins is worthy of the title, father of pastoral care in the Southern Baptist Convention. His involvement in formation of the new Department of Psychology of Religion and Pastoral Care involved more than mere logistics. The department was created to fulfill the theoretical vision he had for the modern church and the professional pastor. In this chapter the motivation for the birth of a new department will be revealed. Dobbins was the primary actor and Wayne Oates became a significant figure in the genesis of clinical pastoral training at Southern Seminary. The chapter will close as I demonstrate the trajectory of pastoral counseling under Oates's leadership as he fulfilled the vision of Gaines Dobbins.

THE FATHER OF PASTORAL CARE IN THE SBC

To describe Dobbins as the father of pastoral care in the Southern Baptist Convention is to make a contrary claim, since most historians have identified Wayne Oates as the proprietor of this title, due to his voluminous work in the field.[1] The supposition is understandable considering Oates's influence lasted for half a century in the field of clinical pastoral care.[2] Indeed, Oates is most recognized ecumenically as the Baptist representative who sustained and promoted Clinical Pastoral Education and pastoral counseling during the mid to late twentieth century.[3] In spite of these accomplishments, Oates should not be considered the father of pastoral care in the Southern Baptist Convention.

Long before Oates became involved in the clinical training of pastoral students, Dobbins had been gradually shifting the pastoral duties toward a professional paradigm. Oates was the first professor dedicated to the

1. Moore, "Counseling and the Authority of Christ," 6. Thornton, *Professional Education for Ministry*, 155.

2. Thornton, *Professional Education for Ministry*, 153–59. Thornton uses Dobbins simply to introduce Oates and the called Oates the, "primary actor" in pastoral care and counseling at Southern Seminary. Oden, *Care of Souls in the Classic Tradition*, 30. In Oden's critique of modern pastoral care, he identified Oates as a primary contributor to the discipline, the only Southern Baptist he named.

3. Oden, *Care of Souls in the Classic Tradition*. See Holifield, *A History of Pastoral Care in America*, 307–30. Holifield demonstrated that Oates was a major contributor to pastoral care and pastoral counseling.

specialty training of pastors in CPE. Holifield claimed that "Long before there were any chairs of pastoral counseling in the Protestant seminaries, religious educators began to teach the subject."[4] Pastoral counseling was defined in terms of the psychological model, and no one knew this model in theological seminaries better than the religious educators. This was certainly true in the Southern Baptist denomination and particularly at Southern Seminary.[5]

Dement began using genetic psychology in his Sunday School pedagogy course.[6] Gardner introduced sociology and psychology into preaching and education at Southern Seminary.[7] Once ecclesiology was combined with religious education and pastoral theology under Dobbins in the new Department of Practical Studies, the effort to utilize the new science became concentrated. The influence of psychology, under Dobbins's leadership, was confined no longer to religious education, but permeated ecclesiology and pastoral theology. The new science was infused into every aspect of ministerial and ecclesiastical life. Dobbins had been teaching the psychologically dependent paradigm of pastoral ministry since at least 1930.[8]

Dobbins's work in pastoral care predated that of Oates considerably. Thornton said, "Interest in clinical training at the Seminary preceded Oates by several years. Seward Hiltner visited the Louisville school in 1937 on the invitation of professors Dobbins and Carver."[9] Dobbins pursued this type of training before 1937, however. Anton Boisen had been invited before 1930 to give lectures to Dobbins's classes and to provide a conference for interested students in the new methods of therapeutic prevention and cure

4. Holifield, *A History of Pastoral Care in America*, 226.

5. Southwestern Baptist Theological Seminary, *Southwestern Baptist Theological Seminary Bulletin*, Vol. 1, No. 3, 21. See the Religious Education and Christian Sociology course offerings. Principles of Religious Education and Methods of Religious Education course descriptions provide proper evidence for course content which reflects the use of psychology as a foundational science for the teaching of Religious Education. Maguire, *J. M. Price: Portrait of a Pioneer*. A cursory study of the work of J. M. Price revealed the impact of psychology in his teaching.

6. Southern Baptist Theological Seminary, *Catalogue of The Southern Baptist Theological Seminary, Forty-Eighth Session, 1906–1907*, 36.

7. Southern Baptist Theological Seminary, *Catalogue of The Southern Baptist Theological Seminary, Fifty-Eighth Session, 1916–1917*, 38. See Weatherspoon, "Charles Spurgeon Gardner," 190.

8. Based on his course notes, one could date Dobbins's teaching on the new pastoral care back into the mid-late twenties. The course catalog description indicated that Psychology of Religion became a major course of study in 1930. Southern Baptist Theological Seminary, *Catalogue of The Southern Baptist Theological Seminary, Seventy-First Session, 1916–1917*, 82–83.

9. Thornton, *Professional Education for Ministry*, 153.

in pastoral care.[10] Luther A. Weigle, of Yale University, gave the Norton Lectures, at the request of Dobbins, on "Psychology of Religion" during the 1927–1928 academic year.[11]

Holifield claimed that the influence of Dobbins upon pastoral care at Southern Seminary began upon his arrival, "And at Southern Baptist Theological Seminary in Louisville, Gaines Dobbins, who had studied with both Coe and Dewey, in 1920 began a long campaign to 'capture psychology for Christ.'"[12] Holifield recognized that the departments of religious education became the seedbed of psychology in theological institutions:

> A professor of "Religious Education and Church Efficiency," Dobbins tried to convince the faculty apart from the study of Scripture, psychology was 'the most important single subject which should be mastered by one who all his life must deal first hand with people.' His courses in religious education introduced the new pastoral theology into southern conservatism. By 1927, the theological seminaries were offering a number of courses on 'personality,' but most of the instruction in counseling took place in the religious education classes."[13]

Among Southern Baptists, Holifield attributed to Dobbins the primary responsibility of the paradigm shift in pastoral care toward a psychological model. While others recognized his contribution to pastoral care, it is often overshadowed by his contributions to church administration and religious education.[14] Wayne Oates did not diminish the contribution of Dobbins to pastoral care because he knew first-hand the recognition that Dobbins deserved for the new approach to pastoral care.

During the time of Dobbins's transitional work in pastoral care at Southern Seminary, Oates was a pastor of a rural church in North Carolina.[15] Oates had been called to ministry as a college student at Mars Hill. He later attended Wake Forest College and Duke University prior to moving to Louisville, Kentucky to attend Southern Seminary in 1943.[16] During the

10. Dobbins, Zest for Living, 64.

11. Southern Baptist Theological Seminary, Catalogue of The Southern Baptist Theological Seminary, Sixty-Ninth Session, 1927–1928, 60. The four lectures were categorized into, "Behaviourism, Auto-suggestion, Psycho-analysis, and Freudianism."

12. Holifield, A History of Pastoral Care in America, 227.

13. Holifield, A History of Pastoral Care in America, 227.

14. Graves, "Gaines Dobbins—Mr. Church Administrator," 383. Ryan, "Gaines S. Dobbins—Author," 409–10. Edge, "Gaines S. Dobbins—The Teacher," 371–76.

15. "Man of the Month," Pastoral Psychology, 8 and 65. Thornton, Professional Education for Ministry, 154.

16. "Man of the Month," Pastoral Psychology, 8.

time of his rural pastorate, the story is told that Oates was called upon to minister to a suffering woman.[17] The medical doctor had already told the woman he could do nothing further to help her. Oates listened to the woman describe her sufferings and then prayed for her, but he felt overwhelmed by the complexity of the situation. Later, Oates became acquainted with the doctor who cared for the woman and advised him, saying:

> We are entering upon a whole new understanding of the nature of disease. I believe this will draw the minister closer to the work of the doctor. You train yourself for this. I don't know where you will get the training, but wherever you find anybody who knows anything about it, listen to him.[18]

This moment sparked in Oates an interest in clinical training, "The first man Oates found to listen to on the subject was Gaines S. Dobbins of Southern Baptist Seminary."[19]

Oates was introduced to Dobbins in 1943 as a student in his "church administration course and an elective called 'psychology of religion.'"[20] Oates explained the content of the psychology of religion course as he reflected, "We explored the relationship between religion and medicine, psychotherapy and the Christian faith, and a Christian apologetic in the fact of the clinical discoveries of psychoanalysis. This was uncharted territory."[21] Oates acknowledged three important facts in this description. First, the course was an intentional attempt to integrate secular psychology and religious faith. Second, the clinical model of training and learning were encouraged as a part of this course. Third, this was a new concept in theological education. This was the type of clinical training Oates had come from North Carolina to find, and Dobbins provided the paradigm.

As a part of the psychology of religion course, Oates participated, with other students, as a psychiatric aide at a Louisville hospital.[22] Dobbins said that this need arose after doctors, nurses and orderlies were drafted to serve in the U. S. military during World War II.[23] The seminary students were

---

17. The story was originally told in Scherzer, *The Church and Healing* , 242–43. The story appeared next in May 1951 as the editorial "Man of the Month," in *Pastoral Psychology*, 65, and then in Thornton, *Professional Education for Ministry*, 153–54.

18. "Man of the Month," *Pastoral Psychology*, 65.

19. Thornton, *Professional Education for Ministry*, 154.

20. Oates, "Gaines S. Dobbins," in Dobbins, *Great Teachers*, 89.

21. Oates, "Gaines S. Dobbins," in Dobbins, *Great Teachers*, 91.

22. Dobbins, *Zest for Living*, 64–65. Oates, "Gaines S. Dobbins," in Dobbins, *Great Teachers*, 94.

23. Dobbins, *Zest for Living*, 64.

exempt from the draft and seemed worthy candidates to perform this type of duty. In this opportunity, "[Dobbins] saw a whole new educational methodology in clinical pastoral education. He saw in this both a challenge to the old presuppositions of the theological education and an effective channel into which to direct the rebelliousness of a considerable number of students on the campus at that time."[24]

Several factors culminated in the practice of clinical training at Southern Seminary. First, the need had been expressed by current students and alumni that more practical training was necessary. Eager to provide more practical training, Dobbins acted upon the opportunity that provided students with clinical experience. Dobbins had adopted the group methodology from Harrison S. Elliot, which he implemented by encouraging student participation. Oates also reported that the problem-solving skills of John Dewey and E. L. Thorndike were encouraged.[25] There were opportunities for the students to practice the new educational methodologies in order to re-learn the theoretical material taught in the traditional classroom.[26] He believed this would better prepare the students for the modern challenges they would face in the pastorate.

Second, the opportunity presented by the hospital created an ideal scenario for his educational methodology to blossom. His vision for pastoral ministry training was driven by his educational methodology. Incidentally, his educational methodology was guided by the modern social sciences. In the aggregate, pastoral theology, particularly pastoral care, was eclipsed by the psychological model. This was due, in part, to the fact that the student's pastoral training was facilitated by doctors, psychiatrists, psychologists, and social workers. The new environment demanded professional training and adoption of the anthropological paradigm, including the language and methodology of the professionals in the hospital.

24. Oates, "Gaines S. Dobbins," in Dobbins, *Great Teachers*, 94.

25. Oates, "Gaines S. Dobbins," in Dobbins, *Great Teachers*, 96.

26. Oates, "Organizational Development and Pastoral Care," 351. Oates explained the benefit of clinical training in what he called, "re-learning." He said, "Supervisors regularly would go with the student in the pastoral call or invite them into pastoral counseling sessions. Reporting and reflecting upon one's actual work with persons provide the data base for developing principles of pastoral care inductively. Comparisons of these with data from biblical studies, ethical studies, theological studies, and historical studies causes the data from these fields to come alive in a re-learning process. As one who teaches both theological students and medical students now, I see the same thing happening to the medical student in the clinical years of medical education as the student relearns material from anatomy, biochemistry, pharmacology, I both theological and medical education the re-learning synthesis takes place in the clinical context.

Dobbins's innovative work in curriculum design and his implementation of the clinical training model should be recognized. Proper credit should be given for his work in pastoral care at Southern Seminary and in the SBC. Oates is typically granted this commendation, but even he testified, as an eyewitness to the pioneering work of Dobbins, "Dr. Dobbins organized the present Department of Psychology of Religion and Pastoral Care. *He started this work.*"[27]

For these reasons it was proper for Oates to declare the degree of Dobbins's influence upon pastoral care. In a *Festschrift* dedicated to Dobbins as a pioneer, Oates said, "The unique genius of Gaines Dobbins as the father of the pastoral care movement at Southern Baptist Theological Seminary lay in his tireless ability in organizational development."[28] Oates was correct in his declaration regarding Dobbins as the father of pastoral care in the SBC, but the implications should not be overlooked. Contrary to many historians in the SBC, Oates admitted he was not the father of pastoral care. This is not to diminish Oates's contribution to pastoral care and counseling or to clinical training in the SBC. If Dobbins is the owner of this title, was pastoral care non-existent prior to Dobbins? Pastoral ministries and pastoral theology were taught at Southern Seminary, as demonstrated by its academic catalogues.[29] Oates's declaration is more than a simple proclamation of Dobbins as the father of pastoral care, but that he had recreated a framework of pastoral theology established upon the psychological model, rather than on a theological, biblical, and Christological foundation. Therefore, a more appropriate title may be proposed—Dobbins was the father of *modern* pastoral care in the SBC.

THE NEW DEPARTMENT

The introduction of a new Department of Psychology of Religion and Pastoral Care in 1947 was not the first appearance of the social sciences into theological education at Southern Seminary. In 1899 Professor Dargan

27. Oates, "Gaines S. Dobbins," in Dobbins, *Great Teachers*, 98 and 109. Emphasis added.

28. Oates, "Organizational Development and Pastoral Care," 349.

29. The catalogues demonstrated that Pastoral Theology and/or Pastoral Ministries were taught until around 1919. The primary texts according to Dobbins for those men who taught before him were Washington Gladden and Richard Baxter. Mueller, *A History of Southern Baptist Theological Seminary*, 61. Mueller stated, "Dr. Boyce's theology still had some of 'the intellectual defenses of historic Puritanism.'" The declaration by Oates indicated that Dobbins's methodology for pastoral theology was a departure from the puritanical model of pastoral ministry.

offered a "Special Study Course" in Practical Theology called, Sociology.[30] Incidentally, this is the same year E. Y. Mullins came to SBTS as president. Based on the catalogue record, there was not another course offered like it until B. H. Dement taught the inaugural course in Sunday School Pedagogy, which considered Psychology of Religion and genetic psychology.[31] During the three academic years spanning 1912 to 1915, Dement offered a Special Study Course at the graduate level on Psychology of Religion.[32] Also in 1915, the president of Carson and Newman College, J. M. Burnett, presented the Gay Lectures on the subject, "Some values in the Newer Psychology for Preachers."[33] Gardner continued to offer Psychology of Religion as a Special Study Course from 1915–1918, promoting psychology's benefit to preaching.[34]

The influx of the social sciences increased at the close of the decade prior to Dobbins's arrival as a professor. The 1920 series of the Norton Lectures were presented by Professor H. R. Mackintosh of Edinburgh, Scotland entitled, "Theology in Light of Modern Philosophy and Psychology."[35] Dobbins entered the seminary in an environment saturated with intrigue for the social sciences. After a disappointing first year, however, he accelerated the influence of the newer sciences through both efficiency and religious education. The behavioral sciences began to dominate his ecclesiology under the course title, Church Efficiency. Psychology of religion, genetic psychology, and educational psychology directed his religious education courses during his first decade as a professor.

During the 1927–1928 academic year, at Dobbins's request, Luther A. Weigle presented the Norton Lectures, with a primary focus upon the psychology of religion and, secondarily, secular psychology. Around the same time, Dobbins had also become acquainted with Boisen and had him present the newly developed ideas of clinical training to his students.[36] It seemed

30. Southern Baptist Theological Seminary, *Catalogue of The Southern Baptist Theological Seminary, Forty-First Session, 1899–1900*, 45.

31. Southern Baptist Theological Seminary, *Catalogue of The Southern Baptist Theological Seminary, Forty-Eighth Session, 1906–1907*, 36.

32. See *Fifty-Third, Fifty-Fourth,* and *Fifty-Fifth* sessions of the *Catalogue of The Southern Baptist Theological Seminary*.

33. Southern Baptist Theological Seminary, *Catalogue of The Southern Baptist Theological Seminary, Fifty-Fifth Session, 1914–1915*.

34. See *Fifty-Sixth, Fifty-Seventh,* and *Fifty-Eight* sessions of the *Catalogue of The Southern Baptist Theological Seminary*. Gardner, "Syllabus of Lecture on Homiletics: Third Quarter." Also see Gardner, *Psychology and Preaching*.

35. Southern Baptist Theological Seminary, *Catalogue of The Southern Baptist Theological Seminary, Sixty-First Session, 1919–1920*, 47.

36. Dobbins, *Zest for Living*, 64.

as though these lectures were preparation for the seminary to introduce a new course of study into the curriculum. In 1929, listed under the Religious Education and Ecclesiology Department, Psychology of Religion could be chosen as a major course of study at Southern Seminary.[37]

In the 1920s, the social sciences continued to influence Dobbins's ideas of theological education. During that decade, Church Efficiency and Religious Education were his primary focus. The clinical training of Anton Boisen was born around 1925 and Dobbins was aware of its development. He would later become more than a fringe observer. As clinical training and pastoral psychology progressed in the decade of the 1930s, it had almost immediate impact upon the curriculum at SBTS.[38] Dobbins continued to introduce students to key framers of the field of clinical pastoral training and the new pastoral theology. During the 1939 academic year, William Sadler of Chicago delivered the Norton Lectures on Pastoral Psychology, which was indicative of the seminary's new direction in pastoral care.[39]

Dobbins, with keen awareness, had been gathering data from students to determine the need for clinical pastoral training, "In the development of a ministry of pastoral care, Gaines Dobbins used a more prophetic approach and less bureaucratic approach to needs assessment." He conducted what Oates called "'a listening-in campaign' among former students and present students in the years between 1937 and 1943."[40] Oates recalled that Dobbins listened patiently to the students to determine the perceived need for clinical pastoral training, taking into consideration the modern context.

Apparently, the response to Dobbins's questionnaires to students gathered remarkable response. The students acknowledged a desire to have more practical and professional training in preparation for their pastoral work. Oates said, "On the tidal wave of this demand, the Seminary embarked upon the development of a program in pastoral care under the leadership of Gaines Dobbins. The need was there and would not be denied."[41] Dobbins began to amass a plan that involved multiple resources and opportunities for students to train, which he believed would meet their needs.

Dobbins had been preparing for the clinical breakthrough that came just after 1940. Scherezer claimed that Dobbins "had for years been giving

37. Southern Baptist Theological Seminary, *Catalogue of The Southern Baptist Theological Seminary, Seventy-First Session, 1929–1930*, 82–83.

38. Thornton, *Professional Education for Ministry*, 152–53. Scherzer, *The Church and Healing*, 243–44.

39. Southern Baptist Theological Seminary, *Catalogue of The Southern Baptist Theological Seminary, Eighty-First Session, 1939–1940*, 46.

40. Oates, "Organizational Development and Pastoral Care," 349.

41. Oates, "Organizational Development and Pastoral Care," 349.

such 'textbook' guidance as he could to men in the field of psychology and a 'person-minded ministry.'"[42] In the words of Edward Thornton, "The fullness of the time had surely come in the postwar years for clinical pastoral education to emerge from a movement into full professional identity. Pastoral counseling skills were becoming increasingly salable in churches as in society in general."[43] Dobbins sought local infirmaries and hospitals as venues for clinical training according to the model by Boisen, Cabot, and Weigle. According to Scherzer, Dobbins had already enlisted Chaplain Ralph Bonacker, of Norton Memorial Infirmary, "to teach a small group of men interested in a clinical approach to pastoral work."[44]

Norton Memorial was not the only institution he attempted to mobilize for his clinical vision. Thornton said, "The seminary was prepared to establish a clinical training program in the Louisville General Hospital as soon as the Council for Clinical Training could provide a supervisor. But no supervisor was available."[45] It is true that the seminary was prepared to establish a clinical training program, but Dobbins described other concerns:

> The Council for Clinical Training had rendered invaluable pioneering service. Yet, their summer program, detached from the regular curriculum of the Seminary had many disadvantages. Its appeal was necessarily limited to a few students; it was not related to the "body of divinity;" it was not under control and so could not command support of Seminary faculty and administration. To us there came the clear conviction that this discipline should become an integral part of the curriculum, open to all interested and qualified students as a regular part of their equipment for pastoral office.[46]

Dobbins's primary concern was that the faculty and school administration would not approve a program that operated outside of the purview of the seminary. Further, there was doubt that the faculty would accept the clinical training as a legitimate subject matter for graduate work.[47] The perception was given, however, that the faculty was fully on board with the clinical method of training. Scherzer reported that Dobbins had the full confidence of the faculty and board of trustees demonstrated by a vote to

42. Scherzer, *The Church and Healing*, 243.

43. Thornton, *Professional Education for Ministry*, 114.

44. Scherzer, *The Church and Healing*, 243.

45. Thornton, *Professional Education for Ministry*, 153.

46. Dobbins, "An Historical Description," in Fuller et al., *A Tenth-Year Report*, 5.

47. Scherzer, *The Church and Healing*, 244–45.

accept the program into the curriculum.[48] According to Dobbins's "Oral History Interviews" with Badgett Dillard, the faculty did not approve the clinical method of training so willingly.

This was about the same time in the life of the seminary when Sampey retired and Ellis Fuller became president. Dobbins said the response to Fuller's election was, "not very favorable in the faculty" because Fuller was not a scholar, at least in the minds of many of the faculty.[49] The trustees, however, believed Fuller to be the man who would "shore up the seminary's flagging reputation for orthodoxy."[50]

The timing of Fuller's election was fortuitous for Dobbins's vision of clinical pastoral training and religious education. The postwar environment had presented needs within the hospitals for theological students to minister. Coupled with the surveys Dobbins had been accumulating from students since 1937, this seemed like the perfect opportunity to begin the clinical pastoral training. Wills reported, "In early 1943 Fuller sketched out his plans. To train leaders in religious education, he wanted to create a two-year program consisting of basic courses in the Bible, church history, and theology, as well as specialized courses in religious education, church administration and church finances."[51] Contrary to the way Wills presented Fuller's involvement, this was not a new direction for Dobbins. Rather, he had been strategically moving in this direction for more than a decade. Fuller was a voice calling for the same modern needs as Dobbins had been asserting, but as president, Fuller had the authority to implement the clinical training. Fuller stated, "The need and value of clinical training for a limited number of students is impressed upon us in many ways."[52] He recognized the need for professional training for pastoral assistants due to his experience as a pastor of Atlanta First Baptist Church. Wills said, "Fuller had been frustrated at his inability to find a qualified and able man to assist him in these areas of church work."[53] He had evidently been practicing the efficiency model of ecclesiology that Dobbins had promoted, or at least a similar model; therefore, he appointed Dobbins to oversee this aspect of the curriculum.

48. Scherzer, *The Church and Healing*, 245.

49. Dobbins, "Oral History Interviews," 57.

50. Wills, *Southern Baptist Theological Seminary*, 326.

51. Wills, *Southern Baptist Theological Seminary*, 326.

52. Fuller and Oates, "An Official Statement of Policy," in Fuller et al., *A Tenth-Year Report*, 1.

53. Wills, *Southern Baptist Theological Seminary*, 327.

In a document written in 1953, Fuller reported his sentiments toward clinical training a decade prior, when the program began during his presidency under the direction of Dobbins:

> The Southern Baptist Theological Seminary in not even remotely interested in training workers for the ministry which ignores or makes incidental the Christian gospel. But we are convinced that ministers need the resources which come from a better understanding of human nature and conduct, from an acquaintance with the techniques which psychiatrists and psychologists have developed for dealing with human problems and needs in sickness and in health, and from familiarity with the workings of hospitals and other institutions in which they will have opportunities to minster to those who need their Christian message and service. For these reasons we feel that it is wise to pursue our venture in giving to our student body such training in this area as may be possible under our limitations.[54]

Specialization was the need of the time and clinical pastoral training would be the tool to satisfy the need. Fuller emphasized that the understanding of human nature would come from secular psychiatrists and psychologists.

Based upon the new change in curriculum, Dobbins was granted permission to begin his practical training in the hospitals. Fuller's curriculum sketch was implemented in 1944 as evidenced by introduction of a course entitled Clinical Training taught by Dobbins.[55] The course in clinical training augmented the psychology of religion course that Dobbins had taught for some years. It should be noted that psychology of religion was a prerequisite course for the new clinical training. Due in part to his responsibilities

---

54. Fuller and Oates, "An Official Statement of Policy," in Fuller et al., *A Tenth-Year Report*, 1–2.

55. Southern Baptist Theological Seminary, *Catalogue of The Southern Baptist Theological Seminary, Eighty-Sixth Session, 1944–1945*, 53. Professor Dobbins: Clinical Training: Course Description: "The aim of this course is to equip the student with insight into the functions of personality, with techniques of pastoral counseling and case-work, and with an understanding of the use of community institutions in the reorientation of maladjusted persons. The course will consist of a seminar in which actual case-histories will be discussed and to which doctors, psychiatrists, and social workers will be invited to lecture. The seminar will be augmented by four hours per week of closely supervised work in the Juvenile Court—Children's Center, the Psychopathic Ward of General Hospital, and a local private hospital. Thus the moral, mental and psychosomatic aberrations of personality will be studied clinically in order that the student may understand more clearly and deal more adequately with the problems of his parishioners."

in church administration and religious education, Dobbins did not offer a full course of study in the new pastoral training.

The courses were offered as a major under the Department of Religious Education, or as electives, until 1947. Before a new department could begin, Dobbins identified the need for two men to provide leadership in the program—someone to organize the student volunteers. "In the class," Dobbins said, "was an exceptional student, Wayne Oates."[56] Dobbins patiently waited to begin the program until he found men he believed worthy to lead. Dobbins later said, "Wayne Oates was the man I had been looking for to lead in Southern Seminary a systematic program of clinical training."[57]

During the summer of 1945 Oates studied with Ralph Bonacker at Norton Memorial, under the direction of Dobbins.[58] The following academic year, Oates began as a teaching fellow under Dobbins. He taught the clinical training course and a newly added course entitled Pastoral Counseling.[59] The professional psychotherapeutic model, taught theoretically in psychology of religion and practiced experientially in clinical training, was aligned with pastoral counseling.[60] Clinical training and pastoral counseling were limited to twenty-one students that first semester and had to be taken in conjunction with one another. Dobbins boasted that "these courses became almost embarrassingly popular."[61]

Dobbins introduced Oates to Anton Boisen, a founder of Clinical Pastoral Education. The following summer of 1946, Oates studied with Boisen in Elgin, Illinois in order to implement the clinical training at Southern Seminary.[62] Dobbins, Fuller, and Oates had not been content with the simple addition of elective courses and wanted to begin a dedicated department. With the addition of Oates to the faculty, Dobbins believed the department was sustainable. Fuller described the benefit in expanding this program for pastoral students:

56. Dobbins, *Zest for Living*, 65. Richard Young was the other student from that class. Young would later become the chaplain of North Carolina Baptist Hospital and teacher of counseling at Wake Forest University.

57. Dobbins, "An Historical Description," in Fuller et al., *A Tenth-Year Report*, 4.

58. Dobbins, "An Historical Description," in Fuller et al., *A Tenth-Year Report*, 4. Oates, "Gaines S. Dobbins," in Dobbins, *Great Teachers*, 102.

59. Southern Baptist Theological Seminary, *Catalogue of The Southern Baptist Theological Seminary, Eighty-Seventh Session, 1945–1946*, 53–54.

60. Southern Baptist Theological Seminary, *Catalogue of The Southern Baptist Theological Seminary, Eighty-Seventh Session, 1945–1946*, 53–54.

61 Dobbins, "An Historical Description," in Fuller et al., *A Tenth-Year Report*, 5.

62. Oates, "Gaines S. Dobbins," in Dobbins, *Great Teachers*, 102. Dobbins, "An Historical Description," in Fuller et al., *A Tenth-Year Report*, 4.

Every minister would clearly profit from some training in this field. Through the years a certain amount of work has been offered as a feature of other courses. We recognize that such study can now well be expanded. To this end four courses are being added, by vote of the faculty, for students who want further specialization in this field. In addition, it now seems timely for some students, called of God to be ministers of the gospel, to fit themselves for specialized services in eleemosynary institutions, where they will have peculiar opportunities for the specialized ministry usually referred to as the chaplaincy. There is a growing demand for this type of ministry, and the need is felt for specialized clinical training of certain students who will be fully equipped to furnish leadership in this field."[63]

In Dobbins's mind "This sort of training is analogous to the externe [sic] and interne training of the doctor."[64] In the same way a doctor, lawyer, or psychiatrist needed professional training, so did the pastor.

The addition of Oates as a regular faculty member in 1947 allowed the school to begin the new Department of Psychology of Religion and Pastoral Care. Training for pastoral care and counseling was not directly associated with church authority or affiliation, but instead students became accountable to clinical facilities as accepted members of the "healing team."[65] The development of the program training was centered "within the hospital or social welfare institution."[66] The jurisdictional confusion was noticed after the program had been in operation for five years. The changes made to correct the problem of jurisdictional blending seemed only semantic and nuanced in order to appease the faculty and administration. Dobbins said, "the terms 'clinical training' and 'pastoral counseling' began to give way to 'pastoral care.'"[67] The term was used to promote a deeper affiliation with the church, but neither the training model nor psychological paradigm for pastoral preparation changed.

The popularity of the program grew on the Southern Seminary campus. The program was attractive to pastoral students who expressed discontent with the previous method of pastoral training in the modern context. Another reason was the growing popularity of the new pastoral theology that

63. Fuller and Oates, "An Official Statement of Policy," in Fuller et al., *A Tenth-Year Report*, 2.

64. Fuller and Oates, "An Official Statement of Policy," in Fuller et al., *A Tenth-Year Report*, 3.

65. Dobbins, "An Historical Description," in Fuller et al., *A Tenth-Year Report*, 5.

66. Dobbins, "An Historical Description," in Fuller et al., *A Tenth-Year Report*, 5.

67. Dobbins, "An Historical Description," in Fuller et al., *A Tenth-Year Report*, 5.

became mainstream through the work of Hiltner, Niebuhr, Williams, and the ecumenism of the Council for Clinical Training.[68] A decade after beginning, the program would extend to incorporate all interested students for clinical training, rather than only a select few.[69] Thornton testified that the professional model of education expanded beyond the seminary's campus in Louisville and into other theological schools, "Positive attitudes toward clinical pastoral education evidenced by The Southern Baptist Theological Seminary were duplicated by seminaries in every region of the country by the mid-fifties."[70]

Spread of Professional Pastoral Care

In the words of Duke McCall, "Gaines Dobbins really is 'Mr. Southern Baptist.'"[71] The impact Dobbins had upon pastoral training and pastoral counseling extended beyond Southern Seminary to a large portion of the churches within the convention. This was primarily accomplished by training leaders to take positions in theological institutions who taught the altered paradigm of pastoral care. While Oates was the primary beneficiary of Dobbins's pioneering spirit in professional pastoral training, many others were impacted: "[Dobbins] influenced other seminaries in that direction."[72] Oates explained the spread of this movement within the seminaries and attributed the organizational development to Dobbins.[73] He believed it was not enough to simply educate men in this paradigm, but that these educated men must become the educators. The following lengthy excerpt from Oates is meant to demonstrate the depth and breadth of Dobbins's impact in the area of pastoral training and pastoral care:

> The organizational development skills of Gaines Dobbins became an inheritance to us all. Richard Young went to North Carolina Baptist Hospitals in Winston-Salem, N.C. and spent his life organizing and developing an extensive school of pastoral

68. Thornton, *Professional Education for Ministry,*153–71. Thornton explained the "warming climate" of theological education to the clinical model of pastoral care. He also gave special attention to the merger of several institutions of pastoral care in favor of the ecumenical Council for Clinical Training.

69. Fuller and Oates, "An Official Statement of Policy," in Fuller et al., *A Tenth-Year Report*, 2.

70. Thornton, *Professional Education for Ministry*, 158.

71. McCall, "Editorial Introduction," 335.

72. Oates, "Organizational Development and Pastoral Care," 349.

73. Oates, "Organizational Development and Pastoral Care," 355.

care. Upon Young's disability retirement, Andrew Lester, a more recent graduate, took up the continuation of this program. Upon his returning to the Seminary as a professor, now Mahan Siler, another graduate, is continuing to develop that program. Similarly, Myron Madden has developed a program of great outreach and depth in Southern Baptist Hospital in New Orleans. E. Augustus Verdery has developed the program at the Georgia Baptist Hospital in Atlanta. These three programs are of long standing and have deep roots in their communities. They provide a continuing flow of pastors of churches an opportunity for clinical pastoral education in conjunction with their personal duties. It needs to be noted also that the Institute of Religion in Houston, Texas was initially developed and continued to be sustained by Samuel Southard, Joe Knowles, Kenneth Pepper, and Edward Thornton . . .

Another focus of placement of leaders has been in theological schools as faculty members. Many of these graduates went to schools where hitherto there had been no curriculum or program in pastoral care. They went through the very difficult process of building a program. They had to exercise skill and patience in organizational development. James Lyn Elder went to Golden Gate Theological Seminary and has created a curriculum and an array of clinical resources. Edward Thornton and Albert Meiburg developed the program at Crozer. They were vital persons in the merger of Crozer with Colgate Rochester and Bexley Hall. Liston Mills went as a professor at Vanderbilt Divinity School and has developed a plexus of clinical relationships to the medical and social service resources of the community. In addition to this he has been very active in the shaping of the whole curriculum at Vanderbilt. Richard Hester took a position at the Phillips University Graduate School of Theology. He pioneered a curriculum in that school before moving to Southeastern Baptist Theological Seminary at Wake Forest, N.C. Until his coming to the faculty there, Southeastern Seminary had depended upon part-time personnel, but has a full-time person in him. Roy Woodruff left his position as a faculty member at the Medical College of Virginia to become professor of pastoral care at Midwestern Baptist Theological Seminary in Kansas City, Missouri. William Van Arnold, a Presbyterian, has become a "second generation" faculty member alongside William Oglesby at the Union Theological Seminary in Richmond, Virginia. Grayson Tucker, another Presbyterian, is the dean at the Louisville Presbyterian Theological Seminary. In addition to the theological seminaries, doctoral graduates of pastoral care/

psychology of religion at the Southern Baptist Seminary have become professors in departments of religion in colleges and universities. Robert Crapps has been such a professor at Furman University for over twenty years. O. William Rhodenhiser has similarly served with distinction at the University of Richmond. Wallace Denton, who took his Master 's Degree in this program, is Professor in Family and Child Development at Purdue University after having received his doctorate at Columbia University Teachers' College. David Edens similarly took his Master's Degree at this school and his doctorate at Columbia University Teachers' College. He now teaches at Stephens College.[74]

Psychology of Religion for Pastoral Care

The psychology of religion had become the foundation for pastoral theology. The new discipline had flourished as the theoretical bedrock of clinical pastoral training at SBTS. Psychology of religion was considered as an empirically grounded view of the doctrine of man that proposed significant ontological implications.

Health defined physiologically and psychologically, according to pragmatic stimulation, became the base of anthropology in the psychotherapeutic model. Religion, or its experiences, was not criticized if it aided a person to the scientifically proposed definition of health. As Philip Reiff argued, "A man can be made healthier without being made better—rather, morally worse. Not the good life but better living is the therapeutic standard."[75] The psychoanalytic therapy that was learned from the philosophical standards of psychology of religion proposed remedies consistent with the therapeutic man, and religion became merely one of many stimulants to obtain a healthy personality. Theology was not the basis for understanding anthropology any longer. Thus, theology did not provide the methodological remedies pertinent to the health of the new man. "Psychological man is," Reiff said, "more native to American culture than the Puritan source of that culture would indicate."[76]

The moral demands placed upon a person from a puritanical system were said to be self-defeating and guilt-ridden. The therapeutic system sought to end the discouraging demands of moral behavior and the resulting guilt. The theological foundations of Protestants, Dobbins and Oates

74. Oates, "Organizational Development and Pastoral Care," 353–55.

75. Reiff, *The Triumph of the Therapeutic*, 48.

76. Reiff, *The Triumph of the Therapeutic*, 48.

included, were compromised and replaced with therapeutic aims. Religious consciousness and religious experiences became the means by which to achieve therapeutic health in the new theologically veiled pastoral care movement. The interpretation of man from the secular and therapeutic sources can lead the theologian to think in terms of non-Christian causality and cure of souls.[77]

The therapeutic focus in psychology of religion upon religious experiences and consciousness turned inward to a focus upon understanding the self as the highest form of health. Reiff recognized this shift in focus when he said, "In the age of psychologizing, clarity about oneself supersedes devotion to an ideal as the model of right conduct."[78] Oates attempted to theologize this concept with Martin Buber's "I-Thou" proposition.[79] Oates concluded, "Until man encounters God in Christ, his own efforts to understand himself and to define the nature of his own personality go unaided and fraught with ambiguities and contradictions."[80] Appealing to the theological mind, this statement is intriguing, but Oates had merely used the encounter with God to achieve personal understanding. Oates simply used the encounter with God as a means to satisfy the innate needs of man in order to gain self-satisfaction and self-discovery.[81] Oates affirmed "the religious life as a pilgrimage in which the merging dynamic self of an individual is called out of one stage of development into another by faith."[82]

The effects of the theories of psychology of religion had a profound impact upon the ministerial training at Southern Seminary. As the basis behind clinical pastoral training, the theory of psychology of religion began to redefine anthropology. As a result, salvation could now be obtained by self-realization, and God could be the stimulant to illicit such desired religious experiences.[83] In 1970, Thornton acknowledged the distortion in theology due to the influence of the therapeutic:

> Neo-orthodoxy had already buried the liberalism of the twenties. Neo-orthodox realism about sin proved to be a belated discovery for many theologians of the irrationality of unconscious

77. Oates, *The Religious Dimensions of Personality*, 48–49.

78. Reiff, *Triumph of the Therapeutic*, 46.

79. Oates, *The Religious Dimensions of Personality*, 50.

80. Oates, *The Religious Dimensions of Personality*, 50.

81. Oates, *The Religious Dimensions of Personality*, 85–136.

82. Oates, *The Religious Dimensions of Personality*, 152.

83. Holifield, *A History of Pastoral Care in America*. Holifield argued that traditional protestant redemptive salvation endured dramatic alteration in favor of a therapeutic form of self-realization for deliverance.

mental processes on which Freud had built his understanding of man. Existentialism was the new thing in postwar theology. The language of psychology became the language of theology, too. Even systematic theologians began to struggle with the correlations between sin and neurosis, temptation and anxiety, sanctification and maturation, vocation and individuation. The identity crisis of the times was matched by subjectivism in theology as well as in clinical pastoral education.[84]

Educational Departure

Psychology of religion and its practical counterpart, clinical training, adjusted the form of theological education. Dobbins's disinclinations with transmissive learning were satisfied by the practical, more professional approach to pastoral education. As with training religious educators, he also believed that training pastors in pastoral care should be different in the modern context. Dobbins said that "for most theological schools, the teaching and learning of pastoral care represents an educational departure."[85]

The educational departure could be described as both physical and philosophical. The clinical model was practiced on-site at various local medical facilities. Dobbins said, "The development for pastoral care called for moving out of the confines of the campus to arenas of human need."[86] The clinical training model relegated jurisdiction of pastoral work into the government and hospitals, outside of the realm of the local church. The seminary was training more than pastors for ministry. Southern Seminary was committed to training specialists in varied forms of psychoanalytic therapy.

Not only was this a movement away from the church in physical location, but also in philosophical underpinnings. The puritanical method of pastoral care was being replaced. Dobbins implemented the new paradigm of pastoral care by turning "to the writings of students of human nature in the fields of theology, sociology, psychology and medicine."[87] As a part of

84. Thornton, *Professional Education for Ministry*, 113.

85. Oates, "Organizational Development and Pastoral Care," 350.

86. Oates, "Organizational Development and Pastoral Care," 350.

87. Dobbins, *Gaines S. Dobbins*, 86. Dobbins's biographer included a sample list of the men and works which he synthesized in implementing the new pastoral care: John Dewey, George Albert Coe, Anton Boisen, Luther Weigle, Karl Menninger, Seward Hiltner, Carroll Wise, Carl Rogers, Gordon Allport, Karen Horney, Russell Dicks, and Richard Cabot.

the clinical training, "Social workers were enlisted as a part of the teaching team, along with psychologists, nurses, penologists, and institutional administrators. Data from their fields germane to problems presented to the theological student by patients, inmates, clients were made part of the student's search for understanding the whole person."[88] The authority of the pastoral counselor was mitigated further, defaulting to the scientifically informed fields of medicine, psychology, psychiatry and social work for directives in health and healing, in body and soul.

The drift in methodology from scriptural indicatives does not seem coincidental. The methodological deferral in pastoral care to social scientists had its effect upon a belief in the sufficiency of Scripture. As Thornton recognized, "Theological liberalism prepared the way for the initial acceptance of clinical pastoral education in seminaries."[89] Scripture became less relevant for the work of pastoral ministry, excused by the demands and complexity of modernity.[90]

Dobbins was not exempt from the tendency toward theological liberalism. When asked by Dillard regarding his views on William James's *Varieties of Religious Experience*, Dobbins expressed that James's masterpiece took the point of view that the "Bible is great literature. It has stood the test of time. It has grown in the estimation of unscholarly as well as scholarly people, and that is the test of a classic."[91] As Dobbins continued, he described the Scripture as a classic in the same manner as Shakespeare's work had also become a classic. Dobbins concluded this portion of the discussion by saying, "When I am asked, Do you believe in the inspiration of the Bible? Why sure I believe it. It inspires me. I never get tired of teaching it."[92] This

88. Oates, "Organizational Development and Pastoral Care," 350.

89. Thornton, *Professional Education for Ministry*, 27.

90. Oden, *Care of Souls in the Classic Tradition*, 40. Purves, *Pastoral Theology in the Classic Tradition*, 5. Oden claimed that modern pastoral care lost its biblical grounding. Purves claimed that modern pastoral care was more constrained by the psychological model than theology or doctrine.

91. Dobbins, "Oral History Interviews," 43.

92. Dobbins, "Oral History Interviews," 43. Dobbins, *The Improvement of Teaching in the Sunday School*, 37. Dobbins's stated belief regarding the inspiration of Scripture often sounded orthodox. He said, "The Bible is a divinely inspired record of truths and experiences, given for human guidance into all truth and experience." Dobbins believed God to be the divine author who wrote through men by the inspiration of the Holy Spirit, but his explanation was focused upon the experiences of men as the truth. Men's experiences confirmed the truth and, in this way, "the Bible becomes truly a living Book." Dobbins's practice did not always correspond to his stated belief as he often promoted and sought experience as a measure of truth that could be equivalent to the Scripture.

view of Scripture allowed him the freedom to be eclectic in choosing varied theories and methodologies.[93]

WAYNE OATES

Dobbins's influence within the discipline of pastoral care and counseling has been both magnified and overshadowed by the work of Oates. Dobbins appointed Oates as his primary disciple in pastoral care and believed that he could further the discipline in a worthy direction. Dobbins was a man of great vision, but could not carry out each specialized discipline to its idealized end. It was a common practice for Dobbins to choose able men to carry on the work he had begun in a particular specialized discipline. Allen Graves studied with Dobbins and was chosen to be the succeeding Dean of the School of Religious Education at Southern Seminary. He supplemented the work of Dobbins in the area of administration. Findley B. Edge studied with Dobbins and became his protégé in the area of Religious Education.[94]

In like manner, Wayne Oates was the individual chosen by Dobbins to fulfill the vision he cast for pastoral care and counseling.[95] Dobbins said, "Wayne Oates was the man I had been looking for to lead in [sic] Southern Seminary in a systematic program of clinical training."[96] The story culminates with Dobbins's selection of Oates to lead the program of Psychology of Religion and Pastoral Care. Oates became the face of pastoral care and counseling through his prolific writing, as well as his dedication to psychology of religion and the counseling task of the pastor. Dobbins continued to support Oates's work, long after he left SBTS. In a letter to Oates on October 18, 1962, Dobbins shared a portion of his affection and support. He wrote, "Wayne, we could not be prouder of you if you were our own son—as indeed we like to think you are!"[97]

The expansion of specialization in pastoral care and counseling flourished under Oates's leadership at Southern Seminary.[98] Thornton called

93. Dobbins, *Gaines S. Dobbins*, 62.

94. John Milburn Price Collection, Box 10, File 1454. "Naturally the work in religious education in general and counselling [sic] in particular is rooted in psychology just as is true in schools of education in universities. And, of course, the work works on out to its application in organizations, methods, and arts."

95. Dobbins, *Zest for Living*, 65–66. Dobbins, "An Historical Description," in Fuller et al., *A Tenth-Year Report*, 4–5.

96. Dobbins, "An Historical Description," in Fuller et al., *A Tenth-Year Report*, 4.

97. Dobbins Papers, Box 8, Folder 42.

98. Fuller et al., *A Tenth-Year Report*, 2, 5, 6.

Oates "the principal actor in the Louisville story."[99] Thornton confined Dobbins's contribution to pastoral care at Southern Seminary and consistently presented Oates as the one man responsible for clinical training at SBTS, even though Thornton clearly acknowledged that clinical training preceded Oates by several years at the seminary in Louisville.[100]

Thornton did, however, identify the trajectory of clinical pastoral training once Oates became its leader: "The openness of the Seminary to clinical pastoral education is as remarkable as the energy and ability of Oates and his colleagues. Both missionary motivation and commitment to the professional model for theological education were involved."[101] As far as Thornton was concerned, "[Oates] had succeeded in developing a clinical program that was seminary-controlled, academically respectable within the context of a graduate school of theology, and to a considerable degree integrated into the total curriculum of the Seminary."[102] Thornton had forgotten or overlooked Dobbins's struggles for over a decade to begin the program. The change finally came early in Ellis Fuller's presidency and the program was placed in Dobbins's care.

Another of Thornton's assertions was the degree to which the program had become academically respectable. The faculty seemed discontent with the program and demonstrated their caution in faculty meetings and in personal altercations with Dobbins and Oates. Dobbins said that the faculty wanted a "body of divinity" and that the School of Music and School of Religious Education did not belong in the curriculum. His recollection of the faculty discontent was captured in a 1978 interview:

> And particularly they objected to this idea for a school of religious education and a school of music. That's not in the body of divinity. And so they said to me, frankly, Get [sic] you a spot over here on the other side of the road, of Lexington Road. Get a lot, and build a house, and let that be the School for Lay Members of the Seminary, and that was said to me frankly. What you are doing is not in the body of divinity. It'll weaken us, water us down and we don't want that.[103]

Dobbins said he was "ousted" by their efforts that led, eventually, to his retirement and move to Golden Gate Baptist Theological Seminary in 1956.[104]

99. Thornton, *Professional Education for Ministry*, 155.

100. Thornton, *Professional Education for Ministry*, 153.

101. Thornton, *Professional Education for Ministry*, 155.

102. Thornton, *Professional Education for Ministry*, 155.

103. Dobbins, "Oral History Interviews," 64.

104. Gray, "Dobbinology," 2–3. See Dobbins, "Oral History Interviews," 62–67.

Oates continued to endure some of those same pressures after Dobbins left.[105] The two men kept in touch via correspondence and Oates expressed the ebb and flow of seminary tensions. Oates's withdrawal from the faculty can be attributed, in some degree, to consistent murmuring from other faculty about the clinical program. Dobbins was asked about Oates's decision to resign from the SBTS faculty:

> Yes, I was opposed to his withdrawal. I wrote Duke [McCall] about it. I wrote to Wayne. I said, I think you're making a mistake. What you are doing is needed here. Now somebody else may do it, but you have the training, you have the background, you have the conviction, you have the technique, you have the standing and I think right here is where you belong. And then he wrote that he felt unaccepted, and he'd had a run-in with one of the professors who said, What [sic] teaching doesn't belong to a theological school, and he said it made him so angry he caught the man by the shoulder and shook him.[106]

Oates left the work at Southern Seminary and began teaching at Louisville Medical School in 1974.

THE EFFICIENT CHRISTIAN PASTOR[107]

Oates's works were more confined to pastoral care and counseling than were Dobbins's. The latter added pastoral counseling as an addendum to the duty of the efficient pastor, progressively making it more prominent in his writings. As professional training became refined, the pastoral duty of soul care became narrower in function until its definition was altered. Pastoral care was the work of the pastor within the confines of the local church, but his work was constricted as professionalization increased. Pastoral counseling was a competitive psychoanalytic system in which religious language was

105. Dobbins, "Oral History Interviews," 67–72. Dobbins claimed that the discontent of the faculty did not subside and ha attributed a portion of the 1958 controversy of the seminary to their murmuring about the practical disciplines.

106. Dobbins, "Oral History Interviews," 71.

107. My intention is not to present an exhaustive study of Wayne Oates's work. The brief attention to his work is intended to place him within the new pastoral care movement introduced by Dobbins. The title of this section is a combination of Dobbins synthesis of the social sciences utilized to redefine pastoral duties and professionalize pastoral counseling training with Oates's systemic explanation of pastoral counseling. The combination of the efficient pastor from Dobbins and the professional pastoral counselor from Oates is suggested "The Efficient Christian Pastor" as a more appropriate title for his book entitled, *The Christian Pastor*.

borrowed to describe the therapeutic discoveries, "Wayne Oates, in his *Pastoral Counseling*, insists that *pastoral* need not limit counseling to ordained pastors but 'becomes *pastoral* when the counselee or the counselor focuses the relationship upon the relation of God to the process of their lives."[108] Dobbins correctly represented Oates, but failed to mention the reason pastoral counseling is not necessarily performed by ordained pastors. The counseling specialists were trained primarily in the therapeutic model and adopted the shepherding overtones to maintain religiosity. Pastoral counseling was viewed in the greater category of pastoral care, but it could be performed by more than just pastors.

It wasn't until Oates's revised version of *The Christian Pastor* in 1982 that there was further distinction in the meaning of pastoral counseling and pastoral care. The distinctions seemed to be ambiguous, but the source of training remained psychotherapy for all forms of pastoral care, pastoral counseling, or pastoral psychotherapy.[109] Pastoral care was the category reserved for less formal counseling and everyday pastoral work. But, Oates said, "Every pastor needs to know what to do when called upon for more complex and detailed pastoral counseling which might be characterized as one of the "nonmedical forms of psychotherapy.""[110] He continued the explanation by saying:

> Pastoral counseling, in this book, refers to the multiple-interview counseling done by a parish pastor, a teacher in a college or seminary, a service chaplain, etc., i.e. a *generalist*. Pastoral psychotherapy refers to specialized and controlled therapy done by the exception rather than the rule in the pastorate. Today this is a highly disciplined subspecialty of the ministry.[111]

Oates may have recognized the danger in the specialization of pastoral care. Rather than remove the professionalized model from the work of the pastorate altogether, he created what may be called varied levels of pastoral care. Each operated at varied levels of specialized training and need.

Based upon the theory and practice of Gaines Dobbins, Oates redefined the paradigm of pastoral care and counseling. In Oates's mind *The Christian Pastor* was intended to modernize the work of Washington Gladden. He said, "The warm rays of the influence of this great pastor have given light and inspiration to me. I am indebted to him for his title, but I have

108. Dobbins, *Zest for Living*, 61.

109. Each of these categories represented varying levels of specialization, but each category operated based upon a psychotherapeutic model of care.

110. Oates, *The Christian Pastor*, 191.

111. Oates, *The Christian Pastor*, 191.

sought to interpret the subject entirely afresh in the light of this generation's resources and needs."[112]

The synthesis of the social sciences for pastoral duties by Dobbins's coupled with Oates's work in clinical training has transformed the identity of pastoral care in the SBC. A more appropriate title for Oates's *The Christian Pastor* could be *The Efficient Christian Pastor*. This title better represents the demarcation of pastoral duties from the previous understanding of pastoral care found in Gladden and Baxter. The variations in resources between those two generations, comparatively, were the social sciences and questions of scriptural authority from theological liberalism.

Levels of Pastoral Care

Oates declared that the pastoral duty was to be engineered into separate levels of pastoral care.[113] The levels of pastoral care in *The Christian Pastor* most clearly and concisely portrayed the movement initiated by Dobbins toward specialized pastoral care.[114] These levels are designed by Oates to meet the parishioner at their level of Christian experience, "in terms of their movement toward spiritual maturity."[115] The levels were divided into five categories consisting of friendship, comfort, confession, teaching, and pastoral counseling.[116] According to Oates, these five levels of pastoral care were consistent with traditional roles of the pastor.

Oates added complexity to the roles of the pastor, persistent with the age of specialization. He predicted that "pastoral care in the future will continue to develop more specialization. The direction it will take is that of specializing in recurrent problem areas of peoples' lives."[117] Oates justified his *deeper levels* of pastoral care with his claim that "neotraditional expectations have been focused upon a pastor's responsibility to be more technically competent."[118] This is consistent with Dobbins's model demonstrating that complexity demands specialization. The first of the deeper levels of pastoral care was known as brief dialogue. Basic spiritual conversations are common

---

112. Oates, *The Christian Pastor*, 12.

113. Wayne E. Oates Papers, Box 1, Folder 40. Oates, *The Christian Pastor*, 194.

114. Oates, *The Christian Pastor*, 194.

115. Oates, *The Christian Pastor*, 194.

116. Oates, *The Christian Pastor*, 190–218.

117. Oates, "Organizational Development and Pastoral Care," 360.

118. Oates, *The Christian Pastor*, 219.

sense to the pastoral duty. Oates considered this stage preliminary to any long-term counseling performed by the pastor.[119]

Pastoral counseling and psychotherapy was another deeper level of pastoral care classified by Oates. He deduced that there were people suffering from "deep inner conflicts over which they have no control."[120] In those cases he said, "They stand in need of a minister who has psychological foundations and knowledge of psychotherapeutic skills as well as the healing power of God."[121] Even at this level of deeper pastoral care, the question was posed by Oates, "How far should a pastor go in 'deeper-level counseling'?" He responded by saying:

> You should go as far as your training has equipped you to accept responsibility for the outcome of your treatment. You should go as far as the uncontrolled environment in which you work will permit you to accept responsibility for the person's life. And, finally, you should go as far as the limitations of your time and social role will permit you to give yourself to the needs of the individual.[122]

The final level presented in Oates's system was called the ministry of referral. In the third edition of *The Christian Pastor*, he revised the phrase to the ministry of introduction.[123] At any of the preceding levels of pastoral care in which the pastor did not feel the relationship was beneficial or he believed himself limited, he was encouraged to refer to another counselor. Oates argued a similar pattern in *Religious Factors in Mental Illness*. Dobbins reviewed the book and said, "[Oates] shows how religion functions at the point of diagnosis, at the point of referral, and in the process of treatment of mental disturbances."[124]

Pastoral Bases of Authority in Counseling

As a result of the complex levels of pastoral care, pastoral authority comes into question. Traditionally, pastoral authority was based upon the biblically infallible explanation of his office as an undershepherd of Christ who

119. Oates, *The Christian Pastor*, 220.

120. Oates, *The Christian Pastor*, 223.

121. Oates, *The Christian Pastor*, 223.

122. Oates, *The Christian Pastor*, 228.

123. Oates, *The Christian Pastor*, 263.

124. Dobbins, *Religious Factors in Mental Illness*, 385. This is the same book that Dobbins said, "marks a milestone in the progress of pastoral care as an applied science." He identified pastoral care as an applied science, no longer an art or a ministry.

is the head of the church.[125] Oates argued, however, that "The meaning of authority is to be shaken loose from authoritarianism, the irrational and unjust use of power."[126] The bases of pastoral authority existed no longer as an ambassador of God or in his trustworthy revelation.

Oates said pastoral authority began with the credibility of the counselor as he pursued an exemplary spiritual life.[127] The second base of pastoral authority identified by Oates was, "the pastoral counselor's competent knowledge of his or her basic data of his or her discipline." The third base was in accumulated fidelity over the many crises of the counselee's life. Oates likened this to Erik Erikson's "epigenetic principle."[128] As the pastor gained experience through different developmental stages of the ministry, he would also add to his authority. The final base for pastoral authority in counseling "rests in the intuitive awareness that he or she has of the Presence of God."[129] These bases of authority are striking due to that which is lacking. The role of the pastor was not centered upon God or his word as the ultimate authority.

A LOST IDENTITY

Pastoral theology incurred dramatic revisions from Dobbins's synthesis of efficiency, educational psychology, and psychology of religion. The duty of pastoral care had been adjusted to fit the psychological model as ushered in by the psychology of the religious educators. At Southern Seminary, Dobbins was responsible for this crossover in disciplines that redefined and retooled pastoral care. The ideological influence of efficiency tended the pastoral duties toward specialization. Each duty eventually required professional training for competency. The pastor was still required to have

125. 1 Peter 5:1–4.

126. Wayne E. Oates Papers, "Pastoral Basis of Authority in Counseling," Box 2, Folders 8, 1.

127. Wayne E. Oates Papers, "Pastoral Basis of Authority in Counseling," Box 2, Folders 8, 1.

128. Wayne E. Oates Papers, Box 2, Folders 8, 3. Erikson, *Identity*, 92–93. Erikson asserted that we develop through an unfolding of our personality in predetermined stages. He said, ". . . the *epigenetic principle* which is derived from the growth of organisms *in utero*. Somewhat generalized, this principle states that anything that grows has a ground plan, and that out of this ground plan the parts arise, each part having its time of special ascendency, until all parts have arisen to form a functioning whole . . . Personality, therefore, can be said to develop according to steps predetermined in the human organism's readiness to be driven toward, to be aware of, and to interact with a widening radius of significant individuals and institutions."

129. Wayne E. Oates Papers, Box 2, Folder 8, 4.

compassion and calling for ministry, whereas, he would be equipped like professional psychologists for soul care, with the clinical training method.

For Southern Baptists, pastoral identity had been compromised due to new professionalized methodologies. Dobbins acknowledged that the new pastoral care he implemented grew more specialized under the leadership of Wayne Oates, "During the next five years of Dr. Oates's leadership the terms 'clinical training' and 'pastoral counseling' began to give way to 'pastoral care.'"[130] Oates began to extend the meaning of pastoral care and counseling as each required deeper levels of specialized training. The professionalization, then, continued until the work of pastoral care became less of a duty and more defined by pastoral identity.

Other have recognized the dramatic shift in pastoral theology and pastoral care during the first half of the twentieth century. Thomas Oden claimed, "[Pastoral counseling] cannot boast of its biblical grounding, historical awareness, or theological clarity."[131] Andrew Purves also recognized the modern distinction of pastoral theology from the classic tradition of pastoral care when he said, "Unlike most twentieth-century pastoral practice, dominated by psychological theory and oriented towards self-realization, classical pastoral care was much more obviously constrained by matters of theology—indeed, by matters of doctrine."[132] Oden identified what he believed to have occurred in the redefinition of pastoral theology that rearranged the parameters of pastoral care—inept theology "has offered pastoral counseling a fleshless Christ, a *logos asarkos*, coupled with a diluted ideology of general ministry that makes no distinction between the ordained ministry and the ministry of the laity, and therefore easily loses track of the specific scriptural entrustment to ordained ministry."[133] Oden's concluding point demonstrated the connectivity between the duty of the ordained minister as contrary to what was being promoted as pastoral theology, pastoral counseling, and pastoral care. The duties of the pastor were not built upon the Scripture, as before; instead, a Christianized image of the psychotherapeutic was practiced.

John Henry Edgar helped to capture the adjustments made to pastoral identity in his dissertation, "Pastoral Identity in the Thought of Wayne E. Oates."[134] He argued in the beginning of his work that the identity of the pastor had changed, "The increasing complexity of American society

130. Dobbins, "An Historical Description," in Fuller et al., *A Tenth-Year Report*, 5.

131. Oden, *Care of Souls in the Classic Tradition*, 40.

132. Purves, *Pastoral Theology in the Classic Tradition*, 5.

133. Oden, *Care of Souls in the Classic Tradition*, 42.

134. Edgar, "Pastoral Identity in the Thought of Wayne E. Oates."

within religious and cultural pluralism affected the status of the Protestant pastor."[135] He also identified the impetus to this change in pastoral theology and, subsequently, in pastoral identity:

> Increasing secular specialization has contributed to the emergence of specialized ministries. Institutional growth in America has led to various types of ministry within institutions such as chaplains in hospitals, prisons, military and industry. The development of modern psychology within the last century includes a psychology of religion and increased scientific concern for the whole person within the ministry of pastoral care and counseling.[136]

Edgar's summary truly captured the work of Dobbins as he introduced the ideas of psychology of religion, church as business institution, and scientific concerns to the theological education of the pastor. The demands of modernity became the stimulant for change in pastoral identity. Edgar said, "The choice of a pastoral identity is made in the context of the cultural environment."[137]

Modernity, in the time of Oates and Dobbins, demanded a specialist, "The generalist pastor who was all things to all people was being replaced or supplemented by the greater competence and professionalism of secular specialists."[138] Edgar's assertion was realized in Dobbins's work, but he also acknowledged this same specialization and professionalism in the thought of Oates. The result was that pastoral identity was no longer grounded in knowing God and his Word. Edgar identified that "A consistent pastoral identity theme of Oates was that pastors needed to understand and accept themselves."[139] Oates believed that as the pastor understood himself better, he would be better fit for the pastoral task. Oates explained this idea in *The Christian Pastor:*

> With clarity of identity and integrity of being, you as a Christian pastor do and do not do many things. *What* you do is not determined by the other-direction of the most recent demand laid upon you. Your functions are determined by your inner sense of identity and integrity or lack of it. The major thrust of your dialogue in prayer with God, in conversation with yourself and your family, and in interaction with your faith community of the

135. Edgar, "Pastoral Identity in the Thought of Wayne E. Oates," 3.
136. Edgar, "Pastoral Identity in the Thought of Wayne E. Oates," 4.
137. Edgar, "Pastoral Identity in the Thought of Wayne E. Oates," 268.
138. Edgar, "Pastoral Identity in the Thought of Wayne E. Oates," 6.
139. Edgar, "Pastoral Identity in the Thought of Wayne E. Oates," 229.

church is, then, the clarification of your identity and the focus
of the integrity of your "personhood" under God. From this you
draw your guidance as to the nature of your task.[140]

Pastoral identity was not grounded in the absolutes of Scripture and the calling by God to an office, but it was relative to the discovered personality of the individual. The reader can identify the ambiguity and relativity of pastoral identity in Edgar, as he explained, "Due to the personal factors of pastoral identity, each individual minister brought his or her distinct personal identity to the definition of pastoral identity."[141] Oden recognized the impact that modern psychology had upon pastoral identity and pastoral duty. He said, "So pastoral theology has become in many cases little more than a thoughtless mimic of the most current psychological trends."[142] He continued to express his concern for the transition of pastoral theology and pastoral care upon the tide of psychological philosophy. He concluded, "We can no longer afford ourselves the luxury of allowing contemporary psychotherapies to define for us what pastoral care is."[143] Oates was aware of Oden's critique and attempted a rebuttal.[144] Oates did not deny most of the charges of Oden. He simply attempted to clarify that he had not abandoned the classic tradition of pastoral care, but he was trying to incorporate the progressive understanding that psychology had provided.[145]

CONCLUSION

I attempted to convey several important factors in this chapter. First, clarity in scholarly research was needed to properly identify the father of pastoral care in the SBC. It is often assumed that Wayne Oates deserved that title for his abundant contributions to the discipline. Oates, however, declared Dobbins to be the father of pastoral care in the Southern Baptist Convention. Second, Dobbins's involvement in the development of the new Department

140. Oates, *The Christian Pastor*, 128–29.

141. Edgar, "Pastoral Identity in the Thought of Wayne E. Oates," 265–66.

142. Oden, *Care of Souls in the Classic Tradition*, 33.

143. Oden, *Care of Souls in the Classic Tradition*, 37.

144. Wayne E. Oates Papers, "A Response to Tom Oden's Article *Recovering Lost Identity*," Box 2, Folder 30.

145. Wayne E. Oates Papers, "A Response to Tom Oden's Article *Recovering Lost Identity*," Box 2, Folder 30, Oden responded to Oates's rebuttal and effectively answered Oates's concerns. Oden's point was simply a warning that the modern shift in pastoral theology and pastoral care had drifted from theology and the classic tradition of pastoral care that had been established prior to 1850.

of Psychology of Religion and Pastoral Care demonstrated his vision. The new clinical model of pastoral training began to spread in the Southern Baptist Convention through theological educators and practitioners who had studied under Dobbins at Southern Seminary.

Any discussion of pastoral care in the Southern Baptist denomination must include Wayne Oates. The purpose of this section is to also demonstrate the trajectory of professionalized pastoral care. Dobbins organized and developed the vision for the new pastoral theology and Oates became the individual he chose to carry it out. Therefore, Oates's work, *The Christian Pastor,* is examined to demonstrate further specialization in pastoral care and counseling. Oates desired to present a modification to Gladden's work called by the same title, but Oates's approach was clearly distinct based on his uses of modern psychological theory and technique. A new title is proposed for Oates's book that more properly associates his work with Dobbins and modern pastoral care, *The Efficient Christian Pastor.*

The final section of this chapter is intended to demonstrate the fruit of Dobbins's work as revealed in Oates as distinct from classical pastoral care. Pastoral identity shifted due to the redefining of pastoral theology. Using the work of Oden, questions are raised regarding the dependence of Oates upon modern psychology. The conclusion is that pastoral identity in Oates reflected the thrust toward professional and specialized pastoral care organized and synthesized in Dobbins. Oden is justified in his warning that modern pastoral care is more reflective of modern psychotherapies than orthodox theology.

Chapter 5

Conclusion

SUMMARY

Discussion surrounding the nature and practice of pastoral care remains relevant among twenty-first century Southern Baptists. The therapeutic culture offers an explanation for moral and psychological conditions and often the church responds with an uncritical acceptance. The SBC ratified a resolution in 2002 that called its churches to "reaffirm" the sufficiency of Scripture for soul care. Yet, the secular therapeutic explanation of mental health reverberates from the pulpits and throughout the pews of many Southern Baptist churches. There are divided responses to issues of soul care that create confusion and doubt concerning the authority and validity of Scripture as competent for such modern concerns.

The existence of such quandaries confirms that alternate systems and methods of soul care were once introduced into Baptist practice. As one studies modern soul care, it becomes evident that the roles of the church and pastor in soul care have diminished, or at least have drastically altered. Obviously, a shift in preparation and practice of pastoral care took place in the early decades of the twentieth century, and the chronological examination presented in this work revealed its impact upon Southern Baptists through Gaines Dobbins.

The Southern Baptist Theological Seminary began in 1859, but its growth was hampered by the start of the Civil War. The determined founders of the institution established a curriculum in which the chief objective was to prepare "its students for the most effective service as preachers of the gospel and pastors of the churches."[1] Boyce's theology was bent toward puritanism and the curriculum was reflective, in that every part of theology ought to be biblically oriented.[2] Since theology was viewed as the queen of the sciences it should inform practice as well as doctrine.[3]

The challenges of modern science prior to 1900 had a gradual effect upon the seminary's curriculum. The theory of evolution, historical criticism, and matters of Baptist origins created controversies at the young school, in which the inspiration and authority of the Scripture were questioned. E. Y. Mullins came to the presidency amid these controversies, but seemed to be a peaceful and stabilizing figure. Discontent with traditional teaching methods and a desire for more practicality prompted a shift in the curriculum.

Mullins employed pragmatism to satisfy the modern ambition for practicality. His pragmatism, informed mostly by William James, permitted his use of unorthodox epistemological sources. Religious experience came into vogue about this same time and it was believed that truth could be discovered from within. Truth known through religious experience began to compete with the Scripture as authoritative. If truth could be discovered from within, then it became imperative to understand the nature of humanity in order to stimulate religious experiences.

The social sciences gained recognition as a credible means to empirically comprehend the nature of man. Psychology and sociology became essential to understanding human nature. Gardner used psychology as a means of enhancing preaching that would stimulate the congregation. He also taught the first regular curriculum course in Christian Sociology at Southern Seminary. The social sciences were not simply a means of understanding human nature, but a foundation of the curriculum that informed practice. Dement relied heavily upon genetic psychology to structure Sunday School pedagogy according to stages of development.

Throughout Mullins's administration, the social sciences gained prominence in the curriculum at Southern Seminary. Ecclesiology, and its corollary pastoral theology, was not exempt from the influence of the new sciences of human nature. At the request of Mullins in 1920, Gaines Dobbins

1. Wills, *Southern Baptist Theological Seminary*, 27.
2. Mueller, *A History of Southern Baptist Theological Seminary*, 55 and 61.
3. Mueller, *A History of Southern Baptist Theological Seminary*, 53–54.

became the professor of Church Efficiency and Sunday School Pedagogy. Church Efficiency was a new paradigm of ecclesiology that amended the role and function of the church and its pastor. The new ecclesiology produced a pastoral theology contrary to a traditional explanation.

In his first year, Dobbins believed himself to be a dismal failure, but with Mullins's encouragement he continued. Mullins supplied him with a title for a new book, *The Efficient Church*, which would redefine ecclesiology in terms of business efficiency and scientific management. Inspired to persevere, Dobbins was directed to study with modern educationalists to enhance his teaching methods. Dobbins adopted more than simple teaching methods. The methods were based upon the new social sciences; however, these sciences were not philosophically indifferent but were built upon philosophies of Darwinian biology, pragmatism, or theological liberalism. Coe's philosophy was based upon psychology of religion and creative, person-centered, learning. Psychology of religion explained human nature from a psychological point of view that highlighted religious experiences as a means to self-discovery and self-actualization.

Dewey, desiring to rid education of sectarian religion, presented an educational theory that was pragmatic and dictated according to societal norms, rather than traditional ethics. The demands of sectarian religious ethics reliant upon Scripture were replaced with an experientially based discovery of truth. The tests and measurements of Thorndike were perceived as empirical insight into laws of human nature. It was thought that persons could be stimulated as mechanical or instinctive responders to stimuli in order to achieve desired experiences. Dobbins synthesized these social sciences and employed them as a means of growth and learning in a religious context. Dependence upon Coe's religious education, Dewey's progressive education, and Thorndike's educational psychology provided a framework for Dobbins to comprehend human nature.

The accumulation of business efficiency and the theories of the modern educationalists led to Dobbins's professional approach to ministry. Business efficiency created the paradigm necessary to professionalize the functions of the church and the pastoral duties. The complex demands of modern society required the laity to specialize in their fields of expertise. As the church grew in complexity, the organization and structure of specialized ministries were necessary. The duties of the pastor also became specialized, requiring more professional training. The minister of education became the first of the pastoral duties to be specialized by Dobbins, but others were soon to follow.

The modern educationalists provided the paradigm to understand human nature according to a secular psychological model. Dobbins and other religious educators were known as the psychologists of the seminaries. As the pastoral care function of the pastor became more specialized, clinical training was the preferred method of preparation. Clinical Pastoral Education, made possible by theological liberalism, was adopted into the seminary curriculum and held a firm place in theological education at Southern Seminary for more than sixty years.

Dobbins was the man responsible for the new structure of ecclesiology and the new expression of pastoral duties. He organized the Department of Psychology of Religion and Pastoral Care in 1947: a department that had unofficial beginnings by at least 1937. Dobbins specifically chose Wayne Oates to further specialize the "new" pastoral function of pastoral care. As Oates flourished under Dobbins's tutelage, pastoral care became more specialized, requiring pastoral counselors for *deeper levels* of care, and pastoral psychotherapists for even deeper levels. While Oates is known as the father of pastoral care in the SBC, he acknowledged that the work of Dobbins earned him the rightful title.

IMPLICATIONS

This study provides historical context for modern controversies. First, the adoption of the psychological model of soul care through clinical pastoral training served to change the Church's view of mental illness. The Church began to adopt the language and explanations of the psychological model regarding human nature and remedy for the subsequently defined human problems. However, the Church is neither obligated nor advised to use the language of the world to understand human nature. As the Church adopted the language of the psychological model for pastoral care and counseling, the language of remedy was not to be found in Scripture. The philosophical underpinnings of the varied psychological models of pastoral care and counseling provide completely divergent explanations of the world and the interpretations of ultimate reality. The explanation of human nature was altered from its scriptural basis and a conglomerate definition, filled with psychological jargon and alleged empirically devised propositions replaced biblical anthropology. This tends to bind the theological approach to the modern topic of mental illness, because the language and paradigm adopted then dictates any remedial theories—theological or otherwise.

Second, the authority of the Church has been compromised in its responsibility to provide soul care. The psychological model of pastoral care has disconnected the church's mission and ability to minister to those who are in emotional and psychological turmoil. The Reformation doctrine of jurisdiction or sphere sovereignty raises questions and provides parameters by which to study the biblical view of authority, responsibility, and role of the Church in pastoral care and counseling.[4] What authority, if any, should the government have in soul care? What responsibility does the Church have, according to Scripture, to care for souls?

The significance of this topic within the modern context is related to the submission of Christian Licensed Professional Counselors (LPC) to the government statutes. Some states, such as California and New Jersey, are limiting the moral parameters for the LPC. The issues regarding religious liberty in counseling—such as Conversion Therapy—will be informative and serve as a necessary warning to believers contemplating submission to the government's paradigm for the care of souls: knowing that their Christian faith will be forcibly compromised.

Third, the motivation to be missional in an approach to counseling was demonstrated to be a detriment to biblical fidelity. Dobbins was motivated by desire to be missional as he organized clinical training for pastors.[5] Similar arguments are made today, but the historical experiment of clinical training should serve as a warning.[6] First, the jurisdiction of counseling and soul care is transferred outside of the church and under the purview of the government. Second, the results of clinical training encouraged the professionalizing of pastoral duties. The pastor became subservient to psychologists, psychiatrists, and doctors in order to truly understand human nature and his practice of soul care. Third, as Allan Bloom said, "Modern psychology at its best has a questionable view of the soul."[7] Following the psychological model as a means for pastoral theology in general and pastoral care in particular provides an impoverished understanding of the soul: the goal of man, being powered from within, is to self-actualize in order to grow in personhood. Bloom argued that "Psychologists are the sworn enemies of guilt."[8] If the soul is understood in terms of the psychologists, then following the psychological model removes guilt and, therefore, the need of redemption in Christ. An approach built upon these premises, therefore, is not missiological in the biblical sense of the Great Commission.

4. Calvin, *Institutes of the Christian Religion*, 799–804.

5. Oates, "Organizational Development and Pastoral Care," 351.

6. Williams, "Counselors as Missionaries," 28.

7. Bloom, *The Closing of the American Mind*, 121.

8. Bloom, *The Closing of the American Mind*, 121.

RECOMMENDATIONS FOR FURTHER RESEARCH

There are several intriguing topics resulting from the present study. Many of the topics could not be covered exhaustively in this work because they were not essential to the thesis. As an interesting aspect of this study, my interest was piqued by the attention Soren Kierkegaard received in the literature of the progressive pastoral care movement. Seward Hiltner, Carl Rogers, Wayne Oates, and Paul Tillich are among the men who were indebted to the work of Kierkegaard. There seemed to be an abstraction in Kierkegaard that endeared him to a wide range of theological convictions—conservatives, liberals, and agnostics interact with his work and quote it positively. What aspects of Kierkegaard's work gained him favor with those who advanced the theory and methodology of Clinical Pastoral Education?

A second topic related to this body of research is the formation of Religious Education in the Southern Baptist Convention. John Milburn Price, of Southwestern Baptist Theological Seminary, is credited with beginning the first School of Religious Education in the Southern Baptist denomination. Similar to Dobbins, Price was dependent upon the social sciences to formulate his approach to religious education. Price and Dobbins were both students of B. H. Dement, who introduced them to the theory of genetic psychology in his course on Sunday School Pedagogy. A complete biography of Price is not necessary since Clyde Maguire has written one. Philip Briggs wrote a dissertation that evaluated Price's philosophy of religious education. The work of Briggs should be expanded to include an evaluation of Price's philosophy compared to Southern Baptist theological distinctives and doctrine. This recommended work may also raise the question: What is biblical education? The answer may then be contrasted with the identified philosophy of Price.

The perplexing state of pastoral care in the SBC demands further research in order to place it in proper historical context. Early on Southern Baptists held to a high view of Scripture as the source and rule for both faith and practice. However, the convention and its agencies—especially the seminaries—struggled during the middle of the twentieth century to maintain biblical fidelity. As biblical fidelity was lost, church practices became dependent upon other sources. Reliance upon alternative sources for methodology continued to erode the doctrine of the sufficiency of Scripture, placing those resources as more important or at best equal to the Scripture in authority. The Conservative Resurgence is evidence that fidelity to the Scripture had been compromised, due to the need for it to be reinstated as authoritative and inerrant within Southern Baptist doctrine. The question that remains is whether the Scriptures are sufficient for all matters of practice.

As a practice of the church, pastoral care must find its doctrine, philosophy, and method from the Scripture. However, the modern language of psychology has commandeered the theory and practice of soul care. Subsequently, as churches attempt to respond to issues of soul care, they do not associate the modern language, often adopted from the *Diagnostic and Statistical Manual of Mental Disorders*, as reflected in Scripture. The descriptive labels and the corresponding jargon often misguide the conclusion that the Scripture does not address the modern problems of soul care. The obligation of the church is to provide a biblical understanding of *soulish* anguish and offer not only a biblically informed, but a biblically dependent approach to the care of souls.

Therefore, future studies should include a biblical theology of personhood as rooted in Trinitarian theology. The biblical study of personhood and personality should be contrasted with the personality theory of Wayne Oates. Oates's understanding of personality was derived almost exclusively from the psychological model, simply adding religious dimensions. A modern study of theology may find profound significance in proposing a biblical theology of personhood as it relates to counseling and soul care.

Appendix

A Tenth Year Report: Curriculum Development, Department of Psychology of Religion and Pastoral Care[1]

_____

1. The document presented in the appendix has been used by special permission from the Special Collection & University Archives/Wake Forest University. The document is located in the Wayne E. Oates Papers, Box 9, Folder 37.

169

A TENTH-YEAR REPORT

C U R R I C U L U M   D E V E L O P M E N T

DEPARTMENT OF PSYCHOLOGY OF RELIGION AND
PASTORAL CARE

SOUTHERN BAPTIST THEOLOGICAL SEMINARY

Louisville, Kentucky

November 1953

I. AN OFFICIAL STATEMENT OF POLICY

Ellis A. Fuller and Wayne E. Oates (1946)

Dr. Ellis A. Fuller recently made a series of chapel talks on "The Issues of Preaching." He began these talks by deploring the fact that the average graduate of the Seminary is disillusioned to the point of despair by the things he confronts in his face-to-face ministry to people in his first pastorate. Then Dr. Fuller spent the rest of his four chapel talks in describing the testing situations of the practical pastoral ministry that the students are to face. In effect he said that the issues of preaching are the issues that a man faces in his pastoral ministry to human beings in acute personal need.

Not only did Dr. Fuller choose to warn his students of the process of disillusionment that faces the average Seminary graduate, but he and the faculty of the Seminary set forth a plan whereby the Seminary curriculum now includes courses and procedures that will help the student to get some first-hand, supervised, and controlled guidance in dealing with acutely needy people while the student is in his formative period. Dr. Fuller wrote the following statement of policy.

The need and value of clinical training for a limited number of students is impressed upon us in many ways. We are coming into an era in which people generally will seek hospitalization in sickness of all kinds. The denominations are building hospitals, communities are building hospitals, and the federal government is in the business of building hospitals. Plans for insurance for individuals and groups which will provide hospital care for great numbers make certain greatly increased admissions to hospitals. There is a widespread interest in better health for all people. The place of religion in the prevention and cure of sickness is being recognized widely by men of science as well as by Christian ministers.

Communities and churches are becoming more aware of the importance of institutions for the mentally ill, for delinquents and criminals, and for the promotion of social welfare through specialized agencies. Ministers and churches have a large part in the development of these means for the conservation of human life. Obviously the churches have a very great stake in this matter.

The Southern Baptist Theological Seminary is not even remotely interested in training workers for a ministry which ignores or makes incidental the Christian gospel. But we are convinced that ministers need the resources which come from a better understanding of human nature and conduct, from an acquaintance with the techniques which psychiatrists and psychologists have developed for dealing with human problems and needs in sickness and in health, and from familiarity with the workings of hospitals and other institutions in which they will have opportunities to minister to those who need their Christian message and service. For these reasons we feel that it is wise to pursue our venture in giving

- 2 -

to our student body such training in this area as may be possible under
our limitations.

Every minister would clearly profit from some training in this
field. Through the years a certain amount of work has been offered as
a feature of other courses. We recognize that such study can now well
be expanded. To this end four courses are being added, by vote of the
faculty, for students who want further specialization in this field.
In addition, it now seems timely for some students, called of God to be
ministers of the gospel, to fit themselves for specialized services in
eleemosynary institutions, where they will have peculiar opportunities
for the specialized ministry usually referred to as the chaplaincy.
There is a growing demand for this type of ministry, and the need is
felt for specialized clinical training of certain students who will be
fully equipped to furnish leadership in this field.

The aim of these courses and procedures is to systematize the experience of
seasoned pastors in such a way that the young minister may be more effective and
less subject to disillusionment in the beginning of his ministry. The aim of this
sort of training is to focus the theoretical pursuits of the students in such a way
that his "book learning" will come alive to him in the testing situations of a
face-to-face ministry to people under the guidance of a more skilled and seasoned
teacher.

This type of training is called "the clinical pastoral training of theological students." The training is based upon the conviction that the reason for pastoral
failure and disillusionment is that the student's theoretical learning overbalances
his emotional development and maturity which comes only from experience and the
acceptance of responsibility for the care of people. Furthermore, this sort of
training is based upon the conviction that the most reliable way of learning is
the study of "living human documents" of people who are in acute personal need of
the gospel of Christ. In this way the student's ideals are harmonized with reality,
and he more readily becomes a servant of Christ who can see the world as it is
without despair, and who can see the possibilities of his people in Christ without
too much optimism.

If the student is to confront people who are in crisis life-situations, he
must be led to places where most of such people are. Experience has shown that
hospitals and other humanitarian institutions are the most densely populated
places where people of every condition and creed are gathered. Therefore, the
cooperation of hospitals, doctors, nurses, psychiatrists, and social workers has
to be sought in the development of such a program. Clinical training is aimed to
equip the minister with such insights and skills that he may not be "ashamed of
the gospel" in the presence of the people of those other professions also dedicated
to the service of mankind. Positively it is aimed to help the minister in the
process of understanding, of cooperative inquiry into human problems, and of
combining of resources with sincere, devoted men and women of science.

The clinical training of students is in no wise an effort to take over the
function of other professional people. Rather it seeks to afford these men the

- 3 -

resources that a carefully trained minister of the gospel has to offer them and to relieve the doctor and the psychiatrist of the necessity of having to take over the functions of the minister. Any good doctor will appreciate the sense of well-being that comes from knowing that his patient has a minister who knows how to cooperate with a doctor in his ministry.

Finally, the central motive of this sort of training is to strengthen, enlarge, and make more effective the missionary interest and enthusiasm of the student. The untouchables of American society are the mentally ill. Authoritative sources tell us that at least seventy-five per cent of these people are suffering from the failure of their inner resources in the press of life in a real world. Until now the only answer to their needs has been curiosity, pity, and sixty cents a day from the taxpayers for their custodial care. A handful of overworked and underpaid psychiatrists have labored at their tangled emotions, twisted ideas, and shattered hopes. It is our conviction that this handful of men need the intelligent cooperation of Christian ministers. But more than that, it is our conviction that these people "who sit in regions of darkness" are people "for whom Christ died," and His redemptive grace can make them whole again.

In this ministry to people, both of prevention and of cure, we join hands with the men and women of science in order that all available resources may be brought to bear upon human need. This is essentially an educational task in which the "know how" of a practical ministry is the material for teaching. This sort of training is analogous to the externe and interne training of the doctor. Indeed, it is a "theological interneship." No person would want a surgeon dealing with him who had only read books on surgery! The surgeon so trained might faint at the sight of real blood! Even so, we feel that many ministers faint in their well doing when they see the wounds inflicted by grief, hate, fear, anxiety, sorrow, tribulation. Many are stricken mortally by the sight and never finish their ministry. The clinical training of students, therefore, aims to put on the feet of the young minister the shoes of "the equipment of the gospel of peace."

The Expectation of Students

Accepting a student for work in the general field of psychology does not in any way obligate the Department to use the student in clinical work. Clinical work involves the Seminary's relationship to the cooperating hospitals, and a student will be selected in cooperation with the chaplains of these hospitals with the view to his fitness for dealing with physically and mentally ill people. Experience has taught that many students seek work in courses in psychology and seminars in clinical training in order primarily to get theoretical teaching about emotional problems that they themselves are facing. Experience has likewise taught that these students become all the more unhappy in clinical work. Reading books and hearing lectures and attending seminars on psychology are not primarily aimed at the therapy of the student, but of the patient. Therefore, therapy of the student is secondary to service to the patient with whom he is working. Such emotional help comes, not as an objective but as a by-product, of the course. Therefore, the primary prerequisite for entrance into this sort of work is an emotionally mature, socially successful, and spiritually productive servant of Christ. The academic excellence required by the Seminary for entrance into the graduate school will be

- 4 -

augmented in this department by preference being given to men who have shown
qualities of leadership, social concern, spiritual originality, and capacity to
accept and discharge responsibility. All of the above prerequisites must be
augmented with a sense of mission that is clear-cut, and a singleness of mind that
is evident. A calm and intelligent compassion for people is of paramount importance.

II. AN HISTORICAL DESCRIPTION OF THE
DEVELOPING PROGRAM OF PASTORAL CARE

Gaines S. Dobbins

In my student days nearly half a century ago the course in Pastoral
Theology dealt helpfully with many practical matters which then confronted the
pastor. The text was Washington Gladden's _The Christian Pastor_, which was supplemented by lectures from a venerable and experienced pastor-teacher.

I went out into my first pastorate wholly ignorant of the psychological
approach to the work of the pastor, and had to stumble through to the solution of
problems which I had never dreamed I would face. Called soon thereafter to teach
in Southern Seminary, I determined to introduce students to the developing field
of psychology of religion. It was my early good fortune to have some courses with
John Dewey of Columbia and Harrison Sackett Elliot of Union. About this time I
came to know Anton Boisen, father of the movement for clinical training of
theological students, and Karl Stolz, who was attracting graduate students in
psychology of education in Hartford. Increasingly I became committed to this
experiential and person-centered philosophy of education and practice of pastoral
care.

When World War II broke upon us, I was teaching a well-attended course in
psychology of religion, with major emphasis on counseling. One day a call of distress
came from the superintendent of the Louisville General Hospital. He explained the
shortage of orderlies and attendants, due to war conditions, and asked if some
arrangement could be made to secure the services of theological students on a
part-time basis. A call for volunteers brought hearty response from the class. In
the group was a student of unusual maturity and discernment, with rare combination
of insight and practicality. He was assigned supervision of the work of fellow
students in the hospital. Apart from the valuable service rendered, two discoveries
were made: The study and viewpoint of the students involved were amazingly
vitalized; Wayne Oates was the man I had been looking for to lead in Southern
Seminary in a systematic program of clinical training.

During the first summer Mr. Oates studied with Ralph Bonacker, Chaplain at
Norton Memorial Infirmary. The next summer he went to Elgin, Illinois, where he
spent a summer under the direction of William Andrew and Anton Boisen. Returning,
he was appointed part-time chaplain in a near-by church-related hospital. Next
summer he continued his clinical training, taking with him a few selected fellow
students.

- 5 -

The Council for Clinical Training had rendered invaluable pioneering service. Yet their summer program, detached from the regular curriculum of the Seminary, had many disadvantages. Its appeal was necessarily limited to a few students; it was not related to "the body of divinity;" it was not under control and so could not command support of Seminary faculty and administration. To us there came the clear conviction that this discipline should become an integral part of the curriculum, open to all interested and qualified students as a regular part of their equipment for the pastoral office. By this time Dr. Oates had become a regular member of our faculty and the announcement of his clinical courses brought enthusiastic student response. Local clinical facilities became immediately available and soon students came to be recognized in near-by general and mental hospitals as acceptable members of the "healing team." To the program of study during the session was added the opportunity for a summer program under Dr. Oates' direction and in other approved clinical training centers.

For the first five years of this development, the training center was largely within the hospital or social welfare institution. The life and work of the typical minister, however, must gather about a church. Again, pressure of need brought us to a change of emphasis from the chaplaincy to the pastorate, from the hospital to the church. To our delight we found that everything we had sought to teach on an institutional level could be easily translated into pastoral care. The student pastorate became a source of infinitely varied clinical materials. "Case studies" could be made along the same lines and for the same purposes as in hospitals or other institutions. Supervised experiences in counseling could be made to enrich greatly the student's pastoral service, his theological and homiletical studies, and his own personal life.

During the next five years of Dr. Oates' leadership the terms "clinical training" and "pastoral counseling" began to give way to "pastoral care." Offered always as electives, these courses became almost embarrassingly popular. Students discovered that they were not only intensely practical, but were also intellectually demanding and personally enriching. Faculty and administration began to "point with pride" to the outcomes of this new department of theological study and life with its vitalizing consequences in all areas of Seminary practice and thought. Hardly less valuable than the courses themselves were the concomitant values as students came to better self-understanding and to the resolution of their own personality problems. Much time has been given by Dr. Oates and his associates to the practical counseling of students, as a result of which disasters have been averted and students saved to usefulness who otherwise might have cracked up.

Perhaps no better statement of viewpoint could be given than that furnished in a directive prepared by Dr. Oates for a group of students. In this statement it is pointed out that clinical pastoral training is an educational departure.

  (1) It is a departure in its concept of the materials of education as
       being participation in interpersonal relationships rather than merely
       a psychological or theological balcony view of life.

  (2) It is a departure in education in that it focuses attention upon
       the living teacher-student relationship rather than on knowledge as

- 6 -

a dead-level extraction.

(3) It is a departure in that it is a protest against mass education and emphasizes the values to be derived from a type of theological education in which one instructor focuses his full attention upon a group of selected students.

(4) Finally, it is a departure in that it embodies the features of a common life shared among students, persons, and instructors.

When the Seminary School of Religious Education was established in March, 1953, in line with the policy adopted the several courses in pastoral care and counseling were transferred to its curriculum. In the School of Education are enrolled students preparing for various phases of an educational ministry. These students are required to take about one-third of their courses in the School of Theology. In like manner, basic courses in religious education are required of the theological students. Thus there is vital cross-fertilization of curriculum and experiences, the idea being that the pastor and the educational worker will constitute a team, each contributing to the effectiveness of the other.

On the graduate level, students may pursue courses leading to degree of Master of Theology or Doctor of Theology. Dr. Oates thus describes opportunities for research in this field:

The Psychology of Religion focuses around the study of the religious consciousness. We study the literature on the origins of the religious consciousness, comparing the work of Tyler, Schmidt, Radin, and Müller with that of Freud, Jung, Rank, and Reik on their concepts of the origins of the religious sentiment. We study the literature on the development of the religious consciousness, comparing the works of Freud, Abrahams, Sullivan, and others with that of Kierkegaard, Sherril, and Kunkel on the growth of the religious personality. We study the works of Saul, English and Pearson, Preston, and others on the Mature Personality in relation to works by Buber, Otto, Oman, and others on religious experience at its best. Finally, we move into a study of the distortions of the religious consciousness, moving the base of our study from the literature to the sphere of the State Hospital. We spend two days a week in the hospital setting, concerning ourselves with our own and the patients' problems in establishing interpersonal relationships at the religious level of reality.

It will thus be seen that in the course of ten years the psychological approach to pastoral care, religious education, theological and Biblical interpretation, and religious experience has moved out into a secure place in the curriculum of Southern Baptist Theological Seminary. The way ahead challenges to new adventures and to creative thought and experience. Theological education can never be the same in the light of these progressive developments.

- 7 -

III. A DESCRIPTION OF THE PRESENT CURRICULUM

The curriculum constitutes three distinct but mutually interdependent emphases:

A. The Psychology of Religion, which provides theological and psychological foundations for the work in counseling and clinical pastoral training. The materials and principles for a psychology of Christian personality are explored, evaluated, and integrated. The relation between modern psychotherapy and a Christian view of man is studied through research in the primary sources in the psychology of personality and psychotherapy.

We offer three courses in this specific area.

P.R. 151 — An introductory course in the psychology of religion. It meets twice a week for one 15-week semester. The use of the psychological method in other fields than religion, the use of the psychological method in religion, the foundational principles of psychology of Christian personality, and the growth, maturity, and disintegration of personality are considered through lectures, group conferences, and class discussions. We have three sections of this course, with an average of about sixty students.

P.R. 154 — Christianity and Contemporary Psychology. Psychotherapy as it involves a Christian view of man is the heart of this course. The student is aided in the careful examination of the primary sources of psychologists on their conceptual models of personality and the teachings of theologians on their doctrine of man. Correlations and contradictions are explored. After a preliminary historical survey by the instructor, groups of students present their research on the contributions of various schools of psychotherapy and of various theologians. Presentations are under careful supervision and personal guidance. Usually about thirty-five students enroll for this course. P.R. 151 is prerequisite.

P.R. 651 — The Psychology of Religious Experience. A graduate seminar on research problems in the psychology of religious experience. The phenomenology of religion, the development of religious experience, the normative approach to religious experience, and the psychopathology of religious experience are the four focal points for research. The Th.M. student takes this as a means of correlating his findings into an adequate theological world-view, and of devising a Christian answer to psychological criticisms of Christian faith and practice. The Th.D. student tends to take this as one means of preparation for his preliminary examinations. One year we taught the first half of this course in the Seminary and the other half at Central State Hospital in actual clinical research on the psychopathology of religious experience.

B. Pastoral Work and Personal Counseling. This is designed to meet the needs of the average pastor and other religious workers for training to function within the context of the church itself. Field work techniques, "on-the-job" training techniques, case conferences on student pastoral problems, and

- 8 -

under-graduate introductions to types of clinical training on "one-day-in-the-institution" bases are used here. This work is predicated upon two objectives:

(1) To provide a larger number of students with an attitudinal orientation for counseling with their people and for doing an effective job of prevention of the need for counseling through sounder theological instruction, more wholesome evangelism, wiser church administration, and increased awareness of the importance of interpersonal relationships. Likewise, this part of the curriculum comes to grips with the facts: (a) that students in great numbers do not want clinical training of an intensive kind, (b) that students are not all temperamentally fitted to do intensive counseling with people, (c) that clinical training facilities are available only for a few selected and advanced students, and (d) that the intensive clinical training of students is best viewed as advanced, graduate research work, the results of which need to be passed on through experienced interpreters to larger numbers of people.

(2) To provide an introduction and to stimulate concern on the part of the student to go on further in the field. These courses, of an introductory nature, affect the attitudes--even though superficially--of all of the students on the campus. As a result, the student who does take intensive clinical training is more at home with his fellow students, seems less of an "unusual" person on the campus, has more acceptance after summer training, and is much less likely to form an "in-group" clique of the "initiated", who "glow" with their new found knowledge in clinical groups. Such an introduction provides the necessary intellectual and emotional preparation for intensive clinical work so that the majority of time in a summer or winter clinical program can be spent clinically rather than in lectures, discussions, and group and individual counseling with students. The procedure used in most clinical centers outside a seminary curriculum can in a large measure be done apart from a hospital or other type of institution. The only reason for having a program in an institution and not in a seminary classroom or a spiritual life retreat is that the student spends most of his time with patients and with other professional people. Introductory courses in the seminary can serve to intensify the distinctly clinical work of the student, and enable the instructional staff to determine which students are most fitted to take intensive clinical work.

We have three courses here, taught on a semester basis. Two of these are classified in the School of Religious Education because of (a) the intrinsic relation of their subject matter to the work of the pastor as an administrator of the church and its group organization and (b) because of a growing tendency within our faculty to interpret practical and implementation courses as "non-theological" subjects, unrelated to the "body of divinity." We do not agree with this latter opinion, but consented to this classification of these two courses because of our desire to keep counseling integrated with the administration of the church and its educational work. We felt that the functional realities are inseparable from theoretical discussions about those realities.

R.E. 435 -- The Theory and Practice of Counseling. This course attempts to do three things: (1) help the student to discover the strengths and weaknesses in his already learned methods of dealing with persons who present problems to him. (2) help the student to become thoroughly acquainted with the trends in contemporary counseling theory and practice. (3) help the student through field work placement

- 9 -

to practice the principle of informal, non-professional personal counseling, and to begin using community resources. His use of community agencies, other professional persons, and the lay leadership of the church develops what Maxwell Jones calls "the therapeutic community" in the church.

A layman in the city has donated a special gift to the Seminary whereby we have been able to place the ninety students in this course in fourteen different institutions. Their field work has four facets: (1) research as to the nature and function of the institution through conferences with administrators and staff members, (2) observation and analysis of the work of the Committee on Institutions of the Louisville Council of Churches, (3) at least two hours of visitation each week with the patients or inmates of the institution, (4) library research and reports of group activities. This work is supervised in complete detail by the professor, two half-time field work supervisors, and the fellow in the course.

The teaching in this course begins with the division of the class into groups of 3-10 according to the institutions in which students choose to work. These students take case materials, prepare reports on visitation, sit together during the class period and serve as "buzz-session" groups. They present materials on the special needs of persons such as the dependent child, the delinquent child, the aged, the mentally ill, the physically ill, etc. Students write up reports of pastoral problems when they need special attention given to their work as student pastors. These cases are discussed individually with the student when he feels sufficient pressure to ask for it. Likewise, statistical and interpretative analyses of these are presented to the whole class by the professor.

The spontaneous elements in the group formations are most interesting. For instance, students working on the same secular job often form discussion groups in their jobs. Some of the couples in the class formed a "breakfast club." Students who were confused about their vocational objectives found themselves meeting outside class to reflect upon their sense of mission in life and to help clarify each other's motives.

Lectures in this course are quite formal during the first two or three weeks. However, the professor soon begins to dramatize counseling experiences in which he has participated. He chooses one student after another as a "silent counselee" to whom he addresses the drama. Then students themselves are drawn into role playing with the professor, and then re-enact dramatic roles in counseling with each other. These dramatic techniques are followed by critical discussions. It is an easy shift from this to impromptu presentations of "live counseling" material which is current to the student. Some of them spontaneously bring in tape recordings. Others bring "thumb nail sketches" of "jams" they have encountered in actual work in their institutions and pastorates.

As the term moves toward the half-way mark, the groups begin class presentations. Resource persons -- psychiatrists, social workers, superintendents of institutions, probation officers, judges, as well as other professors on our own faculty -- are asked to participate in the class discussions.

P.R. 153 -- The Ministry to the Sick and the Bereaved. This course for B. D.

- 10 -

students is an introduction to pastoral training. Usually the problems of both the physically and mentally ill are dealt with synoptically. We think of this course as particularly valuable for men planning to be military chaplains. Various pastoral problems are discussed from case material supplied by class members and then pastors. The course includes medical and psychiatric information by which the pastor may detect early symptoms of illness and make quick referrals to medical, psychiatric, and social welfare persons. Three objectives of this course are important: (1) to teach the pastor his distinctive role as a man of God, one who skillfully uses the resources of theological, ethical, and Biblical insights to meet specific personal needs of patients as individuals; (2) to teach the pastor his limitations as a counselor by confronting him with the "jammed communications" of acutely sick people; (3) to teach him the ethical imperative and techniques involved in the development of adequate care for the sick and distressed people through his church fellowship community; (4) to train his ability to think "clinically" in terms of pastoral problems.

R. E. 437 -- Marriage and Family Counseling. This is an advanced course organized and operated on the same basis as R. E. 435, which is prerequisite to enrollment in this course. The specific data of the growing profession of marriage counseling are the core of research for this course. The field work students previously enrolled in P.R. 435 continue in a more intensive basis in their same institutions. The locus of concern in the field work, however, is shifted to the families of the inmates, the pre-institutionalization and the rehabilitation of the person after dismissed from the institution.

The class is considerably smaller than R. E. 435. About thirty students are in the course. Here, our supervision is more intense--two field-work supervisors and a fellow, all of whom are clinically trained. We can give close attention to the reports of students in their visitation in homes and in their formal counseling in their pastoral work. Also, we can afford some counseling opportunities as our "grape-vine" contacts with needy people in a city of 500,000 after ten years of contact with them.

C. Intensive Clinical Pastoral Education. These courses are taught at the graduate level for the Master's Degree in Theology. Students take these courses-- one in General Hospital and one in Mental Hospital work--on a master's level because the work requires more time than B. D. students can afford, and as necessary preparation for research in the graduate area of Psychology of Religion. It is not offered at the doctoral level for three reasons: (1) The field is too new to constitute and afford an already accrued body of research data with which inex- perienced students may work. (2) Professors in the field have not perfected research techniques that are reliable and accessible to theological students. (3) The development of such techniques and the growth of such a body of data require inter- disciplinary resources available only in a seminary which is directly related to a university and, therefore, would be more appropriately developed toward the Ph.D. rather than the Th.D. In our theological seminary, research on the psychology of religion is related to contemporary psychotherapy and the psychology of personality, the distinctly religious problems of people related to the counseling work of the pastor and to the ethical, historical, philosophical, and theological assumptions of modern psychologists. These are legitimate areas of doctoral research for the

- 11 -

candidate for the doctorate in Theology.

However, both the Master's Degree and the Doctor's Degree are degrees for more intense specialization. The pastor who takes these degrees should have exceptional interest in the field rather than the general interest expected of every pastor. Also, the person who purports to teach, even as a Chaplain-Supervisor of Clinical Training, should not do so without advanced and specialized degrees that involve clinical research.

The Th.M. courses are given in "Intensive Clinical Pastoral Education." These are: I.R. 653, Clinical Pastoral Training: Mental Hospital Training; and I.R. 654, Clinical Pastoral Training: General Hospital Training. These two courses are taught during the Spring and Fall semesters on a two-day a week basis. They are also offered during the summer on a five-day a week basis for six weeks. The student is taught by chaplains in local institutions. We have used two plans for employing these chaplains' services. First, we have charged fees to the student, and with those employed the chaplain on a "consultation staff" basis. For these courses we charge a fifty-dollar fee, require them for the Th.M. Degree, and look upon them as clinical ground work for the whole Th.M. curriculum. A student who majors in the field of Christian Ethics and writes his thesis in the psychology of religion is expected to have had these courses by the time he begins to write his thesis. Secondly, we have employed more experienced chaplains of the part-time instructors and dispensed with fees.

All of our clinical work is concentrated at the Th.M. level. We look upon this degree as a specialized degree to equip a man (1) as a beginning chaplain in a hospital (2) as a beginning military chaplain (3) as a pastor who wishes to put special emphasis upon pastoral care and counseling (4) as an associate pastor who plans to devote his whole work to a counseling pastoral ministry as a large church staff. The following discussion will outline some of the objectives which we seek to achieve through intensive clinical pastoral training for a Th.M.

IV. OBJECTIVES OF CLINICAL PASTORAL TRAINING

A. Selection of Students

Students should be selected on an academically sound basis, and a relatively even background in education and experience should be sought in that particular group of students. Graduate students should be taught together; B.D. students, pastors with seminary training and pastors without seminary training, persons with different vocational roles in life—all these groups should be taught in separate groups in so far as possible. In other words, homogeneous groups are to be preferred over extremely heterogeneous groups. The previous training of students in psychology courses and field work and orientation to clinical training courses should weigh heavily in the selection of students. One kind of heterogeneity needs to be sought by gathering persons from different denominations, different theological schools, and different races. However, their specific professional development should be relatively even.

At this point attention needs to be given by the Council for Clinical Training

- 12 -

and the Institute of Pastoral Care to the relation between their clinical work and the courses offered by the Seminaries.

B. Integration with Theological Discipline

Clinical training becomes superficial and shallow when it is taught apart from, and in isolation from, the rest of the theological curriculum. The hallmark of our approach to clinical training has always been that it is taught in context of the standard, responsible, and historically validated degrees of a seminary and under the academic administration of a total seminary faculty. The student who is trained in this way gets his ideas tested, his relationships challenged, and his methods tried to a more sufficient degree than by having only one supervisor in his training at a time. He either gets a "sticky" fixation or becomes compulsively hostile when he is "closed up" to one instructor. In our most recent summer training program, those students were assigned to each of two supervisors, and all six students had additional responsibilities to the director of the program. Thus students had the opportunity to relate to each of the three staff members and could observe the team approach of these three interdependent workers.

From the purely professional point of view, it always does a student a disservice to take a year of his life and resources in a type of education that does not afford him an academic degree that increases his acceptance in other institutions and his ability to earn money to support his family. The absence of these degrees makes it very difficult for him to advance in the teaching profession particularly. This is a definite handicap when a person so trained seeks to teach theological students later.

C. Cooperation with Other Agencies

Clinical training should be taught on a cooperative basis with everyone who is working productively in the field. There should be a mutual respect for groups who have differing philosophies and procedures in clinical pastoral education. A loose-knit fellowship such as the National Conference on Clinical Pastoral Education, composed of the Association of Professors in the Practical Field of the American Association of Theological Schools, The Institute for Pastoral Care, the Council for Clinical Training, and the Lutheran Advisory Council on Pastoral Care provides a ground of relationship on which we can all stand to learn from each other.

This cooperativeness most certainly is applicable to the relationship between the various seminaries of the Southern Baptist Convention. It does not behoove the personnel of anyone teaching in the field to seek to become a standard setting agency for the others, or to presume to be the sole repository of training for the others. To the contrary, each seminary should have the right and the encouragement from all the rest to develop its own leadership, its own training resources. This should be according to its own local limitations and institutional objectives and advantages. Whatever resources one faculty can afford another should be on the basis of the cooperative relationship of colleague to colleague and not in the "over-under" relationship of student and teacher.

Likewise, the interchange of students from one seminary clinical setting to

- 13 -

another should be according to the same standards of transfer of academic credit as
are applicable to other courses in the curriculum.

D. Qualifications of Teachers

The person who teaches clinical pastoral training should have pastoral
experience and should have met academic requirements for a teaching degree. He
should have at least a Master's Degree and preferably a Doctor's Degree. Irresponsi-
bility in keeping up with the study of theology, history, exegesis, and research
in his own field perpetuates the real danger of "half-bakedness" among students in
this field. The lack of such standards for instruction waters down the training
into superficiality on the part of persons who take it.

Men who teach in the field of clinical pastoral training should have demonstrated their ability in research in both their own particular speciality and in a
larger field of related theological subjects. These men should keep abreast with
the most recent findings at all times and keep in touch with the research of other
devout men who are giving their whole lives to these same studies. The ultimate
test of their maturity is their ability to learn from each other. Professional
competence is the shortest cut away from professional competition.

E. The Centrality of the Church

The needs of sick and abnormal people are the immediate concerns of those
working in clinical pastoral training. These are related to but not substitutes for
the ways of preventing illness and abnormality through more adequate spirituality
in individuals and a more adequate life of the church as the body of Christ. These
are the primary and enduring concern of the arts of the clinician. The training of
chaplains as a sub-group of the Christian ministry, is a secondary concern to that
of training pastors for local churches and to that of developing a more adequate
kind of teaching of the Christian religion in the context of the church. The local
pastor does his most effective work with sick people before and after their
hospitalization and the hospitalization—particularly in the medical and surgical
patient—is only one point in a long continium which gives the hospital experience
its context of meaning. Therefore, the problem of the ambulatory and convalescent
patient is the primary concern of the pastor. It is the patient whom the psychiatrist and surgeon have not yet seen or have already discharged to whom the pastor
can mean most in an enduring way. Clinical training should be aimed toward streng-
thening the pastor's adequacy at these points rather than pushing him into the role
of diagnostician and psychotherapist while leaving undone his distinctive task as
a minister of reconciliation in the enduring relationships of the individual pastor.

The task of a pastor and that of a chaplain is a multiple task of preaching,
worship, teaching, administration, public relations, pastoral care, and personal
counseling. To train him as if his only concern is psychosomatic medicine and formal
counseling is to train him for a task that is only one facet, however important, of
his total task. Therefore, the curriculum of most clinical pastoral training needs
radical re-thinking and revitalization. The training should be in terms of the
unique dynamics of a total Christian ministry. To develop a program which centers

- 14 -

purely in the counseling function of the student's ministry alone, is to lead to distortions equalled only by those types of theological educations that omit the pastor's work in interpersonal relations and healing entirely.

At the same time, our clinical supervision is centered in the students' relationships to patients. This speeds up the learning process by confronting students with present realities that will help him to think in terms of interpersonal relationships. A careful review of verbatim recordings of interviews demonstrates specific difficulties in personal relations. The supervisors also check student interviews to protect patients from hostility which may be transferred by the student from supervisor to patient. At the same time, the student receives emotional support through talking over his anxieties in the context of his professional relationship to patients. Finally, such supervision is designed to foster clinical thinking. That is, students discuss their work in terms of specific interviews rather than in terms of their generalized ideas of what "ought to be."

F. Clinical Training and Therapy for Students

A supervisor cannot ethically accept unlimited therapeutic responsibility for students. For him to define the goal of clinical training as being predominantly that of therapy for the student is to jeopardize the educational objectives of the courses. The relationship of the student to the patient as a professional worker is the relationship that needs the heaviest accent. Particularly is this evident and obvious if the supervisor or the professor later has responsibility for placing students and may be destined to become a colleague in a specific ministry with this person. The confidences revealed to him prejudice his later relationships to the student. We operate on the assumption that the production of specific results in pastoral work and research is the goal of the life of our group. Group discussions are carried out within the framework of our work as religious persons who will be related professionally as well as personally in years to come. Students are helped to discuss varying opinions as ministers, for in the future they will carry the weight of experienced convictions and administrative responsibility in such inter-professional meetings. We assume that love for the brethren is the basis of our relationships, but honest men may differ on the way in which love is to be translated into action. It is hardly necessary to mention that unrestrained "expressions of hostility," although they satisfy the passive-aggressive needs of some students and supervisors, distort group learning and create an unrealistic expectancy in students. Once out of such a "therapeutic group" hot-house, students cannot stand the heat of living in the realistic pressures of an uncontrolled community that is not as morally indifferent as a hospital.

In a Theological Curriculum, therapy should not be pre-planned, but for therapy when the need arises in any marked way three ways may be devised whereby students may learn--without academic credit--more about their own spiritual needs for maturity. (Actual healing of students' personal psychological problems may occur. Participation in these groups must be voluntary and on the basis of a previously understood agreement. Outside a theological curriculum, it must be pre-planned on a democratic basis.)

(1) In spiritual life retreats, where specifically religious resources of prayer, Biblical study, personal testimony as to need, and spiritual fellowship

- 15 -

between students and faculty as equals are used alongside specific insights from psychotherapy.

(2) In group dynamics workshops where the processes of group life are studied by introspective methods as the group studies its own activity as a group.

(3) In group therapy sessions, under the guidance of a qualified psychiatrist. Here the student recognizes his own need for therapy and voluntarily enters this group apart from his clinical training activity as such. The participation being understood beforehand. It is ethically reprehensible to organize a group on the basis of professional training promised and then expect the student to bare his soul in so-called "therapy sessions" of an unclarified group relationship.

The primary responsibility of the supervisor, therefore, does not lie in the area of group therapy; rather, he is called upon to present the accrued experience of his own study--and that of other research persons--as it relates to specific clinical problems facing individual students. He uses the student's present interest to point the way toward further developments of such problems in the active pastorate or counseling ministry. In this way, the supervisor serves as a prophet to guide students toward future responsibilities rather than as a "high priest" who seeks out and tries to bind up every pathological jot in the student's personality.

This recognition of the future responsibilities of students points toward another emphasis in clinical training. This is the recognition that the future pastor's or chaplain's function as a counselor is only one of many aspects of his profession. Students must be reminded that they will not be faced with the problem of "counseling," as such, but will be faced with such exigencies as: time for counseling, place of counseling in the church program, counseling with authority figures in the church, etc. Prospective chaplains need to be asked such questions as: "Now, if you were counseling with this person in a prison or hospital, how would you relate your own solution of the problem to the problems of the institution as a whole?" In this way we hope to prepare students for the actual situations that will make or break them professionally. The way they set up and administer their counseling program, pass on opinions to deacons or superintendents, and hold their pastoral position in time of interpersonal conflicts, will be more important in the early stages of their professional career than their supposed ability to recognize and resolve an "Oedipus complex" in an individual patient. Administrators will give their chaplains time to develop experience in more serious counseling, but the chaplain who gives some staff member a pontifical interpretation of his--the staff member's--psychological conflicts will have no second chance.

G.   Seminary Responsibility for Clinical Training

Because of the vital relationship of clinical work to the future of ministers, we feel that the Seminary should pay for the supervision of its students. Preferably the chaplains in local institutions who obtain our students should meet all of the standards of doctoral research required of any theological professor, as well as have thorough clinical training. Then, he should be an instructor on the Seminary staff.

- 16 -

Our own experience indicates the necessity of this arrangement:

(1) The Seminary sooner or later will lose control of its own teaching program if it does not finance the program.

(2) The Seminary should not reap advantages of prestige for such a program without accepting responsibility financially for its maintenance.

(3) The students do not feel as responsible to a supervisor who is not a member of the Seminary staff as they do to one who is. They are much more likely to be irresponsible in their criticism of each other, of him, and of the Seminary.

With such a close connection to the seminary, clinical training should be given in the same geographical area of the seminary. (a) Thus institutions and seminary staff can confer easily from person-to-person, ironing out difficulties as they arise. They are mutually obligated to each other in effective, natural ways. Communication is easier. (b) Students do not have to disrupt their economy and family life to get the training. (c) Academic disciplines, such as thesis preparations and library research can be carried on without interruption while clinical work is under way.

We feel that clinical training at its best is set within a graduate framework where objective research can be carried on simultaneously. This keeps the student from developing purely secular interests in psychology apart from his main theological task.

V. THE TH.D. PROGRAM

The general graduate school requirements for entrance to the Th.D. are: (1) an undergraduate average of 88.6, (2) the successful passing of a graduate record examination, (3) a reading knowledge of Greek, Hebrew, Latin, French or German, (4) election by the faculty.

It is assumed that the student who proposes to write his thesis in the psychology of religion already has both pastoral experience and a year of clinical training, or its equivalent, in the use of the empirical method of study in human relations.

The Psychology of Religion is one of the five subjects in the field of Christian Ethics. It is so classified because experience has taught us that the problems of ethics and the doctrine of man are the end results of any serious experience in counseling and psychotherapy. It is so classified because we do not believe that the student is ready to carry the highest degree we offer nor to accept the responsibilities that the degree thrusts upon him until he has integrated his experience in clinical training thoroughly with the historical, Biblical, philosophical, and socio-ethical in such a way as to produce perspective and depth for his total relationship to the persons with whom he is to work. This applies no less to his work as a teacher of students than to his work with counselees.

- 17 -

We feel that a theological supervisor of students in a hospital cannot maintain his students' respect by defending his illiteracy in Biblical, historical, theological, philosophical, and other areas of culture and learning. He will be tossed about by all the latest fads in therapy and have no enduring guideposts to lead him. He will make artificial distinctions between "clinical" and "academic," and he will tend to teach concepts which are themselves rash generalizations that have not been thought through.

The Field of Christian Ethics is composed of the following five subjects:

    (1) Biblical Ethics
    (2) Historical Ethics
    (3) Philosophical and Theological Ethics
    (4) Social Ethics
    (5) Psychology of Religion

A student may take a preliminary exam on each of these five subjects at the end of one year. He must take it at the end of three years on his Th.D. After he has passed these exams, he may choose a subject from the five in which to write his thesis. If he chooses Psychology of Religion, we advise him to write one that has a definite clinical base. One illustration of this is a thesis written on an interview-survey of seventy-five families concerning the relationship in pastoral care and counseling. At this time we are in process of designing a thesis on the psychological counseling of candidates for the parish ministry and mission field.

VI. AUXILIARY ACTIVITIES OF THE DEPARTMENT

1. We function as advisers to the State Department of Mental Health and to the Louisville Council of Churches Committee on Institution and the Kentucky Council of Churches on the maintenance of a Chaplaincy program in local and state institutions.

2. We function as a counseling agency for the Foreign Mission Board of the Southern Baptist Convention in the counseling of prospective missionary appointees. We are given a secretary in return for this service.

3. We function as counselors for the student body on specialized problems in their emotional health and marital and parental happiness. In this we have a psychiatrist as a member of our staff.

4. We led out in the development of a comprehensive child-care and nursery center on the campus. Now we serve as consultants and a referral agency for problem children and their parents.

5. We have completed the first stage of research on the problems of counseling with candidates for church vocations on their vocational difficulties.

6. We have developed a work project for student employment in jobs that are "educationally relevant" for students in this area. We serve as an employment

- 18 -

liaison for three psychiatric hospitals who need psychiatric aides. We also have
students working as part-time social workers, probation officers, orphanage
"house-parents," recreational workers, psychiatrists' receptionists, etc.

7. We participate as executive board members of The Department of Health,
Mental Hygiene Division; of the Health and Welfare Council; of the Children's
Agency; of the Family Relations Center; of the Medical Social Service, General
Hospital.

8. We have functioned in the following summer programs:

(a) We established the chaplaincy program at Kentucky State
Hospital and conducted a research-project on "The Role of
Religion in the Psychoses" in 1947.

(b) We supplied both the student personnel and the clinical
director whereby the program of clinical training at
North Carolina Baptist Hospital, Winston-Salem, N. D.,
was initially established.

(c) The major professor has served as a lecturer in counseling
at Union Theological Seminary in New York in 1951, 1952,
1953, and will do so again in 1954.

Bibliography

1958 Controversy Records, 1958–1961. Archives and Special Collections, James P. Boyce Centennial Library, The Southern Baptist Theological Seminary, Louisville, Kentucky.

Adams, James Luther and Seward Hiltner. *Pastoral Care in the Liberal Church.* Nashville: Abingdon-Cokesbury, 1958.

Adams, Jay. *Competent to Counsel: Introduction to Nouthetic Counseling.* Grand Rapids: Zondervan, 1970.

Aden, Leroy and J. Harold Ellens, eds. *Turning Points in Pastoral Care: The Legacy of Anton Boisen and Seward Hiltner.* Grand Rapids: Baker, 1990.

Allport, Gordon. *Becoming: Basic Considerations for a Psychology of Personality.* New Haven: Yale University Press, 1955.

————. *The Individual and His Religion.* New York: Macmillan, 1950.

Almy, Gary. *How Christian is Christian Counseling: The Dangerous Secular Influences that Kept Us from Caring for Souls.* Wheaton: Crossway, 2000.

Anderson, Herbert. *The Family and Pastoral Care.* Eugene: Wipf & Stock, 1984.

Anthony, Michael J. and Warren S. Benson. *Exploring the History and Philosophy of Christian Education: Principles for the 21st Century.* Grand Rapids: Kregel, 2003.

Athearn, Walter S. *The Minister and the Teacher: An Interpretation of Current Trends in Christian Education.* New York: The Century Company, 1932.

Babler, John, et al. *Counseling By the Book.* Maitland: Xulon, 2007.

Baker, Robert. *Tell the Generations Following: A History of Southwestern Baptist Theological Seminary 1908–1983.* Nashville: Broadman, 1983.

Barnes, William Wright. *The Southern Baptist Convention 1845–1953.* Nashville: Broadman, 1954.

Baxter, Richard. *The Reformed Pastor.* Carlisle, PA: The Banner of Truth Trust, 1999.

Beeke, Joel R. and Randall J. Pederson. *Meet the Puritans: With a Modern Guide to Reprints.* Grand Rapids: Reformation Heritage, 2006.

Bloom, Allan. *The Closing of the American Mind: How Higher Education Has Failed Democracy and Impoverished the Souls of Today's Students.* New York: Simon & Schuster, 1987.

Bloom, Harold. *The American Religion: The Emergence of the Post-Christian Nation.* New York: Simon & Schuster, 1992.

Boa, Kenneth. *From Augustine to Freud: What Theologians and Psychologists Tell Us About Human Nature and Why it Matters.* Nashville: Broadman & Holman, 2004.

Boisen, Anton. *The Exploration of the Inner World.* New York: Harper and Brothers, 1936.

———. *Religion in Crisis and Custom.* New York: Harper and Brothers, 1955.

Boyce, James P. *Abstract of Systematic Theology.* Hanford: Den Dulk Christian Foundation, 1887.

Briggs, Philip H. "The Religious Education Philosophy of J. M. Price." PhD diss., Southwestern Baptist Theological Seminary, 1964.

Brown, Arlo Ayres. *A History of Religious Education in Recent Times.* New York: Abingdon, 1923.

Cabot, Richard. *Social Service and the Art of Healing.* New York: Moffat, Yard, and Company, 1915.

Cabot, Richard and Russell Dicks. *The Art of Ministering to the Sick.* New York: Macmillan, 1952.

Callahan, Raymond E. *Education and the Cult of Efficiency: A Study of the Social Forces that have Shaped the Administration of the Public Schools.* Chicago: The University of Chicago Press, 1962.

Calvin, John. *Institutes of the Christian Religion.* Translated by Henry Beveridge. Peabody: Hendrickson, 2008.

Capps, Donald. *Life Cycle Theory and Pastoral Care.* Eugene: Wipf & Stock, 1983.

Carver, W. O. "Life Factors and Tendencies." *Review and Expositor* 30 (1933) 309–13.

Chapman, Thomas W., ed. *A Practical for Ministry: From the Writings of Wayne E. Oates.* Louisville: Knox, 1992.

Clebsh, William A. and Charles R. Jaekle. *Pastoral Care in Historical Perspective.* Northvale, NJ: Aronson, Inc., 1994.

Clinebell, Howard J. *Basic Types of Pastoral Care & Counseling: Resources for the Ministry of Healing & Growth.* Nashville: Abingdon, 1984.

Clinton, Tim and Jim Ohlschlager, eds. *Competent Christian Counseling, Volume One: Foundations and Practices of Compassionate Soul Care.* Colorado Springs: Water Brook, 2002.

Coe, George Albert. "Contributions of Modern Education to Religion." *Proceedings of the National Education Association* (1903) 341–45.

———. *The Core of Good Teaching: A Sunday School Curriculum.* New York: Scribner's Sons, 1912.

———. *Education in Religion and Morals.* Chicago: Revell, 1904.

———. *Motives of Men.* New York: Scribner's Sons, 1928.

———. "The Outlook for Personal Religion." *Congregationalist* (1904) 641–42.

———. "The Philosophy of the Movement for Religious Education." *The American Journal of Theology* 8 (1904) 225–39.

———. "Present Emergency in Religious Education." *Zions Herald* (January 1904).

———. "Psychological Aspects of Religious Education." *Psychological Bulletin* (June 1909) 15–97.

———. *The Psychology of Religion.* Chicago: The University of Chicago Press, 1916.

———. "Religion and the Subconscious." *American Journal of Theology* (July 1909) 337–49.

———. "Religion as a Factor in Individual and Social Development." *Biblical World* (January 1904) 37–47.

———. *The Religion of a Mature Mind.* Chicago: Revell, 1902.

———. *A Social Theory of Religious Education.* New York: Scribner's Sons, 1917.

————. *The Spiritual Life: Studies in the Science of Religion.* New York: Eaton and Mains, 1900.

————. *What Ails Our Youth?* New York: Scribner's Sons, 1924.

————. *What is Christian Education?* New York: Scribner's Sons, 1929.

————. *What is Religion Doing to our Consciences?* New York: Scribner's Sons, 1943.

Collection of Southern Seminary Examinations, Course Descriptions, and other Material, 1884–1920. James P. Boyce Centennial Library, Southern Baptist Theological Seminary, Louisville, Kentucky.

Collins, Gary. *Can You Trust Psychology?* Downers Grove: InterVarsity, 1988.

————. *Christian Counseling: A Comprehensive Guide, Revised Edition.* Nashville: Nelson, 1988.

————. *Psychology & Theology.* Nashville: Abingdon, 1981.

————. *The Rebuilding of Psychology: An Integration of Psychology and Christianity.* Wheaton: Tyndale, 1985.

Combs, Stephen K. "The Course of Religious Education at the Southern Baptist Theological Seminary 1902–1953: A Historical Study." DEd thesis., The Southern Baptist Theological Seminary.

Conner, W. T. *Revelation in God: An Introduction to Christian Doctrine.* Nashville: Broadman, 1936.

Cox, Norman Wade and Judson Boyce Allen, eds. *The Encyclopedia of Southern Baptists, Vol. II.* Nashville: Broadman, 1958.

Crapps, Robert. *An Introduction to Psychology of Religion.* Macon: Mercer University Press, 1986.

Curti, Merle. *The Social Ideas of American Educators: With New Chapter on the Last Twenty-Five Years.* Patterson, NJ: Pageant, 1959.

Dagg, J. L. *Manual of Theology: A Treatise on Church Order.* Harrisonburg: Gano, 1858.

Dargan, Edwin C. *Ecclesiology: A Study of the Churches.* Louisville: Dearing, 1897.

Deckard, Mark. *Helpful Truths in Past Places: The Puritan Practice of Biblical Counseling.* Scotland: Christian Focus, 2009.

Dewey, John. *A Common Faith.* New Haven: Yale University Press, 1934.

————. *Democracy and Education: An Introduction to the Philosophy of Education.* New York: Macmillan, 1916.

————. *Experience and Nature.* Chicago: Open Court, 1925.

————. *Human Nature and Conduct: An Introduction to Social Psychology.* New York: Holt, 1922.

————. *The Public and Its Problems.* New York: Holt, 1927.

————. "Reflex Arc Concept in Psychology." *Psychological Review* (1978) 337–47.

————. *The School and Society.* Chicago: The University of Chicago Press, 1915.

Dewey, John and Evelyn Dewey. *Schools of Tomorrow.* New York: Dutton & Company, 1915.

Dineen, Tina. *Manufacturing Victims: What the Psychology Industry is Doing to People.* 3rd ed. New York: Davies, 1996.

Dobbins, Austin. "Gaines S. Dobbins: Journalist, Teacher, Administrator. . .Evangelist." *The Review and Expositor* 75 (1978) 337–47.

————. *Gaines S. Dobbins: Pioneer in Religious Education.* Nashville: Broadman, 1981.

Dobbins, Gaines S. *Baptist Churches in Action.* Nashville: Baptist Sunday School Board of the Southern Baptist Convention, 1929.

———. *Building a Better Sunday School: Through the Weekly Officers and Teachers' Meeting.* Nashville: Convention, 1957.

———. *Building Better Churches: A Guide to the Pastoral Ministry.* Nashville: Broadman, 1947.

———. *Can a Religious Democracy Survive?* New York: Revell, 1941.

———. *The ChurchBook: A Treasury of Materials and Methods.* Nashville: Broadman, 1951.

———. "The Contribution of The Southern Baptist Theological Seminary to Religious Education," *Review and Expositor* 53 (1956) 174–86.

———. *Deepening the Spiritual Life.* Nashville: The Sunday School Board of the Southern Baptist Convention, 1937.

———. *The Efficient Church: A Study of Polity and Methods in the Light of New Testament Principles and Modern Conditions and Needs.* Nashville: Sunday School Board of the Southern Baptist Convention, 1923.

———. "An Efficient Church in a Modern World." *Review and Expositor* 17 (1920) 375–88.

———. *Evangelism According to Christ.* Nashville: Broadman, 1949.

———. "Facing Pastoral Problems: Capturing Psychology for Christ." *Review and Expositor* 33 (1936) 427–36.

———. "Facing Pastoral Problems: Case Studies in Solution of Pastoral Problems." *Review and Expositor* 30 (1933) 434–43.

———. "Facing Pastoral Problems: The Method and Value of the Case-Study." *Review and Expositor* 31 (1934) 98–105.

———. "Facing Pastoral Problems: The Minister Learning from the Psychiatrist." *Review and Expositor* 34 (1937) 60–71.

———. "Facing Pastoral Problems: The Pastor Studying His Church Membership." *Review and Expositor* 31 (1934) 216–22.

———. "Facing Pastoral Problems: Planning the Church Program." *Review and Expositor* 38 (1941) 286–96.

———. "Facing Pastoral Problems: The Problem of Pastoral Visiting." *Review and Expositor* 34 (1937) 218–25.

———. "Facing Pastoral Problems: The Psychological Approach to Religion." *Review and Expositor* 32 (1935) 442–51.

———. "Facing Pastoral Problems: Some Studies in Pastoral Diplomacy." *Review and Expositor* 30 (1933) 296–308.

———. "Facing Pastoral Problems: A Suggested Course of Reading for the Person-Minded Minister." *Review and Expositor* 37 (1940) 408–15.

———. "Facing Pastoral Problems: Theological Education in a Changing Social Order." *Review and Expositor* 32 (1935) 181–96.

———. "Facing Pastoral Problems: Wanted–An Adequate Philosophy of Religious Education." *Review and Expositor* 33 (1936) 53–61.

———. "Facing Pastoral Problems: What Shall We Do about the New Teaching Methods?" *Review and Expositor* 33 (1936) 188–95.

———. *Good News to Change Lives: Evangelism for an Age of Uncertainty.* Nashville: Broadman, 1976.

———. *Great Teachers Make a Difference.* Nashville: Broadman, 1965.

———. *Guiding Adults in Bible Study.* Nashville: Convention, 1960.

————. *The Improvement of Teaching in the Sunday School.* Nashville: Convention, 1973.

————. *Learning to Lead.* Nashville: Broadman, 1968.

————. *A Ministering Church.* Nashville: Broadman, 1960.

————. "My Sixty Years of Involvement in the Convention." *Baptist History and Heritage* 5 (1970) 135–43, 169.

————. "The Pastor and His Post-War Ministries." *Review and Expositor* 43 (1946) 50–59.

————. "Pastor as Counselor." *Review and Expositor* 50 (1953) 421–29.

————. "Religious Factors in Mental Illness." *Review and Expositor* 52 (1955) 384–85.

————. *Teaching Adults in the Sunday School.* Nashville: Broadman, 1936.

————. *Vitalizing the Church Program.* Nashville: Broadman, 1933.

————. *Winning the Children.* Nashville: Broadman, 1953.

————. *A Winning Witness.* Nashville: Sunday School Board of the Southern Baptist Convention, 1938.

————. *Working Together in a Spiritual Democracy.* Nashville: The Sunday School Board of the Southern Baptist Convention, 1935.

————. *The Years Ahead.* Nashville: Convention, 1959.

————. *Zest for Living.* Waco: Word, 1977.

Drakeford, John W. *Psychology in Search of a Soul.* Nashville: Broadman, 1964.

Eavey, C. B. *History of Christian Education.* Chicago: Moody, 1964.

Edgar Young Mullins Papers. James P. Boyce Centennial Library, The Southern Baptist Theological Seminary, Louisville, Kentucky.

Edgar, John Henry. "Pastoral Identity in the Thought of Wayne Oates (Ministry, Care, Counseling)." PhD diss., The Southern Baptist Theological Seminary, 1985.

Edge, Findley B. "Gaines S. Dobbins–The Teacher." *Review and Expositor* 75 (1978) 371–82.

————. *The Greening of the Church.* Waco: Word, 1971.

————. *A Quest for Vitality in Religion: A Theological Approach to Religious Education.* Nashville: Broadman, 1963.

————. *Teaching for Results.* Nashville: Broadman, 1956.

Edwin Charles Dargan Papers. Southern Baptist Historical Library and Archives, Nashville, Tennessee.

Ellis, William E. *A Man of Books and a Man of the People: E. Y. Mullins and the Crisis of Moderate Southern Baptist Leadership.* Macon, GA: Mercer University Press, 1985.

Emerson, Harrington. *The Twelve Principles of Efficiency,* 5th ed. Industrial Management Library. New York: Engineering Magazine Company, 1919.

Erickson, M. J. *Christian Theology,* 2nd ed. Grand Rapids: Baker, 1998.

Erikson, Erik. *Identity: Youth and Crisis.* New York: Norton & Company, Inc., 1968.

Findley B. Edge Papers, Archives and Special Collections, 1948–1990. James P. Boyce Centennial Library, The Southern Baptist Theological Seminary, Louisville, Kentucky.

Flake, Arthur. *Building a Standard Sunday School.* Nashville: Sunday School Board of the Southern Baptist Convention, 1919.

Foote, Henry Wilder. "Psychology and Preaching." Book review in *Harvard Theological Review* 13 (1920) 202–4.

Francisco Clyde T. "John R. Sampey: *Samuel Redivivus.*" *Review and Expositor* 63 (1966) 459–68.

Freeman, Curtis W., et al. *Baptist Roots: A Reader in the Theology of a Christian People*. Valley Forge, PA: Judson, 1999.

Fuller, Ellis, Wayne Oates, and Gaines S. Dobbins. *A Tenth-Year Report: Curriculum Development, Department of Psychology of Religion and Pastoral Care*. Southern Baptist Theological Seminary, Louisville, Kentucky, November 1953.

Gaines Stanley Dobbins Papers. Southern Baptist Historical Library and Archives, Nashville, Tennessee.

Gaines Stanley Dobbins: Oral History Interviews, Badgett Dillard, Interviewer, August 7, 8, and 9, 1978. Archives and Special Collections, James P. Boyce Centennial Library, The Southern Baptist Theological Seminary, Louisville, Kentucky.

Gangel, Kenneth O. and Warren S. Benson. *Christian Education: Its History and Philosophy*. Chicago: Moody, 1983.

Gardner, Charles Spurgeon. *Psychology and Preaching*. New York: Macmillan, 1918.

———. "Syllabus of Lecture on Homiletics: Third Quarter." Louisville: Baptist World, 1912.

Geisler, Norman L. *Christian Apologetics*. Grand Rapids: Baker, 1976.

———. *Systematic Theology: In One Volume*. Minneapolis: Bethany, 2011.

George, Timothy and David S. Dockery, eds. *Baptist Theologians*. Nashville: Broadman, 1990.

———. *Theologians of the Baptist Tradition, Revised Edition*. Nashville: Broadman & Holman, 2001.

Gibbs, Eugene S., ed. *A Reader in Christian Education: Foundations and Basic Principles*. Grand Rapids: Baker, 1992.

Gladden, Washington. *The Christian Pastor*. New York: Scribner's Sons, 1902.

Gould, Stephen Jay. *Ontogeny and Phylogeny*. Cambridge: Belknap, 1977.

Graves, Allen W. "Gaines S. Dobbins–Mr. Church Administrator." *Review and Expositor* 75 (1978) 383–95.

Gregory A. Wills Collection, History of The Southern Baptist Theological Seminary, 1859–2009. Archives and Special Collections, James P. Boyce Centennial Library, The Southern Baptist Theological Seminary, Louisville, Kentucky.

Grinder, Robert, ed. *A History of Genetic Psychology: The First Science of Human Development*. New York: Wiley and Sons, 1971.

Grudem, Wayne. *Systematic Theology: An Introduction to Biblical Doctrine*. Grand Rapids: Zondervan, 1994.

Gutek, Gerald L. *Historical and Philosophical Foundations of Education: A Biographical Introduction*. 4th ed. Upper Saddle River, NJ: Pearson Prentice, 2005.

Hacker, William Joe. "A Study of the Learning Theories of E. L. Thorndike and Evidence of Their Similarities as Reflected in Southern Baptist Adult Curriculum Materials, 1964–1965." PhD diss., Southwestern Baptist Theological Seminary, 1966.

Hall, G. Stanley. *Adolescence: Its Psychology and its Relations to Physiology, Anthropology, Sociology, Sex, Crime, Religion and Education, Vol. I & Vol. II*. New York: Appleton & Company, 1904.

———. *Jesus, The Christ in the Light of Psychology*. Vol. II. New York: Doubleday, 1917.

Hammett, John S. *Biblical Foundations for Baptist Churches: A Contemporary Ecclesiology*. Grand Rapids: Kregel, 2005.

Hardin, John Curran. "Retailing Religion: Business Promotionalism in American Christian Churches in the Twentieth Century." PhD diss., University of Maryland, College Park, 2011.

Harris, R. L., et al., eds. *Theological Wordbook of the Old Testament*. Chicago: Moody, 1980.

Harrison, Everett F., et al., eds. *Baker's Dictionary of Theology*. Grand Rapids: Baker, 1960.

Harvey, Hezekiah. *The Pastor: His Qualifications and Duties*. Philadelphia: American Baptist, 1879.

Henderlite, Rachel. *Forgiveness and Hope: Toward a Theology for Protestant Christian Education*. Richmond: Knox, 1962.

Hight C. Moore Papers. Southern Baptist Historical Library and Archives, Nashville, Tennessee.

Hight C. Moore Papers. Z. Smith Reynolds Library Special Collections and Archives, Wake Forest University, Winston-Salem, North Carolina, USA.

Hiltner, Seward. *The Counselor in Counseling*. Nashville: Abingdon, 1976.

———. *Pastoral Counseling*. Nashville: Abingdon-Cokesbury, 1949.

———. *Preface to Pastoral Theology*. Nashville: Abingdon, 1958.

———. *Protestant Religious Work in Mental Hospitals*. American Protestant Hospital Association, 1944.

Hobbs, Herschel and E. Y. Mullins. *The Axioms of Religion*. Revised ed. Nashville: Broadman, 1978.

Hofstadter, Richard. *Anti-Intellectualism in American Life*. New York: Random, 1966.

Holifield, E. Brooks. *A History of Pastoral Care in America: From Salvation to Self-Realization*. Eugene: Wipf & Stock, 1983.

Honeycutt, Roy Lee. "Theological Education: Retrospect and Prospect." *Review and Expositor* 75 (1978) 423–32.

Hunter, James Davison. *The Death of Character: Moral Education in an Age Without Good or Evil*. New York: Basic, 2000.

Isaac Jacobus Van Ness Papers. Southern Baptist Historical Library and Archives, Nashville, Tennessee.

Jackson, Walter C. "A Brief History of Theological Education Including a Description of the Contribution of Wayne E. Oates." *Review and Expositor* 94 (1997) 503–20.

James, William. *Varieties of Religious Experiences: A Study in Human Nature*. New York: Modern, 1902.

Jeane, Martin Keller. "An Analysis of Wayne Edward Oates' Phenomenological Method of Diagnosis in Pastoral Counseling." PhD diss., Southwestern Baptist Theological Seminary, 1986.

John Albert Broadus Papers, 1844–1895. Archives and Special Collections, James P. Boyce Centennial Library, The Southern Baptist Theological Seminary, Louisville, Kentucky.

John Milburn Price Collection. Archives, Roberts Library, Southwestern Baptist Theological Seminary, Fort Worth, Texas.

Johnson, Eric. *Foundations of Soul Care: A Christian Psychology Proposal*. Downers Grove: IVP Academic, 2007.

Johnson, Eric, ed. *Psychology & Christianity: Five Views*. 2nd ed. Downers Grove: IVP Academic, 2010.

Johnson, Inman. *Of Parsons and Profs*. Nashville: Broadman, 1959.

Joncich, Geraldine M. ed. *Psychology and the Science of Education: Selected Writings of Edward L. Thorndike*. Richmond, VA: Byrd, Inc., 1962.

Kemp, Charles F. *Physicians of the Soul: A History of Pastoral Counseling.* New York: Macmillan, 1947.

Kilpatrick, William Heard. *Philosophy of Education.* New York: Macmillan, 1951.

Knight, George R. *Philosophy & Education: An Introduction in Christian Perspective.* 4th ed. Berrien Springs, MI: Andrews University Press, 2006.

Lambert, Heath. *The Biblical Counseling Movement After Adams.* Wheaton: Crossway, 2012.

Landrum Pinson Leavell Collection. Southern Baptist Historical Library and Archives, Nashville, Tennessee.

Landry, Sabin P. "The Master Teacher of Evangelism." *Review and Expositor* 75 (1978) 397–408.

Lankard, Frank Glenn. *A History of the American Sunday School Curriculum.* New York: Abingdon, 1927.

Larsen, Timothy, ed. *Biographical Dictionary of Evangelicals.* Downers Grove: InterVarsity, 2003.

Leo T. Crismon Records, 1938–1971. Archives and Special Collections, James P. Boyce Centennial Library, The Southern Baptist Theological Seminary, Louisville, Kentucky.

Lewis, C. S. *The Abolition of Man.* New York: Macmillan, 1947.

Lewis, Gordon R. and Bruce A. Demarest. *Integrative Theology.* Grand Rapids: Zondervan, 1996.

Lionni, Paolo. *The Leipzig Connection.* Sheridan, OR: Heron, 1993.

Lovegrove, Deryck W., ed. *The Rise of the Laity in Evangelical Protestantism.* New York: Routledge, 2002.

Lucas, Sean Michael. "Christianity at the Crossroads: E. Y. Mullins, J. Gresham Machen, and the Challenge of Modernism." *The Southern Baptist Journal of Theology* 3 (1999) 58–79.

Lundgaard, Kris. *The Enemy Within: Straight Talk about the Power to Defeat Sin.* Phillipsburg: P & R, 1998.

Maguire, Clyde Merrill. *J. M. Price: Portrait of a Pioneer.* Nashville: Broadman, 1960.

Malony, H. Newton, ed. *Current Perspectives in the Psychology of Religion.* Grand Rapids: Eerdmans, 1977.

McCall, Emmanuel L. "Theological Education and the Black Community." *Review and Expositor* 75 (1978) 417–21.

McCord, James I. "Seward Hiltner's Contributions to the Life of the Churches and to Professional Theological Education." *Pastoral Psychology* 29 (1980) 13–16.

McElrath, Hugh T. "Perspectives on Public Worship in the 1970s." *Review and Expositor* 75 (1978) 361–70.

McGee Family Papers, 1920–1981. Z. Smith Reynolds Library Special Collections and Archives, Wake Forest University, Winston-Salem, North Carolina.

McGee, William Kay. "The Place Of The Bible In The Curriculum Of Religious Education." ThD diss., The Southern Baptist Theological Seminary, 1929.

McNeill, John T. *A History of the Cure of Souls.* New York: Harper & Row, 1951.

Menand, Louis, ed. *Pragmatism: A Reader.* New York: Vintage, 1997.

Mohler, R. Albert. "Baptist Theology at the Crossroads: The Legacy of E. Y. Mullins." *The Southern Baptist Journal of Theology* 3 (1999) 4–22.

Moore, Russell D. "Counseling and the Authority of Christ: A New Vision for Biblical Counseling at The Southern Baptist Seminary." (Booklet prepared for The Southern

Baptist Theological Seminary, Louisville, KY, January 31, 2009); accessed, October 22, 2012, http://www.sbts.edu/documents/Counseling-book-moore.pdf.

Moore, Russell D. and Gregory A. Thornbury. "The Mystery of Mullins in Contemporary Southern Baptist Historiography." *The Southern Baptist Journal of Theology* 3 (1999) 44–57.

Moore, William Gene. "From Biblical Fidelity to Organizational Efficiency: The Gospel Ministry from English Separatism of the Late Sixteenth Century to the Southern Baptist Convention of the Early Twentieth Century." PhD diss., The Southern Baptist Theological Seminary, 2003.

Mueller, William A. *A History of Southern Baptist Theological Seminary.* Nashville: Broadman, 1959.

Mullins, E. Y. *The Axioms of Religion.* Philadelphia: Judson, 1908.

———. "Pragmatism, Humanism and Personalism—The New Philosophic Movement." *Review & Expositor* 5 (1908) 501–15.

———. "A Roman Catholic Party among the Baptists." *Religious Herald* (July 16, 1896) 1.

———. *Why Christianity is True?: Christian Evidences.* Philadelphia: American Baptist, 1905.

Nettles, Thomas J. "E. Y. Mullins: Reluctant Evangelical." *Southern Baptist Journal of Theology* 3, no. 4 (1999) 24–43.

Nietzche, Friedrich Wilhelm. *Beyond Good and Evil.* Translated by Marianne Cowan. Chicago: Regenry, 1955.

———. *Thus Spoke Zarathustra.* Edited by Manuel Komroff. New York: Tudor, 1936.

Norman, Stan. "Fighting the Good Fight: The Struggle for Baptist Identity," *SBC Life* (April 1999) 8–9.

Oates, Wayne. *Anxiety in Christian Experience.* Philadelphia: Westminster, 1955.

———. "Association of Pastoral Counselors: It Values and Its Dangers." *Pastoral Psychology* 15 (1964) 5–7.

———. "Basic Types of Pastoral Counseling." *Pastoral Psychology* 17 (1966) 61–62.

———. *The Bible and Pastoral Care.* Grand Rapids: Baker, 1953.

———. *The Bible in Pastoral Counseling.* Grand Rapids: Baker, 1971.

———. *Christ and Selfhood.* New York: Association, 1961.

———. *The Christian Pastor, Revised and Enlarged Edition.* Philadelphia: Westminster, 1976.

———. "Conceptions for Ministry in the Pastoral Epistles." *Review and Expositor* 56 (1959) 388–410.

———. "Contribution of Paul Tillich to Pastoral Psychology." *Pastoral Psychology* 19 (1968) 11–16.

———. "Counseling and the Human Predicament: A Study of Sin, Guilt and Forgiveness." *Review and Expositor* 87 (1990) 536–37.

———. "The Cult of Reassurance." *Review and Expositor* 51 (1954) 335–47.

———. "Gospel and Modern Psychology." *Review and Expositor* 46 (1949) 181–98.

———. *Grace Sufficient.* Nashville: Broadman, 1951.

———. *Introduction to A. Graham Ikin: New Concepts of Healing Medical, Psychological, and Religious.* New York: Association, 1956.

———. *An Introduction to Pastoral Counseling.* Nashville: Broadman, 1959.

———. *The Minister's Own Mental Health.* Great Neck: Channel, 1961.

————. "New Emphases in Psychiatry and Religion: DSM III." *Pastoral Psychology* 36 (1981) 141–47.

————. *Nurturing Silence in a Noisy Heart.* New York: Doubleday, 1979.

————. "Organizational Development and Pastoral Care." *Review and Expositor* 75 (1978) 349–60.

————. *Pastoral Counseling in Social Problems: Extremism, Race, Sex, Divorce.* Philadelphia: Westminster, 1974.

————. "Pastoral Counseling in the Free Church Tradition." *Pastoral Psychology* 12 (1961) 21–34.

————. "Pastoral Psychology and Faith Healing." *Pastoral Psychology* 5 (1954) 27–40.

————. "Pastoral Psychology: The Next 20 Years in Relation to Theological Education." *Pastoral Psychology* 21 (1970) 49–55.

————. *Pastor's Handbook.* Philadelphia: Knox, 1980.

————. *Premarital Pastoral Care and Counseling.* Nashville: Broadman, 1958.

————. *The Presence of God in Pastoral Counseling.* Waco: Word, 1986.

————. "Professional Education for Ministry: A History of Clinical Pastoral Education." *Review and Expositor* 67 (1970) 385–86.

————. *Protestant Pastoral Counseling.* Philadelphia: Westminster, 1962.

————. *The Psychology of Religion.* Waco: Word, 1973.

————. "Psychosocial Dynamics of Family Living." *Review and Expositor* 75 (1978) 67–74.

————. *The Religious Dimensions of Personality.* New York: Association, 1957.

————. *Religious Factors in Mental Illness.* New York: Association, 1955.

————. "Religious Understanding of Personality." *Pastoral Psychology* 8 (1957) 46–50.

————. "The Role of Religion in Psychosis." *Review and Expositor* 45 (1948) 35–48.

————. *The Revelation of God in Human Suffering.* Philadelphia: Westminster, 1952.

————. "The Significance of the Work of Sigmund Freud for the Christian Faith." ThD diss., The Southern Baptist Theological Seminary, 1947.

————. "Socio-psychological Influences on Personalities Resulting from Social Change." *Review and Expositor* 68 (1971) 339–46.

————. *The Struggle to Be Free: My Story and Your Story.* Philadelphia: Westminster, 1983.

————. "The Theological Context of Pastoral Counseling." *Review and Expositor* 94 (1997) 521–30.

————. *What Psychology Says About Religion.* New York: Association, 1958.

————. *Where to Go for Help.* Philadelphia: Westminster, 1957.

————. *Workaholics: Make Laziness Work for You.* New York: Doubleday, 1978.

————. *Your Particular Grief.* Philadelphia: Knox, 1981.

Oates, Wayne E. and Kirk H. Neely. *Where to Go for Help.* Philadelphia: Westminster, 1957.

Oates, Wayne E. and Wade Rowatt. *Before You Marry Them.* Nashville: Broadman, 1975.

Oden, Thomas C. *Care of Souls in the Classic Tradition.* Philadelphia: Fortress, 1984.

————. *Classical Pastoral Care: Volume One Becoming a Minister.* Grand Rapids: Baker, 1987.

————. *Pastoral Theology: Essentials of Ministry.* San Francisco: HarperCollins, 1983.

Oglesby, William B. Jr., ed. *The New Shape of Pastoral Theology: Essays in Honor of Seward Hiltner.* Nashville: Abingdon, 1969.

Pearcey, Nancy R. *Total Truth: Liberating Christianity from Its Cultural Captivity.* Wheaton: Crossway, 2005.

Pearcey, Nancy R. and Charles B. Thaxton. *The Soul of Science: Christian Faith and Natural Philosophy.* Wheaton: Crossway, 1994.

Person, Peter P. *An Introduction to Christian Education.* Grand Rapids: Baker, 1958.

Plantinga, Jr., Cornelius. *Not the Way It's Supposed to Be: A Breviary of Sin.* Grand Rapids: Eerdmans, 1995.

Powlison, David. *The Biblical Counseling Movement: History and Context.* Greensboro: New Growth, 2010.

Price, J. M. *Jesus the Teacher.* Nashville: Convention, 1946.

Price, J. M., ed. *Introduction to Religious Education.* New York: Macmillan, 1932.

Price, J. M., et al. *A Survey of Religious Education.* New York: Ronald, 1940.

Purves, Andrew. *Pastoral Theology in the Classic Tradition.* Louisville: Knox, 2001.

Reed, James E. and Ronnie Prevost. *A History of Christian Education.* Nashville: Broadman & Holman, 1993.

Reiff, Philip. *The Triumph of the Therapeutic: Uses of Faith After Freud.* Wilmington, DE: ISI, 2006.

Resolution No. 5: "On Mental Health Concerns and the Heart of God." A Resolution Adopted by the Southern Baptist Convention in Houston, Texas, June 2013.

Resolution No. 5: "On the Sufficiency of Scripture in a Therapeutic Culture." A Resolution Adopted by the Southern Baptist Convention in St. Louis Missouri, June 2002.

Rienow, Rob. *Reclaiming the Sufficiency of Scripture.* Nashville: Randall, 2012.

Rockefeller, Steven C. *John Dewey: Religious Faith and Democratic Humanism.* New York: Columbia University Press, 1991.

Rogers, Carl R. *Counseling and Psychotherapy.* New York: Mifflin, 1942.

———. *The International Lesson System: The History of Its Origin and Development.* New York: Revell, 1911.

———. *On Becoming a Person.* New York: Mifflin, 1961.

Rowatt, Wade. "Oates' Theological Model for Psychology and Pastoral Care." *Review and Expositor* 101 (2004) 87–95.

Rufus Washington Weaver Papers. Southern Baptist Historical Library and Archives, Nashville, Tennessee.

Ryan, James. "Gaines S. Dobins–Author." *Review and Expositor* 75 (1978) 409–16.

———. "A Study of the Administrative Theory of Gaines Stanley Dobbins in Relationship to the Scientific Management, Human Relations, and Social Sciences Emphases in Administration." PhD diss., The Southern Baptist Theological Seminary, 1973.

Sampey, John R. *Memoirs of John R. Sampey.* Nashville: Broadman, 1947.

Sanford, Alexander E. *Pastoral Medicine: A Handbook for Catholic Clergy.* New York: Wagner, 1905.

Schaeffer, Francis. *Escape From Reason.* Downers Grove: InterVarsity, 2006.

———. *He is There and He is Not Silent: Does it Make Sense to Believe in God.* Carol Stream, IL: Tyndale, 2001.

Scherzer, Carl. *The Church and Healing.* Philadelphia: Westminster, 1950.

School of Theology Lecture Notes Collection, 1921–1973. Southern Baptist Theological Seminary Archives.

Schreiner, Thomas R. "Editorial: History Matter." *The Southern Baptist Journal of Theology* 3 (1999) 2–3.

Sherrill, Lewis. *Understanding Children.* New York: Macmillan, 1939.

Sinclair, Upton. *The Jungle.* New York: Grosset & Dunlap, 1906.

Sleeper, Ralph. *The Necessity of Pragmatism: John Dewey's Conception of Philosophy.* New York: Yale University Press, 1987.

Southern Baptist Convention Sermon Collection. Southern Baptist Historical Library and Archives, Nashville, Tennessee.

Southern Baptist Theological Seminary Annual Catalogue. Louisville: Seminary Press, 1908–1956.

Spencer, Ichabod. *A Pastor's Sketches: Conversations with Anxious Souls Concerning the Way of Salvation.* Vestavia Hills, AL: Solid Ground, 2001.

Starbuck, E. D. *The Psychology of Religion: An Empirical Study of the Growth of Religious Consciousness.* London: Scribner's Sons, 1899.

Steffens, Lincoln. *The Auto-Biography of Lincoln Steffens.* New York: Harcourt, Brace & World, Inc., 1958.

———. *The Shame of the Cities.* New York: Smith, 1948.

Stolz, Karl. *The Church and Psychotherapy.* New York: Abingdon-Cokesbury, 1941.

Sullivan, Mark. "A Year of the Government," *The North American Review* Vol. 215, No. 796 (1922) 308–21.

———. *Pastoral Psychology.* New York: Abingdon-Cokesbury, 1940.

———. *The Psychology of Religious Living.* Nashville: Cokesbury, 1937.

Sutton, Jerry. *The Baptist Reformation: The Conservative Resurgence in the Southern Baptist Convention.* Nashville: Broadman & Holman, 2000.

Symonds, Percival Mallon. *What Education has to Learn from Psychology.* New York: Bureau of Publications, Teacher's College, Columbia University, 1958.

Tappert, Theodore G., ed. and trans. *Luther: Letters of Spiritual Counsel.* Vancouver, British Columbia: Regent College Publishing, 2003.

Thayer, H. S. *The Logic of Pragmatism: An Examination of John Dewey's Logic.* New York: Humanities, 1952.

Thorndike, Edward L. *Educational Psychology: Briefer Course.* New York: Teacher's College, Columbia University, 1921.

———. *The Elements of Psychology.* 2nd ed. New York: Seiler, 1922.

———. *The Principles of Teaching: Based on Psychology.* New York: Mason, 1906.

Thornton, Edward. "A Critique of Clinical Pastoral Education." ThD diss., The Southern Baptist Theological Seminary, 1960.

———. *Professional Education for Ministry.* Nashville: Abingdon, 1970.

Torrance, E. Paul and William F. White, eds. *Issues and Advances in Educational Psychology.* Itasca, IL: Peacock, 1969.

Towns, Elmer., ed. *A History of Religious Education.* Grand Rapids: Baker, 1975.

Verkuyl, Gerrit. *Christ in American Education.* New York: Revell, 1934.

Vitz, Paul. *Psychology as Religion: The Cult of Self-Worship.* 2nd ed. Grand Rapids: Eerdmans, 1977.

Walters, Orville S. "The Counselor: Values and Cognitive Process Metaphysics, Religion, and Psychotherapy." *Journal of Counseling Psychology* 5 (1958) 243–52.

Watson, Thomas. *The Doctrine of Repentance.* Carlisle, PA: Banner of Truth Trust, 2012.

Wayne E. Oates Papers, MS624. Z. Smith Reynolds Library Special Collections and Archives, Wake Forest University, Winston-Salem, North Carolina.

Wayne Ward Papers, 1951–1991. Archives and Special Collections, James P. Boyce Centennial Library, The Southern Baptist Theological Seminary, Louisville, Kentucky.

Weatherspoon, J. B. "Charles Spurgeon Gardner," *Review and Expositor* 52 (1955) 183–98.

Weatherspoon, J. B. and Gaines S. Dobbins. *The Bible and the Bible School.* Nashville: Broadman, 1935.

Weaver, C. Douglas, ed. *The Axioms of Religion.* Macon: Mercer University Press, 2010.

Webster, Richard. *Why Freud was Wrong: Sin, Science and Psychoanalysis.* New York: Basic, 1995.

Weeks, Noel. *The Sufficiency of Scripture.* Carlisle: The Banner of Truth Trust, 1988.

Wells, David F. *Losing Our Virtue: Why the Church Must Recover Its Moral Vision.* Grand Rapids: Eerdmans, 1998.

Wendell Randolph Grigg Papers. Z. Smith Reynolds Library Special Collections and Archives, Wake Forest University, Winston-Salem, North Carolina, USA.

White, Thomas, ed. *Selected Writings of James Madison Pendleton, Volume II: Ecclesiological.* Paris, AR: The Baptist Standard Bearer, 2006.

Williams, Sam R. "Counselors as Missionaries," *Journal of Biblical Counseling* 26 (2012) 28–40.

Wills, Gregory A. *Democratic Religion: Freedom, Authority, and Church Discipline in the Baptist South 1785–1900.* New York: Oxford University Press, 1997.

———. *Southern Baptist Theological Seminary 1859–2009.* New York: Oxford University Press, 2009.

Wise, Carroll A. *The Meaning of Pastoral Care.* New York: Harper and Row, 1966.

———. *Pastoral Counseling: It's Theory and Practice.* New York: Harper and Row, 1951.

———. *Pastoral Psychotherapy: Theory and Practice.* New York: Aronson, 1980.

———. *Psychiatry and the Bible.* New York: Harper and Brothers, 1956.

Woolley, Davis Collier, ed. *The Encyclopedia of Southern Baptists, Vol. III.* Nashville: Broadman, 1971.

Young, Warren C. *The Influence of John Dewey in Religious Education.* Chicago: Self-Published, 1949.

Yount, William. *Created to Learn: A Christian Teacher's Introduction to Educational Psychology.* Nashville: Broadman & Holman, 1996.

Made in the USA
Las Vegas, NV
07 January 2022

40721213R00118